Current Hi

A Monthly M:

The European War, March 1915

Various

Alpha Editions

This edition published in 2022

ISBN: 9789356784789

Design and Setting By

Alpha Editions

www.alphaedis.com

Email - info@alphaedis.com

Contents

Caldron of the Balkans

But little has hitherto been published in English describing from original sources how the Balkan States, out of which the world conflict arose, resolved, in Kipling's phrase, to "stand up and meet the war." The following documents, taken from authoritative Balkan sources, show for the first time the purely Balkan aspect of the great struggle.

How Turkey Went to War

By Ottoman Authorities

Immediately on receiving official notification of the rupture of diplomatic relations between Austria and Servia, the Turkish Grand Vizier hastened to inform the Diplomatic Corps in Constantinople that Turkey would remain neutral in the conflict. Explaining this official Turkish declaration, the following editorial article appeared early in August in the Ministerial paper, Tasfiri-Efkiar, published in Constantinople:

THE declarations made by the Grand Vizier to the Ambassadors of the powers, in order to reassure them as to the dispositions of Turkey, do not constitute from a legal point of view a declaration of neutrality, according to the stipulations of The Hague Conventions; likewise the Austrian ultimatum to Servia, viewed in the same light, is not tantamount to a declaration of war. In fact, The Hague Conventions demand a formal declaration in both cases. But if the formal declaration of Turkish neutrality cannot be made before she has received an official notification of the existing war, it is nevertheless true that the head of the Government, in his conversations with the Ambassadors, has given them to understand what the opinion of the people is here. And even without this, the efforts of the Turkish Government, the desire, and the policy of Turkey, are so explicit that there is no ground for doubt as to the significance of the declarations of the Grand Vizier.

Turkey has never asked for war, as she always has worked toward avoiding it. But we must not misunderstand the meaning of certain terms. Neutrality does not mean indifference. The present Austro-Servian conflict is to a supreme degree interesting to us. In the first place, one of our erstwhile opponents is fighting against a much stronger enemy. In the natural course of things Servia, which till lately was expressing, in a rather open way, her solidarity as a nation, still provoking us, and Greece will be materially weakened. In the second place, the results of this war may surpass the limits of a conflict between two countries, and in that case our interests will be just as materially affected.

We must therefore keep our eyes open, as the circumstances are momentarily changing, and do not permit us to let escape certain advantages which we can secure by an active and rightly acting diplomacy.

The policy of neutrality will impose on us the obligation of avoiding to side with either of the belligerents, but the same policy will force us to take all the necessary measures for safeguarding our interests and our frontiers.

If it be true, as reported, that the pacificist tendencies of Turkey constitute one of the safest guarantees of peace in the Balkans, then we must hope that on the day when a general settlement of accounts will be made Europe will be willing to recognize the important part played by Turkey in the preservation of peace in the Near East, and will be eager to rectify, if not all, at least one part of the wrongs she has caused to our country.

TURKEY LEARNS OF THE WAR.

Turkish mobilization was still at its first stages when the European war began on Aug. 1, 1914. The Turkish Government in particular and the Turkish population in general were overwhelmed by the unexpected turn of European events, and it was at the height of the crisis that Turkey received the news of her two battleships building in British yards being taken over by England. A correspondent of The Daily Atlantis of New York, writing in Constantinople on Aug. 10, said:

The European war makes the Turks think that this is their golden opportunity for turkifying the empire from the one end to the other. All non-Moslems, mere boys and young men of 25 to 30 years of age and grown men up to 45, are being arrested by the police and secret service force, and dragged to the barracks, like convicts, and if they fail to pay the fifty or eighty pounds Turkish ($230 or $350) for exemption from military service, they are forced to work as "assistant-soldiers."

The soldiers thus designated are not given rifles, nor are they trained for service, but are simply employed as servants to the regular soldiers. It is easy to understand that no one can endure such conditions of military life, the result being that each and every one of these non-Moslems sells whatever property he has in order to pay the ransom and get away from the army, and from Turkey as well. In ten days, since this peculiar recruiting began, fully ten thousand Greeks found a way of escaping from Constantinople, many of them finding a refuge in the free and hospitable United States. This getting away is not so easy, writes the same correspondent, because officials of the various ports are exacting heavy sums from the fugitives before letting them go. Graft and extortion in this case reign supreme, and it costs anywhere from three to fifteen pounds ($13 to $70) to "buy" a police or port official. This process, originating in Constantinople, is widespread in the provinces, and the sums paid in this way by the non-Moslems to escape military service amount to millions. "Let the infidels pay!" say the Turkish officials. "They have taken our ships, and they have to pay for it."

The popular feeling against England in these first days of the European war is fierce. Numerous manifestations, in which the younger element was largely represented, proceeded to attack the British stores and British subjects, and there have been serious attempts against the British Embassy in Constantinople and the British Consulate at Smyrna.

H.R.H. PRINCESS MARIE JOSE

Only Daughter of the King of the Belgians.

(*Photo from Underwood & Underwood.*)

HIS EMINENCE, CARDINAL MERCIER

Archbishop of Mechlin, Primate of Belgium.

CONSTANTINOPLE IN AUGUST.

Another letter from the same source, dated Constantinople, Aug. 6, gives the following picture of the Turkish capital in the early days of the European war:

It is impossible to describe the way in which the Porte is trying to put the country on a war footing, notwithstanding the terrible odds she has to fight against. God only knows what the Turks are expecting if the Austro-Servian conflict turns out according to their desires, or if the European conflict takes the form of a decisive Austro-German victory. We now have ample proof to show that the Turkish mobilization is in such a way conducted as to be ready to act in common with Bulgaria, in a simultaneous attack against Greek and Servian Macedonia, as soon as the Austrians have a first decisive victory over the Servians. This scheme, however, seems to be doomed since the entry of Great Britain into the general war, and there are indications that Turkey, warned by England and Russia, will disband her already mobilized army. On the other hand, the news reaches Constantinople that the Russian forces have crossed the frontier into Turkish Armenia, and occupied Erzeroum, while Enver Pasha was seen yesterday, (Aug. 5,) paying hasty visits to the Russian and British Embassies. While such is the political situation, matters are still worse in the business world of the Turkish capital. It is almost impossible to give an idea of the general upheaval brought about by greedy speculators, who are taking advantage of this anomalous situation, and by the Government itself, requisitioning everything they can lay their hands on, regardless of reason or necessity.

Policemen and Sheriffs, followed by military officers, are taking by force everything in the way of foodstuffs, entering the bakeries and other shops selling victuals, boarding ships with cargoes of flour, potatoes, wheat, rice, &c., and taking over virtually everything, giving in lieu of payment a receipt which is not worth even the paper on which it is written.

In this way many shops are forced to close, bread has entirely disappeared from the bakeries, and Constantinople, the capital of a neutral country, is already feeling all the troubles and privations of a besieged city. Prices for foodstuffs have soared to inaccessible heights as provisions are becoming scarce. Actual hand-to-hand combats are taking place in the streets outside the bakeries for the possession of a loaf of bread, and hungry women with children in their arms are seen crying and weeping in despair.

Many merchants, afraid lest the Government requisition their goods, hastened to have their orders canceled, the result being that no merchandise of any kind is coming to Constantinople either from Europe or from Anatolia.

Both on account of the recruiting of their employes and of shortage of coal the companies operating the electric tramways of the city have reduced their service to the minimum, as no power is available for the running of the cars.

Heartrending scenes are witnessed in front of the closed doors of the various banking establishments, where large posters are to be seen, bearing the inscription: *Closed temporarily, by order of the Government.* The most popular of these institutions is the Wiener Bankverein. This bank, by making special inducements to small depositors and by paying a higher interest than the others, succeeded in concentrating the savings of many people of the working classes, and as this institution is in imminent danger the rush to its doors is exceptionally great and riotous.

The municipality has issued a number of ordinances fixing the prices of all necessary commodities, and the Government, after the first panic, declared that no further requisitions are to be made. At the same time the authorities took special pains in order to induce the various merchants to import goods from abroad, thus relieving the extremely strained situation of the market; but it is doubtful whether such measures will have any calming effect on the scared population.

Immediately after war was declared between Germany and Russia the Porte ordered the Bosphorus and the Dardanelles closed to every kind of shipping, at the same time barring the entrances of these channels with rows of mines. The first boat to suffer from this measure was a British merchantman, which was sunk outside the Bosphorus, while another had a narrow escape in the Dardanelles. A large number of steamers of every nationality are waiting outside the straits for the special pilot boats of the Turkish Government, in order to pass in safety through the dangerous mine field. This measure of closing the straits was suggested to Turkey by Austria and Germany, and was primarily intended against Russia, as it was feared that her Black Sea fleet might force its way into the Sea of Marmora and the Aegean.

TURKISH PARLIAMENT PROROGUED.

On Sunday, Aug. 2, the Medjlissi-Meboussan, or Parliament of Turkey, was urgently called together, and the Speaker of the House addressed the members as follows:

Dear Colleagues: The imperial proclamation ordering the last elections has produced some uneasiness both within and without the empire. It was said at that time that the Chamber was to be convened only to give vent to partisan feeling and to disturb the quiet of the country. The elections, however, proceeded in as orderly a way as possible, and the Chamber performed its duty with great order and solicitude, having voted the budget and many other laws. The country accordingly is convinced that the Chamber has fulfilled its duty with relative calm, in view of the circumstances. We part today in order to meet again in November. The war between Austria-Hungary and Servia has a tremendous importance in the general European situation. While until yesterday Europe was kept in a state of watchful waiting, now we are informed that war has been declared between Germany and Russia. In face of such an international situation, it behooves all us Ottomans to rally in a spirit of harmony around the imperial throne, and to act with the moderation characteristic of our race for the preservation of our country.

Hoping that the great example given by Parliament to the nation as regards the working in a spirit of harmony and order will have its due influence on the country at large, I salute you and bid you farewell.

THE MOBILIZATION.

One of the first schemes of the German General, Liman von Sanders, for the reorganization of the Turkish Army was to provide a system whereby a speedier mobilization of the forces could be made possible. According to this scheme, as far back as the first days of May, 1914, every Mayor and village President of the empire was provided with a sealed envelope, under orders to open it only on telegraphic notice from the Central Administration. These envelopes were opened on Aug. 3, and were found to contain the papers constituting the order of general mobilization, including a large poster in colors, bearing, under the imperial monogram, or "Tougrah," two crossed green Turkish flags, with crossed sword and rifle, and underneath a gun and its carriage, and lastly the imperial edict in large letters, reading as follows:

A general mobilization was ordered to

start on ....

(To be dated on notice.)

Those liable for duty must report at

their respective headquarters. First day

of mobilization is on ....

(To be dated on notice.)

DIPLOMATIC SITUATION AND PRESS OPINIONS.

While Turkey in this way was preparing for war, Talaat Bey, the Turkish Minister of the Interior, and Halil Bey, President of the Chamber, were leaving Constantinople for Bucharest, where they intended meeting the representatives of the Greek Government, in order to find a way of settling the outstanding Greco-Turkish differences regarding the Aegean Islands and the question of refugees. The object of this political move was twofold.

First, Turkey was bent on giving to Europe a proof of her pacific intentions, and, second, she was trying to convince the Hellenic Government of her willingness to reach an understanding regarding their mutual differences, and begin anew the friendly relations of yore. The following extract is from an editorial article published in the Ikdam of Constantinople on Aug. 17:

From today the regeneration of our fleet begins. From today Ottoman hearts must again rejoice. We must work hard now for the strengthening of our navy. We must know that our fleet, which till yesterday was lifeless, is no longer in incompetent hands and under the leadership of lazy minds. New Turkey has intrusted her navy to iron hands. At the head of our fleet is Djémal Pasha, whose naval successes it is unnecessary to mention. The commander of the fleet is the Chief of the Naval Staff, Arif Bey, and in command of the light flotilla is Capt. Muzzafer Bey. Likewise the commanders and the other officers of the two new battleships are chosen among the fittest. This is the beginning of a new era for our navy. In addition to this we must say that we are expecting good results from our political activity. Talaat Bey and Halil Bey have left for Bucharest, where they will try to find a solution of outstanding serious questions. At the same time they will have an opportunity to exchange views with Rumanian statesmen. It is unnecessary, in our belief, to exalt the significance of this mission. We think, however, that a wise and moderate policy, strengthened by a good army and navy, will go far in bringing good results.

On Sept. 10 an official announcement from the Sublime Porte was handed to the representatives of the powers in Constantinople, and communicated to the press. This declaration ran as follows:

As an expression of the sentiments of hospitality and friendship on the part of the Ottoman Government toward the European populations of the empire, there were instituted long ago certain regulations to which Europeans coming to the Levant for commerce would be subjected, these same regulations having been duly communicated to the respective Governments of those Europeans.

These regulations, adopted by the Porte on its own initiative, and considered entirely as privileges, and having been strengthened and made more general through certain acts, have continued to be in force up to this time under the name "Old Treaties," (in Turkish "Ouhout-i Atikah.") These privileges, however, are wholly incompatible with the legal status of recent years, and especially with the principle of national sovereignty. In the first place, they became a hindrance to the progress and development of the Imperial Government, while in the second, by creating misunderstandings in its relations with the foreign Governments, they formed a barrier preventing these relations from becoming more harmonious and more sincere.

The Ottoman Empire continues to advance in the path of regeneration and of reforms, overleaping many obstacles, and in order to acquire the position due to it in the civilized family of Europe, it adopted modern principles of government, and has not deviated from its programme of having the State conducted on these principles.

The founding of the constitutional form of government is in itself a proof that the efforts of the Ottoman Empire for its regeneration have been fully crowned with success. Certain exceptions, however, based on the capitulations, such as the participation of foreigners in the administration of justice, which is an all-important prerogative of national sovereignty, the limitations imposed on the legislative rights of the State, based on the argument that certain laws cannot be applied to foreigners, the injustice inflicted on common right from the impossibility of convicting a delinquent who disturbs the safety of the country merely because he happens to be a foreigner, or because the prosecution against him must be subjected to certain limitations and particular conditions; and likewise the difference in the competency of the various courts dealing with cases where the capitulations are involved; all these constitute impregnable barriers against every effort of the country toward progress in the administration of justice.

From another point of view, the fact that foreigners living in the Ottoman Empire are exempt from taxation, in accordance with the capitulations, makes it impossible for the Sublime Porte to procure the indispensable means for the carrying out, not only of the reforms but of its everyday needs.

The impossibility of increasing the indirect taxation is bringing about the increase of direct taxes, and therefore makes the burden on the Ottoman tax-payers all the heavier. The fact that foreigners who enjoy in the Ottoman Empire every protection and every privilege as well as freedom in their business transactions are exempt from taxation constitutes in itself an intolerable injustice and creates at the same time a situation detrimental to the independence and prestige of the Government.

While the Imperial Government was firm in its resolution to continue its efforts regarding the reforms, the general war broke and increased the financial difficulties of the country in such a degree that all the innovations and all the reforms which have been decided upon and actually begun are threatened to remain without effect.

The Sublime Porte feels convinced that the only way toward salvation for the Ottoman Government lies in the realization of the necessary reforms in the least possible time. In the same way the Porte feels that every encouragement will be shown her in the decisive steps to be undertaken for this end.

Convinced of this, the Imperial Government has decided to abolish, on Oct. 1, 1914, the capitulations, and all conventions, concessions, and privileges emanating therefrom, which have become an iron ring around the State, making it impossible for it to progress.

At the same time the Ottoman Government engages to treat with foreign countries in accordance with the rules of international law. While I have the honor of communicating to your Excellency this decision, which opens a new and happy era in the life of the Ottoman Empire, an event which undoubtedly will please your Excellency, I consider it my duty to add that the Porte in abolishing the capitulations does not harbor any hostile feeling against any of the foreign States, but is acting solely in the highest interests of the empire. At the same time, the Porte is ready to begin pourparlers for the conclusion of commercial treaties in accordance with the principles of international law.

The Turkish press made little mention of the manner in which Europe took notice of the important step taken by the Porte, and the Ministerial Tasfiri Efkiar was the only one to express the feelings of the Government on this occasion, saying:

It is not proper for us to expect a unanimous and speedy satisfaction from all the European powers; but, on the other hand, we must welcome every objection and every discussion from whatever source it comes, as in this way we shall know who are our friends and who our enemies.

APPROACHING THE CRISIS.

The events covering the period from Sept. 10, when the abolition of the capitulations was decided upon, till Oct. 29, when the Turkish fleet attacked Russian ports and shipping in the Black Sea, were confined mostly to hasty and all-absorbing warlike preparations on the part of the Turkish Government, assisted by the German military mission. The Constantinople correspondent of The Daily Atlantis of New York wrote on Sept. 17:

We are daily approaching a crisis. The Government has not swerved from its warlike attitude, and is threatening not only Greece, but Russia and the Triple Entente as well, while, on the other hand, it has failed to secure Rumanian or Bulgarian co-operation in its militant policy. At the same time, the Porte has learned that efforts are being made in the Balkans for common action against Turkey. It also became known that the Governments of London and Petrograd agreed to indemnify Bulgaria by giving her Adrianople and Thrace, while Greece was to have Smyrna, with a considerable hinterland.

During this period the Turkish press maintained an active campaign against England and the Allies. The following extract from an editorial article published in the Terdjumani-Hakkikat thus characterizes the situation:

Everybody knows that the Balkan States are traversing a period of doubts, and that the belligerent parties are doing their best in order to secure the sympathies and the assistance of the Balkan States.

To begin with, the idea of reconstructing the Balkan League came under consideration. In this way the Balkan States think they will become strong enough to impose their will at the final settlement that will follow the war. This idea, however, based as it is on the nullification of the Treaty of Bucharest, and on certain sacrifices on the part of Rumania and Greece, proved to be a failure. In the course of the discussion between the two States it was shown that neither Greece nor Rumania was willing to make any sacrifice in favor of Bulgaria. The Balkan Alliance, being thus unpracticable, the belligerent powers of Europe attempted to attract Rumania and Bulgaria only, and to this end they made every sort of promise to the two Governments of Sofia and Bucharest. The President of the London Balkan Committee, Mr. Noel Buxton, went to Bulgaria and made certain promises to Mr. Radoslavoff, the Bulgarian Premier, in the name of Sir Edward Grey. He promised the restitution to Bulgaria of the Enos-Midia line, including Adrianople. The Bulgarians, however, are not to be fooled in this way by promises at the expense of third parties, and especially when the eventual cost of these gifts might be a heavy one. We must not forget that Bulgaria wants not Thrace, but Macedonia. If Great Britain had promised Bulgaria Macedonia, including Saloniki, and the Bulgarian Government was convinced beforehand of the fulfillment of the promise, then it is certain that the proposal would be accepted. But this is not in line with England's interests, because in that case she would lose her two other customers—Greece and Servia. And so there goes Mr. Buxton making offers out of our own pocket.

But we Turks have been used to injustices; and it has become an axiom in history that whenever there is trouble in any part of the world we must be the ultimate sufferers. It seems that this time, too, "our friends" felt like repeating the same story; but now we are not to be caught napping, and the Government, having in time mobilized the army, is ready for every emergency.

On Sept. 27 a Turkish destroyer having been stopped by a British destroyer outside the Dardanelles, the Turkish Government ordered the straits closed to all shipping.

The Turkish Government tried to justify in the official press of Constantinople the measure of closing the straits by declaring that this important step was undertaken only after a Franco-British fleet had established an actual blockade of the straits to the detriment of Turkish commerce and neutral navigation. The Government organ, The Tasfiri-Efkiar, said:

The powers are trying to justify the mobilization of Switzerland, and are making a great case of Belgian neutrality, but meantime they consider our mobilization as having no other purpose than an aggression against our neighbors.

Now, if the neutrality of Switzerland, which is guaranteed by all the powers, is likely to be endangered, how is it possible for us to remain calm and undisturbed in this universal upheaval, so long as we know that to annoy and continually harass Turkey according to the fancies of Europe has well-nigh become a sort of fashion?

Those powers that are dissatisfied at our mobilization are eager to find our anxiety as without foundation for the mere reason that our territorial integrity remains under the guarantee of all the powers. But where was that guarantee when Tripoli and Cyrenaica were attacked in a way little differing from open brigandage? And was it not the same powers who forgot their guaranties in the Balkan Peninsula when they abolished the famous status quo? With such facts before us is it not ridiculous to speak of European guaranties? While we have now before us what happened to Belgium, why should our mobilization excite such widespread indignation? All we are trying to do is to safeguard and protect our interests and protect ourselves from aggression on the part of the Balkan States.

WAR DECLARED.

On Oct. 29, 1914, the attack of the Turkish forces upon Russia and England was delivered. Following is the official Turkish version of the events leading to the rupture of diplomatic relations between Turkey and the Triple Entente, contained in the first Turkish communiqué of the war, appearing in the Turkish press on Oct. 31, 1914:

While on the 27th of October a small part of the Turkish fleet was manoeuvring in the Black Sea, the Russian fleet, which at first confined its activities to following and hindering every one of our movements, finally, on the 29th, unexpectedly began hostilities by attacking the Ottoman fleet.

During the naval battle which ensued the Turkish fleet, with the help of the Almighty, sank the mine-layer Pruth, displacing 5,000 tons and having a cargo of 700 mines; inflicted severe damage on one of the Russian torpedo boats, and captured a collier.

A torpedo from the Turkish torpedo boat Gairet-i-Millet sank the Russian destroyer Koubanietz, and another from the Turkish torpedo boat Mouavenet-i-Millet inflicted serious damage on a Russian coastguard ship.

Three officers and seventy-two sailors, rescued by our men and belonging to the crews of the damaged and sunken vessels of the Russian fleet, have been made prisoners. The Ottoman imperial fleet, glory be given to the Almighty, escaped injury, and the battle is progressing favorably for us.

The Imperial Government will no doubt protest most energetically against this hostile action of the Russian fleet against a small part of our fleet.

Information received from our fleet now in the Black Sea is as follows: From accounts of Russian sailors taken prisoners and from the presence of a mine-layer among the Russian fleet, evidence is gathered that the Russian fleet intended closing the entrance to the Bosphorus with mines and destroying entirely the imperial Ottoman fleet after having split it in two. Our fleet, believing that it had to face an unexpected attack, and supposing that the Russians had begun hostilities without a formal declaration of war, pursued the scattered Russian fleet, bombarded the port of Sebastopol, destroyed in the city of Novorosiysk fifty petroleum depots, fourteen military transports, some granaries, and the wireless telegraph station.

In addition to the above, our fleet has sunk in Odessa a Russian cruiser and damaged severely another. It is believed that this second boat was likewise sunk. Five other steamers full of cargoes lying in the same port were seriously damaged. A steamship belonging to the Russian volunteer fleet was also sunk, and five petroleum depots were destroyed.

In Odessa and Sebastopol, the Russians from the shore opened fire against our fleet.

The officers and crews of the mine-layer Pruth were subjected to a rigid examination.

Eight or ten days ago the Pruth, lying in the roadstead of Sebastopol, received a cargo of mines and was put under the command of officers who for a number of years past had been training on board the Russian depot ship in Constantinople and therefore had become familiar with the ins and outs of the Bosphorus.

As soon as it became known that a small part of the Turkish fleet went out to the Black Sea, the Russian fleet sailed from Sebastopol, leaving only an adequate squadron for the protection of the city, and on Oct. 27 put to sea, taking a southerly direction with the rest of its forces. On the next day the mine-layer Pruth left Sebastopol and steamed southward.

The Russian fleet, acting in different ways, intended to fill with mines the entrance of the Bosphorus, attack the weak squadron of the Ottoman fleet, at that time on the high seas, and cause the destruction of the rest of the Turkish fleet, which, being left in the Bosphorus, would rush to the assistance of the light flotilla, and, encountering the mines, would be destroyed.

Our warships manoeuvring on the high seas met the mine-layer Pruth as well as the torpedo boats accompanying her, and thus took place the events already known from previous communications.

The rescued Russian officers are five in number, one of them a Lieutenant Commander. The prisoners have been sent to Ismid.

This successful action on the part of our squadron, which only by chance came to be on the high seas at the time of the naval battle, is itself one of the utmost importance for us, as it assures the future of our fleet.

THE SULTAN'S PROCLAMATION.

As soon as war was declared against Russia, England, and consequently France, the Sultan issued the following proclamation to his troops:

To my army! To my navy!

Immediately after the war between the Great powers began, I called you to arms in order to be able in case of trouble to protect the existence of empire and country from any assault on the part of our enemies, who are only awaiting the chance to attack us suddenly and unexpectedly as they have always done.

While we were thus in a state of armed neutrality, a part of the Russian fleet, which was going to lay mines at the entrance of the straits of the Black Sea, suddenly opened fire against a squadron of our own fleet at the time engaged in manoeuvres.

While we were expecting reparation from Russia for this unjustified attack, contrary to international law, the empire just named, as well as its allies, recalled their Ambassadors and severed diplomatic relations with our country.

The fleets of England and France have bombarded the straits of the Dardanelles, and the British fleet has shelled the harbor of Akbah on the Red Sea. In the face of such successive proofs of wanton hostility we have been forced to abandon the peaceful attitude for which we always strove, and now in common with our allies, Germany and Austria, we turn to arms in order to safeguard our lawful interests.

The Russian Empire during the last three hundred years has caused our country to suffer many losses in territory, and when we finally arose to that sentiment of awakening and regeneration which would increase our national welfare and our power, the Russian Empire made every effort to destroy our attempts, either with war or with numerous machinations and intrigues. Russia, England, and France never for a moment ceased harboring ill-will against our Caliphate, to which millions of Mussulmans, suffering under the tyranny of foreign domination, are religiously and whole-heartedly devoted, and it was always these powers that started every misfortune that came upon us.

Therefore, in this mighty struggle which now we are undertaking, we once for all will put an end to the attacks made from one side against the Caliphate, and from the other against the existence of our country.

The wounds inflicted, with the help of the Almighty, by my fleet in the Black Sea, and by my army in the Dardanelles, in Akbah, and on the Caucasian frontiers against our enemies, have strengthened in us the conviction that our sacred struggle for a right cause will triumph. The fact, moreover, that today the countries and armies of our enemies are being crushed under the heels of our allies is a good sign, making our conviction as regards final success still stronger.

My heroes! My soldiers! In this sacred war and struggle, which we began against the enemies who have undermined our religion and our holy fatherland, never for a single moment cease from strenuous effort and from self-abnegation.

Throw yourselves against the enemy as lions, bearing in mind that the very existence of our empire, and of 300,000,000 Moslems whom I have summoned by sacred Fetwa to a supreme struggle, depend on your victory.

The hearty wishes and prayers of 300,000,000 innocent and tortured faithful, whose faces are turned in ecstasy and devotion to the Lord of the universe in the mosques and the shrine of the Kaabah, are with you.

My children! My soldiers! No army in the history of the world was ever honored with a duty as sacred and as great as is yours. By fulfilling it, show that you are the worthy descendants of the Ottoman Armies that in the past made the world tremble, and make it impossible for any foe of our faith and country to tread on our ground, and disturb the peace of the sacred soil of Yemen, where the inspiring tomb of our prophet lies. Prove beyond doubt to the enemies of the country that there exist an Ottoman

Army and Navy which know how to defend their faith, their country and their military honor, and how to defy death for their sovereign!

Right and loyalty are on our side, and hatred and tyranny on the side of our enemies, and therefore there is no doubt that the Divine help and assistance of the just God and the moral support of our glorious Prophet will be on our side to encourage us. I feel convinced that from this struggle we shall emerge as an empire that has made good the losses of the past and is once more glorious and powerful.

Do not forget that you are brothers in arms of the strongest and bravest armies of the world, with whom we now are fighting shoulder to shoulder. Let those of you who are to die a martyr's death be messengers of victory to those who have gone before us, and let the victory be sacred and the sword be sharp of those of you who are to remain in life.

MEHMED-RESHAD.

On the 22 Djilhidje, 1332.
Or October 29, 1914.

VERBATIM TERMS OF THE FETWA

(Sultan's Proclamation of a Holy War.)

The issuance by the Sultan of the Fetwa, or proclamation, announcing a holy war, called upon all Mussulmans capable of carrying arms—and even upon Mussulman women—to fight against the powers with whom the Sultan was at war. In this manner, according to Constantinople newspapers, the holy war became a duty not only for all Ottoman subjects, but for the 300,000,000 Moslems of the earth. The Turkish newspaper Ikdam called upon the people as follows:

Mussulmans, open your eyes! Grasp your weapons; trust to God. Hurl yourselves with full might against the foe! As the Caliph has said, the Divine help will be with us. Forward! Sons of Islam! There is no longer a difference of nationality; there is no longer a difference of culture. All Mussulmans are united and have but a single wish—to destroy our foes!

The wording of the Fetwa itself, however, is less fiery in tone than the impassioned newspaper appeal. The Fetwa reads as follows:

First Question—If lands of Islam are subjected to attack by enemies, if danger threatens Islam, must in that case young and old, infantry and mounted men, in all parts of the earth inhabited by Mohammedans, take part in the holy war, with their fortune and their blood, in case the Padisha declares the war to all Mohammedans? Answer—Yes.

Second Question—Since Russia, England, France, and other States supporting these three powers against the Islamitic Caliphate have opened hostilities against the Ottoman Empire by means of their warships and their land troops, is it necessary that all Mohammedans also who live in the countries named shall rise against their Government and take part in the holy war? Answer—Yes.

Third Question—Under all circumstances, since the attainment of the goal depends upon the participation of all Mohammedans in the holy war, will those who refuse to join in the general uprising be punished for conduct so abhorrent? Answer—Yes.

Fourth Question—Mohammedans who live in lands of the enemy may, under threats against their own lives and the lives of their families, be forced to fight against the soldiers of the States of Islam. Can such conduct be punished as forbidden under the Sheriat, and those guilty thereof be regarded as murderers and punished with the fires of hell? Answer—Yes.

Fifth Question—Inasmuch as it will be detrimental to the Mohammedan Caliphate of the Mohammedans who live in Russia, France, England, Servia, and Montenegro fight against Germany and Austria-Hungary, which are the saviors of the great Mohammedan Empire, will therefore those who do so be punished with heavy penalties? Answer—Yes.

BRITAIN'S ANSWER.

[From The London Times, Nov. 6, 1914.]

A supplement to The London Gazette published yesterday morning contains the following:

NOTICE.

Owing to hostile acts committed by Turkish forces under German officers, a state of war exists between Great Britain and Turkey as from today.

Foreign Office, Nov. 5, 1914.

Following this notice is a proclamation extending to the war with Turkey the Proclamations and Orders in Council now in force relating to the war, other than the Order in Council of Aug. 4, 1914, with reference to the departure from British ports of enemy vessels which, at the outbreak of hostilities, were in such ports or subsequently entered the same.

The Gazette also contains an Order in Council, dated Nov. 5, annexing the Island of Cyprus.

The order, after reciting the Convention of June 4, 1878, the Annex thereto, and the Agreement of Aug. 14, 1878, by which the Sultan of Turkey assigned the Island of Cyprus to be occupied and administered by England, and affirming that by reason of the outbreak of hostilities with Turkey the Convention, Annex, and Agreement have become annulled, asserts that it has seemed expedient to annex the island. His Majesty, with the advice of his Privy Council, has therefore ordered:

From and after the date hereof the said island shall be annexed to and form part of his Majesty's dominions, and the said island is annexed accordingly.

EGYPT'S NEW SULTAN.

The New Sultan of Egypt, Hussein I., made his State entry on Dec. 20, 1914, into the Abdin Palace, in Cairo. The streets were lined with troops and the progress of their new ruler was watched by thousands of enthusiastic spectators. The King of England sent a telegram to the Sultan, to which his Highness replied thanking his Majesty for the promised British support. A new Cabinet had already been formed. Rushdi Pasha retained the position of Prime Minister and the portfolio of the Interior. Following is King George's telegram to the Sultan:

On the occasion when your Highness enters upon your high office I desire to convey to your Highness the expression of my most sincere friendship and the assurance of my unfailing support in safeguarding the integrity of Egypt and in securing her future well-being and prosperity.

Your Highness has been called upon to undertake the responsibilities of your high office at a grave crisis in the national life of Egypt, and I feel convinced that you will be able, with the co-operation of your Ministers and the Protectorate of Great Britain, successfully to overcome all the influences which are seeking to destroy the independence of Egypt and the wealth, liberty, and happiness of its people.

GEORGE R. AND I.

The Sultan telegraphed the following reply:

To his Majesty the King, London.

I present to your Majesty the expression of my deepest gratitude for the feelings of friendship with which you see fit to honor me and for the assurance of your valuable support in safeguarding the integrity and independence of Egypt.

Conscious of the responsibilities I have just assumed, and resolved to devote myself, in entire co-operation with the Protectorate, to the progress and welfare of my people, I am happy to be able to count in this task on your Majesty's protection and on the assistance of your Government.

HUSSEIN KAMEL.

Servia and Her Neighbors

The utterances of Servia's statesmen and people since the war began have not appeared in English. Only accounts of fighting by the nation from which the great conflagration started have been printed. How Servia has judged the issues while conducting her struggle against annihilation, and how the neighboring Balkan States regard her, are authoritatively presented below.

PREMIER PASHITCH spoke in the Skuptschina, or Servian Parliament, on Aug. 4, 1914, and made the following declaration given to the press by the Official Servian Bureau:

Mr. Pashitch laid stress on the fact that the Serajevo affair was used as pretext for the war, desired long ago by the Austrian Monarchy, which did not look on Pan-Serbism with a favorable eye, while the aspirations of other countries of Rumania, Germany, and Italy were tolerated. The Austro-Hungarian Monarchy wished to crush Servian aspirations by curbing the Servian prestige.

In answering the Austrian note, Mr. Pashitch said, we reached the extreme limits of submission to her demands. We did everything in order to avoid the conflict and prove that we were peaceful. Now, all united, we will defend our rights.

We rely on the sympathy and support of great and sisterly Russia, who knows that our foes have been conspiring against our independence and our progress, and who will not permit our prestige to be crushed. At the side of Russia we have other friends.

(Long live Russia! Long live England! Long live France! Long live the Triple Entente!)

I thank the Opposition—continued Mr. Pashitch—because she has united with us in these critical moments, forgetting in the face of danger party lines and the dissension of opinions.

From Nish the following official communication was telegraphed to the foreign press by the Government Bureau on Aug. 9, 1914:

The Servian mobilization was effected with marvelous order, and once more it proved the good military organization of Servia, and how much the country can rely on the patriotic devotion of her soldiers.

Notwithstanding the erroneous statements of a part of the foreign press, notwithstanding the speedy development of events, notwithstanding the season of work in the fields, fully 80 per cent. of the reserves presented themselves on the first day of mobilization, which was completed amid general enthusiasm.

For a long time the Servians knew that the main struggle would be turned against Austria. The Montenegrin and Servian peoples enter the war against the common foe with an equal confidence in their armies. The enthusiasm of these two countries is all the stronger from the fact that they are fighting simultaneously with the aid of the Russians, French, and English. Numerous manifestations have taken place in Servian and Montenegrin cities in favor of Russia, France, and England.

THE BULGARIAN MENACE.

Following is the account of the declaration of the Servian Minister of Commerce, Mr. Paul Maringovich, published in the Bulgarian newspaper Mir of Sofia in November, 1914:

Mr. Maringovich's declarations are characteristic of the Serbo-Bulgarian relations. This Servian statesman at first spoke of the trials of the Servian Nation on account of the war, and then expressed the belief that these trials will pass and Servia will see better days with the realization of her ideals. Mr. Maringovich predicts that the differences between Servia and Bulgaria will be settled in the future and that the two peoples will live in perfect harmony.

Regarding the Serbo-Bulgarian relations Mr. Maringovich said in the Mir:

"I am sorry to hear that Bulgaria demands concessions from us. In exchange for her friendship she demands concessions in Macedonia. But in this case that cannot be called friendship.

"Bulgaria demands this today because we are at war with Austria, and we cannot accordingly oppose her. But in doing this she simply betrays her weakness because it is a certain proof of weakness to strike one from behind while he is struggling with another. If Bulgaria is proud and strong she can measure herself with us as soon as the war with Austria is over. A strong Bulgaria must measure herself with the strong and not with the weak.

"Why do people in Bulgaria today insist on concessions? Do you know how many difficulties there are today in the granting of such territorial concessions? You felt the pain of similar action. Silistria was taken from you while your army was victoriously marching on Constantinople. Do not insist on implanting deep in the Servian heart a mortal hatred against yourselves.

"Do not ask the reason of our dissensions of today, in a difference of interests, because such difference does not exist, but try to find it in the arrogance and the conceit of the two nations. We do not recognize you as a nation. But this recognition must be made with the understanding that you drop your conceit.

"In Bulgaria people think that at this moment we have the support of Russia. But there is a mistake even in this, as we are further than you from Russia. If today Russia offers to us her support she is doing that because we are struggling against Austria and preventing her from invading the Balkans.

"To this argument you oppose the treaty of Bucharest. But that treaty is not our work. By not accepting the Czar's wish in his telegram of May 5, (18,) 1913, you lost his support. This example from the past can show you how far you can go when you oppose Russia. But in no case are you entitled to blame those who are not guilty of your misfortune.

"When Russia undertakes to do something for the Slavs, she always does it in a way beneficial to the party to which she promised her support.

"When this war is over, when the whole of Slavdom shall be freed, when in a special congress all the interests of the Slavs shall be discussed and the services rendered by each and every one of them shall be weighed, Bulgaria must fear that decisions will be taken which will be contrary to her and that her interests will be sacrificed.

"A country must not act always according to her interests. Does not the Bulgarian people have any obligations toward Russia? Duty always stands above mere interest.

"When the war is over an entirely different atmosphere will rule in the souls of the peoples, and it will then be possible to weigh the actual interests with more equanimity and more calm. At least we Servians have this opinion."

The following statement was made by the Servian Minister at Petrograd, Mr. Spalaikowich, in the Russkoye Slovo:

What is Bulgaria going to do in the present circumstances? To which side will she cling? Is not her people going to take the arms against their secular enemy, the Turks?

This solution would be the most satisfactory for Bulgaria. Now a chance is given her to fulfill her obligations to Russia, who made her free. Let the Bulgarian sword be thrust against the secular enemy of Slavdom and the petty differences be forgotten.

Bulgaria, under the Russian wing, will enter the Slav family united, strong, and beloved. If she remains inactive she will drag herself poor and forgotten by all and full of regrets.

A PEASANT'S ANSWER.

As illustrating the popular feeling in Bulgaria the following letter from a peasant to Mr. Maringovich appeared in the official organ of the Bulgarian Government, Echo de Bulgarie, published in French:

Your Excellency: I am a plain peasant from the Danube country. While born on the shores of the beautiful blue Lake of Ochrida, and really, I cannot understand what is the meaning of your factum, (sic.) What have you come to do among us? Nobody knows you any more in Sofia. You are Servian and consequently a foreigner to us Bulgarians. There are certain pains that nothing can alleviate, nor heal, and there are wounds that nothing can cicatrize.

Since your entry in Ochrida, in my father's house, you, the Servian Army, behaved like enemies. You profaned the church, that Bulgarian church where I took my first communion. You have despoiled the archives and burned our libraries; you ordered closed our national school where I learned to mumble the alphabet of my mother tongue.

I have seen the epic struggle of my compatriots against Greeks and Turks, and I took part with them in order to obtain these national institutions. And did you come there in Ochrida, and everywhere in Macedonia protected by our valiant army of Lulé Bourgas and Chataldja, to perform the duty of allies—of Slav brethren?

You established yourselves as conquerors of the country, as vandals, with the manifest purpose of extinguishing every vestige of our national culture. You associated yourselves with the non-Slavs (Rumanians and Greeks) against us, your allies, in order to reach your end. Why, then, do you call us Slavs? We were called Tartars until just before you arrived in Sofia.

You treated as villains our Bishops, whom the Turks and the Greeks were forced to restore us after a struggle of seventy-five years. You burned our Bulgarian books, and you forbade, under penalty of death, our people from calling themselves Bulgars. You tortured my parents with all the refinements of torture that you have invented.

Why, I beg of you? Because you were Servians? I will not go so far as to injure you with the belief that the Servians are capable of crimes against nature. Then, because we were Bulgarians; because those poor people, taking you for their brethren, for Christians, for Slavs, at least had the courage to say they were Bulgarians and to think themselves such.

And this continues today with increased intensity. Ah, Mr. Maringovich! You have committed there and you persist in committing a crime against humanity that nothing will ever efface. You stabbed us to the heart, with premeditation, and the wound is still bleeding; you killed our faith in the Slav brotherhood. You morally assassinated us.

In the face of these crimes, Bregainitza and Slivnitza are pale figures. These odious crimes will not be left unpunished. The day of chastisement will come whether you look for it or not.

Your Excellency, I permit myself to repeat the question: What have you come to do among us?

Really you must have a good cheek—permit me this undiplomatic expression—and a Servian cheek, in order to have the audacity to come here and tell us tales. It is not only this; but you make sport of our sacredest and deepest sentiments, you reopen our wounds, and you purely and simply abuse us. You ought to have thought of all this before you set out for Sofia. Today there is an abyss dividing Serbs and Bulgars. It is an open precipice which will serve for you as a grave. You wish to fill it? To succeed you must employ other means than words.

Sir: You are a foreigner to us; there is not an honest man in all Bulgaria who can consider you a welcome guest. Nobody knows you. For every Bulgar there is only one word and one gesture for you. We stake our liberty in giving you the answer and in making the gesture.

Sir: You may take the train which brought you here from Nish. There is the depot. Farewell! Kindly accept the assurance of my consideration for your person, whom I had not the advantage to know.

THE MINISTRY'S POSITION.

The statement by the new Servian Cabinet in the Skuptschina on Dec. 8, 1914, follows:

The new Ministry has made in the Skuptschina the following declarations: The Government that has the honor to appear before you has been constituted with the purpose of manifesting to the end of this great crisis the union of the wills, the forces, and the intentions of all political parties of our country.

This Government is convinced of the confidence of the Skuptschina, as it puts all of its forces to the service of the great cause of the Servian Nation, and of the Serbo-Croatian-Slovenian family.

The Government considers its first duty to bow low before the heroic sacrifices voluntarily made on the altar of the fatherland.

The Government sends to the entire army and to all the military, from commanders down to simple privates, the expression of its confidence, its admiration and its gratitude for their efforts and their sacrifices to the common fatherland.

Our little and young army, conserving the good reputation it had acquired in the past years, has put itself worthily on the side of the glorious and veteran armies of our great allies, who are struggling together with us for the cause of justice and liberty.

There is no doubt that in the end of these painful days of war our historic nation will be recognized and appreciated.

The Government is convinced that all the Servian people are united until the end of this hallowed war, to defend their hearths and their liberty; that their sole duty is to assure an army proportionate to this great war, which from the very beginning has been a struggle for the emancipation and the union of all our brother Serbo-Croato-Slovaks, who now suffer under foreign rule.

The brilliant success which will crown this war will compensate largely the great sacrifices of the present Servian generation. In this struggle the Servian people have not to choose, because in a question of life and death there is no choice.

This people is forced to struggle and will do its duty with the same unflinching energy of a century ago for the redemption of the tomb of Kossovo.

The Government will try faithfully to represent this national decision; and, faithful to its powerful and heroic allies, it will with confidence await the hour of victory.

The Government, conscious of the pains and hardships suffered by the army and in large part by the nation, will do all that human strength can do for the amelioration of the present situation and will energetically try all measures for refitting the army and bettering the sanitary service, as in this cause no sacrifices shall be spared.

In concert with you, gentlemen, the Government will take all the necessary measures for helping the population to recuperate after the war.

Now, while the enemy is yet at the gates of our country, the Government cries: Forward, with God's help, against the enemy! Forward in the struggle against the enemy!

[All the Deputies, without party distinction, repeated the last words of Premier Nicola Pashitch, and immense applause greeted the manifesto.]

STATEMENT TO GREECE.

The Servian Minister at Athens, Mr. Baluhtchich, caused this announcement to be made on Nov. 29, 1914:

On Nov. 29 the Servian Minister at Athens declared that all talk of Servian concessions of any kind in favor of Bulgaria was premature.

The Servian Government, the Minister said, finds it impossible to proceed to any concession territorial or moral, so long as Servia is in a state of war.

The Bulgarian Government has not made, and it is impossible to formulate, her demands directly to Servia, because it is impossible to foresee the outcome of a struggle so violent and apparently destined to be long. For Servia it is impossible to enter negotiations of indemnity or concessions for the neutrality of Bulgaria before an end is put to the present situation. The only certain thing is that the Governments of the Triple Entente are endeavoring to reconstitute the Balkan League, which is to be made of three Balkan States, namely, Servia, Greece, and Bulgaria.

But, as I had the occasion of stating some time ago, the Bulgarian territorial demands, with regard to the reconstitution of the league, have been so preposterous that neither Greece nor Servia could begin discussions on such a basis.

I deny, in the most emphatic manner, Mr. Baluhtchich said, the news that Servia was to cede, or that Bulgaria directly and formally demanded from my Government, any strip whatever of Macedonian territory, at least for the time being.

Likewise it is untrue that the Bulgarian Prime Minister, Mr. Radoslavoff, demanded from the Ambassadors of the Triple Entente that the compensation for her neutrality be guaranteed to her from now for the future. It is true that a disturbing political ferment is going on now in the Balkan Peninsula, the Servian Minister said in conclusion, but it is a difficult thing to express opinions at this time.

However, before the war is over, neither concessions nor discussion can be made, at least as far as Servia is concerned, and it seems that the Triple Entente concurs in this view.

BULGARIA AND KULTUR.

In the semi-official Servian daily, Samouprava, published in Belgrade and now at Nish, the following editorial article appeared early in the first week of October, 1914:

The Bulgarians are a queer people. Those of the foreigners who sympathize with them are apt to call them realists, positivists, and calculants, but we Servians, knowing them, understand that such definitions applied to them are flattering euphemisms and nothing more. The Bulgarian people are really laborious and thrifty. Unfortunately the cultured members of Bulgarian society, who studied abroad, bear in their social and political life the fundamental characteristics of the German intellect.

The cultured Bulgarians have absorbed the German Kultur, although they do not owe Germany even the hundredth part of what they owe to Russia.

All these are facts that need not proofs. Bulgaria, therefore, could not more wantonly accuse Servia than by saying that we allied ourselves with the enemies of Slavdom. The cynicism of these accusations is proved by the following officially registered Bulgarian actions:

The Stoïlof Ministry has concluded an alliance with Servia and also an understanding which the Bulgarians sold to Turkey for eight Bishoprics in Macedonia.

During the crisis which followed the annexation of Servian Bosnia and Herzegovina to Austria, and when Russia was mortally insulted, Bulgaria, in common understanding with Austria, proclaimed her independence and definitely annexed Oriental Rumelia. These profits Bulgaria secured to the detriment of Servian interests.

During the Balkan war, and notwithstanding all that Servia had done for Bulgaria, the Bulgarian attitude was once more treacherous, culminating in the wanton attack upon her allies at the instigation of Austria.

Today, when Russia fights a life-and-death struggle, Bulgaria is keeping neutral, and every one knows what kind of neutrality is this when such a multitude of Germans is passing through Bulgarian territory in order to arm and lead the Turks against Russia. And, last but not least, immediately after the present war between Austria and Servia, the Bulgarians proposed an alliance to Rumania.

After all this it is a wonder how the Bulgarians dare to invoke Slav sympathies, which they always sold to Austria, and which the Bulgarian press is now trying to sell at auction. Lucky he who buys them.

A YOUTHFUL BELGIAN HERO

Joseph Lessen, a Boy Scout, 18 Years of Age, Who So Distinguished Himself That He Was Decorated on the Field by King Albert.

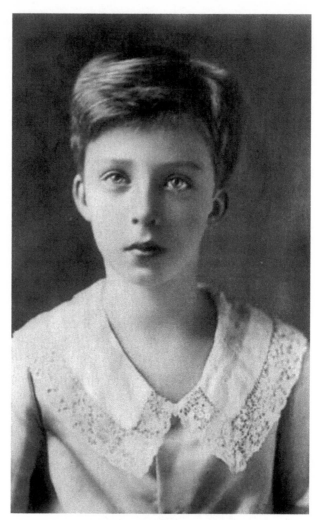

THE CROWN PRINCE OF BELGIUM

H.R.H. Prince Leopold, Eldest Son of the King of the Belgians.

(*Photo from Underwood & Underwood.*)

AFTER FIVE MONTHS' FIGHTING.

On Dec. 17, (30, New Style,) 1914, Crown Prince Alexander of Servia, in his quality of Commander in Chief of the Army, issued the following order of the day to his troops:

Soldiers! It is now five months since the day when the enemy attacked our beloved country. Notwithstanding the fact that we had suffered the trials of two heroic but hard wars, nevertheless firm and undaunted we have stood the attack. Having routed the enemy in Tchar and Zadar we gave him, after heroic and sanguinary battles, the biggest blow of all.

Thousands of prisoners, hundreds of guns, a quantity of war booty, which came to our hands, are witnesses of his defeat and our glory.

Soldiers! I feel proud in announcing to you that not a single enemy remains on the soil of the Servian Kingdom. We cast him out with great losses.

At this sacred moment, when on the heroic City of Belgrade anew waves the victorious Servian flag, I desire to fulfill a great duty of gratitude. In our ranks, in this third war, are fighting our brothers which we have liberated from the Turkish yoke. The soldiers of Kossovo, of Vardar, of Hekligovatz, of Bregalnitsa, of Bitolie, and of Porets, have shown themselves worthy of their brothers of Shumadia and the Danube, of Poutrin and Morava, of Timok and Usjitsa.

They have shown themselves worthy of the heroes Milaten and Dughan, who for long have carried the glory and the good name of the Servian arms.

I want to give to these new soldiers of ours conspicuous proofs of the gratitude of the fatherland. In the face of the undeniable proof of their fulfillment of their duty, in the face of their enthusiasm I declare that these soldiers shall have the political and constitutional rights of Servia, their liberatrix! The Skuptschina, in its first sitting after peace is signed, will take all the necessary measures in order that full liberties be given to our brethren.

Soldiers! The iron ring of our powerful allies is fastening tighter every day around our common enemy. And he, (the enemy,) feeling that his defeat is well nigh at hand and dreading its dire consequences, fights desperately and strenuously. But in vain. The number of their soldiers is diminishing daily, and our allies are strengthened with new troops on the fields of battle.

The end of this gigantic struggle is from now known, although not yet accomplished. We must, therefore, for some time to come, fulfill our difficult duty and stay by the side of our big and powerful allies, who are fighting for us, till our enemy is annihilated on the battlefield.

And then peace will come to crown worthily those who have been sacrificed for our great fatherland, and then our country will be much enlarged, much stronger, and much happier than she ever has been. And for this, oh, my heroic Servia will be grateful to you.

RUSSIAN CONGRATULATIONS.

On Dec. 18, 1914, the new Russian Minister to Servia, Prince Troubetzkoï, presented his credentials to the Servian Crown Prince Alexander, whom he addressed as follows:

Illustrious Sir: I have the honor to hand to your Royal Highness the letter by which his Majesty the Emperor of Russia has deigned to accredit me by his Majesty the King of Servia.

My august master has charged me to express to you the vivid sympathy and the sincere admiration which his Majesty feels for the valiant people of Servia, her heroic army, and her venerable chief.

Allow me to express to your Highness the joy that I feel in fulfilling the imperial commission today when your army has covered itself with immortal glory and has written in Servian history the most beautiful page that a people may desire.

Separated by a long distance, but, attracted by the heart of her elder sister, Servia may say that in this terrible struggle against an enemy, numerically stronger but morally weaker, she is not alone and will not be forsaken.

I pray that this conviction may double the unflinching courage of the Servians and lead them always to new victories.

In assuming today the duties incumbent upon me after the death of my lamented predecessor, Hartwig, I take the courage, illustrious Sir, to express the hope that your Highness will not deprive me of his assistance, which will be absolutely necessary to me in order that I may work to the best of my abilities for the common good of the two countries, and also for the consummation of peace in the Balkan Peninsula, this peace that Russia considers as the essential aim of her efforts and her sacrifices.

Crown Prince Alexander answered as follows:

The expression of the vivid sympathy and admiration which his Majesty the Emperor has addressed through you to the people and army of Servia are so much the more welcome as I personally witnessed the hard conditions under which my valiant army is struggling and the heavy burdens oppressing my brave people.

The fact that, although separated by a long distance from Russia, her elder sister, Servia can find in her bosom a heart having the same sentiments as hers, has encouraged our army and our people to persist in the heroic struggle that they are waging against a more numerous enemy. This certainty will give us new strength to carry the struggle to the end.

In the fulfillment of your mission, after the death of your predecessor, a mission which the late Hartwig performed with such love and such devotion to the true Slav interests, you can rest on my absolute confidence and the continued support of my Government, being sure that the greatness and the power of Servia are in full accord with the greatness and the power of holy Russia.

The lamented Hartwig made many trips for the mutual benefit of both countries, Russia and Servia, and his efforts had resulted in creating stable conditions and securing the peace of the Balkans.

In accepting the letters, by which his Majesty the Emperor has accredited you by his Majesty the King of Servia, my beloved father, I bid you, Mr. Minister, welcome, and I wish you success in your mission.

BULGARIA'S SENTIMENT.

The following Bulgarian view of the Servian victory that resulted in the recapture of Belgrade is presented from an editorial article of the Dnevnik of Sofia:

The Austro-Hungarian action against Servia seems to have failed. It goes without saying that the return of the Servians to Belgrade does not mean yet that the handful of the starving and half-naked Servian Army has been victorious against its strong opponent.

The Servian success, according to latest information, is due to means that are very little laudable in themselves.

The commander of the advance posts of the Austro-Hungarian Army, being a native of Dalmatia, became intimate with the Servians and committed an odious treason. He disclosed to them the dispositions of the Austro-Hungarian forces, and he himself, with the sections forming the guard, surrendered to the Servians.

From the Austrian rearguard one part scattered to various villages, another was sleeping. They were not ready and, caught unexpectedly, were dispersed.

Austro-Hungarian prestige is severely wounded. The shameful treason shows how dangerous is the Pan-Servian propaganda to the integrity of the Austrian Empire, when corruption has reached even the officers standing in high command.

The Austro-Hungarian General Staff, as we are informed, has already taken those measures imposed by the situation. The Generals, Frank and Potiorek, have been recalled and will be probably court-martialed. And it seems that the "brilliant" Servian victories are the beginning of the end of the "Slav Belgium."

GREECE ACCLAIMS.

The following editorial article, headed "A New Marathon" on the Servian victory, appeared in the Greek newspaper Patris of Athens on Dec. 3, (16, New Style,) 1914, expressing the views of the Hellenic Government:

The reoccupation of Belgrade by the Servians is one of those military feats which amount to historical phenomena. The Servians not only contributed the greatest feat of the European war, as far as results are concerned, but won for themselves an immortal page in the world's history.

Greece alone has to show an analogous achievement, although greater, when she expelled the Persian invasion.

Only the achievements of Arhangelovatz, Ouzhitse, and Lazarevats can compare in a certain degree to the brilliancy of Marathon and Plateae. And the Servian achievement appears all the more Hellenic if analogies are to be considered.

The Servians, until yesterday a little people, with an army almost insignificant in face of the masses of the Austrian columns, submissive in times of peace, in the face of the most oppressive demands of Austrian diplomacy—considered like all the small peoples to be living at the mercy of the great—when the hour of supreme defense for altars and hearths struck, and in the face of an enemy threatening to swallow their country, they arose, terrible in their vengeance, and repeated the feat of the routing of Goliath by their small but invincible power.

This was possible because their regiments were not moved by the hope of effectively beating the enemy, which hope springs from the consciousness of numerical superiority, but they were enlivened and strengthened before death by the undying fire of freedom, national pride, and the conviction that they were thrust into the most honored struggle, after which there would not be left for them anything but to live or die.

And the Austrians, who considered their campaign against Servia as mere child's play; the Austrians with their German military organization; the Austrians, who constitute one-sixth of the entire European military power, started against Servia with the same logic, the same haughtiness, the same bombastic prediction of the result of the unequal war with which the Persian masses moved against Greece....

Little Montenegro Speaks

The following Montenegrin message to Italy appeared in La Gazetta del Popolo *of July 21, (Aug. 3,) 1914:*

THIS terrible European war, if one takes away from it the diplomatic ornaments with which the Chancelleries are wont to decorate it, dates from a century back. It is, let us hope, the final revolt of the nations oppressed by the unjust work of the Congress of Vienna.

The nationalities of which the powers of the Triple Entente, and especially Russia, have made themselves the champions have not provoked this bloody struggle. It was imposed on them by the reactionary spirit of the Germanic world, which desired to consolidate its hegemony, based on the sufferings of the weak, impossible to describe, and on the contempt of right, which was proclaimed as a system of government.

The neutrality observed up to now by your august Italian country has been a powerful assistance to the cause of right against the cause of oppression.

We Serbs of Montenegro and Servia are now on the point of conquering that national unity, which our poets, our thinkers, and our sovereigns have sung, implored, and prepared, and, following the trail opened by Mazzini, Cavour, and Garibaldi, we put our confidence in Italy, this mother of civilization, who by her smile embellishes the sun-kissed Slav shores of the Adriatic.

Help us in conquering the place which is awaiting us at the altar of justice! We firmly believe that Italy, when at the price of new sacrifices she shall have all of her exiled sons united under her glorious standard, will inaugurate a new era of friendly and intimate connections with the young Slav world, who from her hands received so many benefits and who in exchange offers her the collaboration of young and enthusiastic people in the great task undertaken by our protectors in the name of civilization and liberty.

Bulgaria's Attitude
Speech From the Throne

By Tsar Ferdinand I.

The following speech by Tsar Ferdinand I. of Bulgaria was read at the opening of the Bulgarian Parliament, called the Sobranje, on Oct. 15, (28,) 1914, by the Prime Minister, Mr. Radoslavoff.

WITH the ending last year of a long and exhausting struggle which we conducted with incomparable self-denial, the Bulgarian people and my Government directed again their efforts toward the healing of the wounds of the recent past and the remodeling of the national forces, and likewise toward creating new resources and prosperity for the country.

Our common peaceful activity was interrupted by the breaking out of the greatest and most terrible of all wars that history has up to this day recorded. In face of this mighty struggle of the European nations my Government has deemed it its duty before the nation, and the course imposed on it, to declare the neutrality of Bulgaria and to maintain this attitude sternly and honestly according to international obligations and the interests of the fatherland.

Thanks to this process, my Government maintains good and friendly relations with all the great powers; has succeeded in giving to our relations with our neighbors a color of greater confidence, so necessary after the crisis of the last year, and in the midst of the events that lie heavy today on the whole of Europe.

A supplemental statement of the royal position was made by the Bulgarian Premier, Mr. Radoslavoff, in the Sobranje at the sitting of Nov. 12, (25,) 1914, which follows:

With the proclamation of the state of siege, taken in accordance with the decision of Parliament, as a measure of further security, everything is moving along according to the laws and the Constitution of the country. And the Government is endeavoring that the internal administration may proceed in as orderly a way as possible.

You remember very well that on the 16th (29th) of July, when war was declared by Austria-Hungary, I came here and told you that the decision of the Government was to maintain strict neutrality.

One day before the closing of the extra session of Parliament I repeated the declarations of the Government, that no matter what kind of political combinations were formed around us the Government is resolved to maintain absolute neutrality to the end.

It was with pleasure that I heard at that time the assurances of all the party leaders that if I were to keep this attitude they would help me maintain the absolute neutrality of Bulgaria.

I do not know why after a few days there have been published various statements signed by the different party leaders.

Nothing in particular had been done on our side up to that time. There was nothing irregular, but, notwithstanding all this, complaints have been lodged against the Bulgarian Government that its neutrality was one-sided, that the Government was favoring one group of the powers while hostile to the other, that through Bulgaria arms and ammunition were sent from a belligerent country [Germany] to a non-belligerent, [Turkey,] and this moved the leaders of the parties to turn to the nation and denounce the sincerity of your Government.

The silence of the nation and the attitude of the powers gave us full justification for the fairness and loyalty with which we keep our neutrality.

Two months ago the nation had witnessed a manifesto, signed by all the party leaders with the exception of the narrow Socialists, which means that the opposition has not been united on this question, as it is said in the manifesto that all the opposition was united in a fear lest the Government abandon its neutrality. In the manifesto addressed to the Bulgarian nation the desire was expressed for the formation of a Ministry in which all the political parties were to be represented.

But the silence of the nation has given ample proof of its confidence in the present Ministry. The declaration of the Government on July 13 (26) holds today, as it held then. We are keeping the strict neutrality of Bulgaria. Those that were supposed to have grievances against us have no proofs to show our breach of neutrality. Every side was satisfied with our assurances.

Notwithstanding the difficulties with which the path of the Government is strewn today, I, supported by the majority of the Parliament, will follow the same policy. Bulgaria has remained neutral, and up to now she is in excellent relations with all neighboring countries.

Bulgaria is in most friendly relations with Rumania, Greece, and Servia, which is at war. Bulgaria keeps the most sincere relations with Turkey. Bulgaria remains neutral and loyal in her position. I make the declaration so that the entire nation may be informed that the present Government has assured the territorial integrity of Bulgaria.

Our policy meets with the approval of all the great powers without exception. If we ever are led by the force of circumstances to enter some arrangement whereby Bulgaria will obtain something more in the way of territory, this will come from the will of the entire Bulgarian concert, with which we desire to remain up to the end in good relations.

This is what I can and what I must say today in the National Parliament. [Cheers and applause.]

BULGARIAN PARLIAMENT REPLIES.

[As voted on Nov. 12, (25,) 1914.]

Your Majesty: The national representation considers it an agreeable duty to express its satisfaction for the statements addressed to it and to offer its collaboration to the Tsar and the Government for the safeguard of the dear interests of the fatherland.

Your Majesty!

The breaking out of the terrible war which today oppresses and exhausts the nations has stopped the peaceful activity in which the Bulgarian Nation and your Government were engaged for the regeneration of the national forces and the creation of new resources for the prosperity of the country and the healing of the wounds of the long and heroic war which the nation, with unflinching self-sacrifice, has waged in the past year.

Your Majesty!

In the face of the momentous and far-reaching events now taking place in Europe and around Bulgaria, the national representation has noted with delight that the Government, having at heart the future of the country when it declared the neutrality of Bulgaria, is maintaining this attitude strictly and loyally, as the international necessities and the most vital interests of the country demand.

Your Majesty!

The national representation has learned with joy that, thanks to this attitude, the Government of your Majesty has preserved good and friendly relations with all the great powers and has improved our relations with our neighbors, which good relations are so necessary for Bulgaria after the crisis of the last year, and during the events of which we are the witnesses.

Your Majesty!

The great events that are shaking Europe are apt to call for our attention, but, in spite of this, they will not stop us in the way of the peaceful development of our culture, to which Bulgaria after the war devoted her energies.

We will carefully examine and heartily approve of all the measures which the Government may take for the progress of the country and will give them our support.

Long live his Majesty the Tsar!

Long live her Majesty the Tsarina!

Long live his Royal Highness the Crown Prince!

Following is the allocution of Tsar Ferdinand I., on Dec. 2, (15,) 1914, to the Delegation of the Sobranje, which brought to him the Bulgarian Parliament's answer to the speech from the throne.

Gentlemen: It has always been agreeable to me to meet the representatives of the National Parliament and exchange with them ideas on the situation and the administration of the country. In the present year, however, during the development of the events around us this contact with the representatives of the people is not without some importance for the Chief of the State.

I desire to hear from you, gentlemen, what are the concerns of the nation and to partake of them with you. The thought that I am nourishing, and my hope is, that, thanks to the stability and the wisdom of the Bulgarians, the country will emerge from the new trials untouched and without being threatened in the future.

I am really proud in duly acknowledging the virtues of the Bulgarian people. When, in 1912, this people, moved by a single impulse, arose and crushed a strong opponent by a force and ardor unsurpassed till now, the whole world recognized its military virtues. But the Bulgarian Nation has also displayed unique virtues in its reverses by valiantly enduring the blows of misfortune.

This nation will warmly undertake its mission in order to achieve its destiny, when it will win more respect on the part of foreigners than it won by its victory; and the hearts of its sons, so devoted to the fatherland, will be warmed anew.

Today, when the whole of Europe is burning and the conflagration is approaching us, when all the nations around us are moving and making ready for action, the Bulgarian Nation, duly appreciating the situation, has established its attitude with an equanimity and a reserve which constitute the undeniable proofs of its wisdom and its political maturity.

The eyes of the Czar and of the people are turned toward you. In the advices that you are giving, in the opinions that you express, I observe your care for the national prosperity and your resolution to sacrifice everything on the altar of the fatherland and for the interests of the nation. This sets me at rest and inspires me with the hope that in the future also complete harmony will prevail between the nation and the Crown, and that from this harmony we shall draw the necessary strength for the assurance of the future of Bulgaria.

May God watch over the fortunes of our fatherland and may He crown with success our common efforts.

BULGARIA'S NEUTRALITY.

In the last sitting of the Bulgarian Sobranje, just before the Christmas holidays, the Premier, Mr. Radoslavoff, made the following statements as they appear in the semi-official organ, Narodni Prava, of Sofia:

Since last July Bulgaria has maintained strict neutrality. Whatever accusations have been addressed to her from abroad as to her alleged breaches of neutrality, on the part of one or other of the belligerent groups, are without any foundation whatever. It is recognized that such insinuations come from our enemies, who have every interest in our breaking neutrality.

The Government maintains and will maintain its neutral policy to the end, and in this case we declare that we will adhere to it, and, supported by the country, we will try to take as much advantage of it as is possible.

Whether we are going to have or not to have a Ministry in which all the political parties will be represented, this does not at all interest those from abroad, where the dignified attitude of our Government is recognized. Do not ask us to negotiate what the Triple Entente is willing to give us, or to say to the central powers—Austria and Germany—"You, what are you going to give us?"

Because in that case they would answer: "Why should we give you anything? For your inactivity? Because you keep tranquil, watching us shedding our blood? Is it for this that we must give you something?"

I, for myself, have repeated on another occasion that during these critical moments, when new States are being founded while others are falling to the ground, to safeguard and preserve the present frontiers of Bulgaria is the greatest service that can be rendered her. We know what we have asked and what was offered to us. But who guarantees that we shall have what was orally promised to us? We ourselves cannot guarantee it. I declare that we are on good terms with our neighbors so long as they respect the interests of Bulgaria. If I knew that we would receive Macedonia and Cavalla and Dobrudja, be sure that I, first among all, would advise the formation of a coalition Ministry.

Representative Tchandref (interrupting)—Go ahead and take them alone.

Radoslavoff—But now we may not, neither in Chataldja nor in Cavalla nor in Dobrudja. The Bulgarian Government is pursuing the absolute preservation of peace and is watching developments. The friends that we have, notwithstanding all evil machinations, have not deserted us. Bulgaria still has friends, but friends and enemies tell us, Keep quiet, Bulgarians! In this lies your safety!

A MILITARY ESTIMATE.

The subjoined statement by the Bulgarian General, Savoff, appeared in the Vienna Reichspost of Dec. 20, 1914:

Taking into account the military operations up to this date, it is easy to conclude that the two central monarchies are holding the advantage of the Allies. Germany has demonstrated to the world her enormous strength, while Austria-Hungary has shown herself to be really a great power. Austria-Hungary must be proud of her army and of the brilliant successes it has won against the colossal Russian military organization.

So far as the neutral States are concerned, Gen. Savoff said:

Bulgaria will keep neutral as long as she can. The responsible factors of the country will face every influence, and will act according to the best interests of the fatherland. We must insist on the correction of the mistakes made by the Treaty of Bucharest. We are resolved, in case this should prove necessary, to take back by force of arms the territories that belong to us and that have been snatched from us. The Bulgarian Army is ready and will do its duty up to the end when the interests of the country demand it.

OPPOSITION PARTY'S STATEMENT.

Following is an editorial article published Oct. 15, (28,) 1914, in the Mir, the organ of the Nationalists, and signed by A. Bouroff, ex-Minister and ex-Vice President of the Bulgarian Parliament, or Sobranje.

The Government knows that the Bulgarian people will never forgive it, should the Ministry let pass the present historical opportunity without securing important advantages for Bulgaria.

These advantages the Government is endeavoring to obtain by keeping a pro-Austro-German neutrality. In order not to disclose this policy, the Government avoids a discussion with Austria and Germany. In order to render service to Austria the Government is courting Turkey, provoking Russia through its action and its press, avoids the constitution of a council of State demanded by the opposition, and objects to the formation of a Ministry in which all the political parties were to be represented. Perhaps the Government would go even further, but it is prevented from doing so, on one hand by Rumania, who maintained a puzzling position, and the probable surprises that her "friendly" Turkey has in store, and on the other by the explicit and general unwillingness of the Bulgarian people to jeopardize its existence through adventurous actions that are so contrary to its national character and sentiments. The result of these contradictory inclinations and influences is shown in our present political weakness, which I am afraid will be fruitless in the end.

What is to be expected from this policy? In case of victory of the Triple Entente, Bulgaria can hope for nothing good. If the Dual Alliance is victorious we shall have certain compensations that to my deep conviction will be far from satisfying our national aspirations. The Austro-German alliance, first of all, will think of itself; that is to say, to realize the greatest ideals of pan-Germanism, the debouching of Austria in the Aegean Sea through Saloniki, which necessarily comprises the occupation by Austria of all Macedonia west of the Vardar. In the second place, Turkey will have to be compensated and strengthened, as in the future her army will be a more obedient organ in the hands of German diplomacy and more amenable than Slav Bulgaria, whose troops, in the opinion of the most prominent German papers, cannot fight the Russians, while Turkey at any time is ready to serve Germany. But Turkey can be compensated in Europe only at the expense of Bulgarian Thrace. To Bulgaria will be given, at most, Istip, Kotchana, Radovich, Serrés Drama, and Cavalla to make good the losses in Thrace.

To obtain such a meagre result, the Government of Bulgaria maintains a policy contrary to popular sentiment and to the racial bonds of the people, and a policy contrary to the further interests of Bulgaria, which are incompatible with the building up of a strong Turkey in the Balkans, a Turkey that would be the bulwark of Germany. The most essential part of it is that this policy is based on a most improbable hypothesis, that is to say, the final triumph of the Austro-German arms. If the Bulgarian Government had left prejudices to one side and looked clearly at the events, they would not have been slow to understand that from the moment England stepped into the war and Italy abandoned her allies, the Austro-German alliance politically lost the game. Each passing day diminishes more and more the hopes of success of the Dual Alliance, and permits England and Russia to expand their inexhaustible forces. It is not difficult to foresee from now the terms of peace that England and Russia will impose. Any policy which expects to profit from the defeat of these two powers is doomed to failure, and because such is the policy of the Bulgarian Government, we think that it is against the interests of the country.

This policy, among its other disadvantages, opens forever a gap between little Bulgaria and great Russia, which power, even if defeated, will never cease to play an active part in the Balkans. Against this policy, which is risking much to obtain little, we propose the policy of coming to an agreement with the Triple Entente, on the basis of a Bulgarian neutrality favorable to it, which surely and without sacrifices is expected to bring to us greatest results. The only thing that the powers of the Triple Entente are demanding from us is to open negotiations with them. This does not abolish our neutrality, because other States, too, such as Italy, Rumania, Greece, and Turkey, are negotiating at the present time.

BALKAN ALLIANCE OPPOSED.

An editorial article which appeared in the Bulgarian paper Volja of the Stamboulovist Party, on Dec. 20, 1914, appears below.

The question has been raised whether in reality negotiations are being conducted between the Balkan States, that is to say, Bulgaria and Servia, Greece and Bulgaria, Bulgaria and Rumania. How much of this is true?

Such negotiations are not being conducted, neither do we believe that it is possible for them to exist, because we do not know what our neighbors demand from us. The only true part of this story is that the powers of the Triple Entente are endeavoring to drag into the war Greece, Bulgaria, and Rumania, a thing that would be not only profitable to them, but even necessary for these same powers of the Triple Entente.

And as long as Bulgaria is not any longer inhabited by imbeciles, who will undertake once more a war for the promotion of the glory and the interests of those who by every means endeavored to ruin us, these powers are thinking today, being moved by some sentiment of humanity, that certain concessions must be made to Bulgaria, but on condition of military support.

And so far as concerns Servia, who only a few days ago was on the brink of the precipice, and who, in a little while from now, will find herself in a worse position, it is apparent that, without the assistance of Bulgaria, her ruin will be certain. This, however, does not prevent Servia as well as the Triple Entente from insisting on giving us as little as possible, and then only after the Serbs have taken Bosnia and Herzegovina.

Rumania and Greece desire an understanding for the sake of their tranquillity. And it was said that Rumania is giving Dobrudja, but Greece does not want even to hear of the cession of Cavalla Drama and Serrés, but, on the contrary, demands, in case Bulgaria gets Servian Macedonia, to obtain for her (Greece's) account Doïrani, Ghevgeli, and Monastir. Greece and Rumania agree on one point—themselves to stay out of the war, while inducing Bulgaria to fight.

But Bulgaria insists on getting compensation, not by war but by her neutrality. The aspirations therefore of the interested States are totally different, and, under such circumstances, no understanding is possible. The object of the Triple Entente is clear. But this is no concern of ours, nor of any of the other Balkan States, with the exception of Servia.

Therefore, to speak plainly, the understanding will be possible only when interests are taken into account. And on this basis some means to an understanding with our neighbors will be found, whether they want it or not.

THE TURK IN EGYPT'S EYES.

[Special Cable to THE NEW YORK TIMES.]

CAIRO, Jan. 31, (Dispatch to The London Daily News.)—In order to understand the bearing of the latest news upon Moslem opinion, particularly in Cairo and Alexandria, it must be borne in mind that Turkey still enjoys considerable military prestige here. Tens of thousands of Egyptians continue to regard her one of the great powers. They never believed the news of her defeat in the Balkans and the reoccupation of Adrianople confirmed them in their skepticism. At the same time, a secret German propaganda for some years before the war did much to spread abroad the doctrine of German invincibility. It is not to be wondered at, therefore, that a section of the population holds entirely erroneous views as to the present balance of power and requires unmistakable evidence of Turkish defeat to open their eyes.

Greece's Watchful Waiting
Grecian Neutrality Defined

[From the Athenae, Athens, July 23, (Aug. 3,) 1914.]

YESTERDAY at 10 A.M. the Council of Ministers met at the Premier's house and took cognizance of a number of dispatches from the Hellenic representatives of the Governments of the great powers relating to the European war which has just begun. At 11 A.M. the Ministers went in a body to the palace, where, under the Presidency of the King, a council was held which discussed the position of Greece in the European conflict. His Majesty, having listened to the Premier, who communicated all the latest news regarding the situation, agreed on all points as to the attitude of Greece in the Austro-Servian conflict, which attitude would be one of absolute neutrality as long as Bulgaria and Turkey remained neutral.

During this council the Chief of Staff of the army, Gen. v. Dousmanis, was sent for, and he gave the Ministers some information of a military character regarding the position of Greece. Gen. Dousmanis assured them that the army was in excellent condition and that all preliminary preparations for a mobilization were already taken.

FRENCH, GREEKS, AND GERMANS.

[Editorial comment of the Athenae of Aug. 9 (Sept. 21)]:

... In Greece there does not exist a discrimination between those who love France and those who do not, because as a rule the entire nation worships France. The Hellenic world, from the most uneducated citizen to the one who represents all the development of intellect, worships France.

It was always with admiration that the discerning Hellenic intellect looked upon the French Nation, which is the leader in every progress. French letters, French art, and French industry have found in Greece sincere admirers and enthusiastic heralds. The French heroism, the devotion that every Frenchman feels for the ideals of the fatherland, the superiority of the French woman, whom certain malevolent writers have so misrepresented to the world; the virtue of the French housewife, the French mother, and the French patriot, have always been splendid examples to those who are apt to think on the world's progress. The birthplace of the forerunners of the modern social and civic spirit and the mother of the most genuine philhellenism, the France of Rabelais, Molière and Voltaire and Béranger and Hugo has always been an object of respectful sympathy for those in Greece who are admirers of the beautiful, the liberal, and the ideal.

Every one of us knows that, if France has not been able to help materialize the Greek's rightful aspirations, this is not due to lack of good intentions on her part, but rather to the French compliance with the interests of the Slav; and we know that France had to cultivate those interests by her own wealth, and contrary to her democratic principles, only in order to have an alliance against her neighboring enemy, against whom she meditated revenge for a defeat and the vindication of her subjugated children.

For the German people, this people of progress and civilization, which has never aspired to a world hegemony by the subjugation of other peoples, outside of the needs of their frontiers, Greece feels the same admiration and sympathy. And when such French patriots as Jules Huret and Georges Bourdon, in voluminous works, have cited the German progress and German social civilization as an example to their own country, it would be almost a reversal of logic if we outsiders were to deny these things, at the sight of two friends who have come to blows.

If there is anything that grieves the Greek soul, which has always been used to appreciate virtue disinterestedly, it is the fratricidal woe of two nations who ought to be, hand in hand, forerunners and co-workers in the great enterprises of science and civilization!

PRIME MINISTRY'S ATTITUDE.

Premier Venizelos set forth the Government's neutral policy in his speech to Parliament on Sept. 15, (28,) 1914. A translation appears below.

After speaking of the Greco-Turkish relations and the efforts being made at the time for the settlement of the outstanding questions of the refugees and the Aegean Islands, Mr. Venizelos said:

Unfortunately the labors of the new session are beginning amid the clangor of the great European war. The Government has declared that during this war Greece is to remain neutral, but at the same time it did not conceal the fact that it has obligations toward one of the belligerents, Servia, and that said obligation it was resolved to fulfill faithfully should the *casus foederis* arise.

Greece, however, wishes nothing more than that such an occasion should not arise, as it desires that the conflagration which is gradually enveloping

Europe should not spread over the Balkans, whose peoples, after two wars, so much need rest.

So far as it depends upon the initiative of Greece, every one may be assured that the European conflagration will not spread in the Balkan Peninsula. And if its other peoples are inspired by the same thoughts, then we can feel sure that peace will be preserved in the Levant up to the end of the war.

But even for the neutrals there are obligations. The position of the neutrals is not so easy as one might think, and the Government has endeavored and is still endeavoring to fulfill as perfectly as possible the various obligations imposed by neutrality. I must acknowledge at this time that my task has been rendered easier by public opinion, which notwithstanding its sympathies, has done nothing to hurt any one of the belligerents. I regret that I cannot say the same as regards the press, because the press, not confining itself to the expression of so many natural sentiments, has often indulged in violent attacks against the belligerents, and especially at the time when, owing to the peculiar psychological condition in which the latter find themselves, every such attack touches them most deeply. And I again entreat you, from this official tribune, to avoid any such attack. I hope my advice will be more willingly complied with at this time.

WHERE GREECE STANDS.

The following statement by Premier Venizelos was published in the Corriere della Sera of Milan on Oct. 29, 1914.

The Greek Government has declared its neutrality and will abide by this policy. Notwithstanding this, she did not deny her treaty obligations to Servia, and is resolved to fulfill all the terms of this treaty should the *casus foederis* arise.

It is understood that Greece does not desire this *casus foederis* to arise.

Our relations with Turkey have been strained for some months. But after the negotiations of Bucharest some agreement was reached regarding the refugees. Those in Europe will learn that the Greeks expelled two hundred thousand persons from Thrace and Asia Minor. One portion of them we have settled in the islands. Besides those there are about fifty thousand Turkish refugees—though not persecuted—in Macedonia. A mixed committee was to arrange the exchange of these refugees at the beginning of the war. As to the question of the ownership of the Aegean islands, the Hellenic Government considers the question settled from an international standpoint, not only by the treaties of London and Athens, but also by the unanimous decision of all the European powers.

The Government declared that it was ready to satisfy Turkey regarding this question, under the *sine qua* condition that the islands would continue to be occupied and administered by Greece in the same way as all the other provinces of the Hellenic Kingdom. After an exchange of views on the subject, it was decided that I should meet the Grand Vizier in Brussels, but the war prevented this.

Afterward, this desire was again expressed, that the negotiations which originally were to take place in Brussels should open elsewhere. To this end both parties sent delegates to Bucharest in order to find some solution of the island question, but again this meeting failed to accomplish anything.

Turkey proposed an adjournment of the negotiations to a more propitious time, alleging that the general conditions in Europe, and her internal troubles, made it impossible for her delegates to continue the discussions on the island question. Unfortunately the plight of the Greek populations in Turkey is becoming worse every day, and large numbers of refugees are coming daily to Greece.

Regarding Bulgaria, I can say nothing, except that she keeps repeating her intention of remaining neutral. At the same time Bulgaria did not mobilize, therefore we have not taken this measure ourselves.

But naturally—and this must be taken in its widest meaning—when the flames of a conflagration are licking one's door one must take all the precautionary measures. Is it not right?

Regarding Epirus, we declared clearly that we have no designs upon Avlona.

OCCUPATION OF EPIRUS.

The subjoined statement by Premier Venizelos appeared in The London Morning Post.

ATHENS, Oct. 27.

In the Chamber of Deputies this evening, in reply to an interpellation, M. Venizelos, the Premier, stated that Greece had reoccupied Northern Epirus solely to restore order and security to those districts already cruelly tried by prolonged bloodshed and anarchy. The Premier emphasized the provisional character of this reoccupation, inasmuch as Greece continued to respect the international agreements regarding Albania.

M. Venizelos was followed by M. Zographos, the late President of the Epirote Provisional Government, and now Deputy for Attica, who, amid profound attention and great enthusiasm, recounted the enormous sacrifices of blood and treasure by the Epirotes for their freedom, and declared that the liberation of Epirus must this time be final. M. Rallis, one of the leaders of the Opposition, declared that Epirus was resolved to remain united with Greece.

I am informed from a diplomatic source that the great powers have received the announcement of the reoccupation in a friendly spirit, and no protests have thus far been received from quarters whence they might have been expected.

RELATIONS WITH BULGARIA.

Following is an editorial article from the semi-official newspaper Patris of Athens of Dec. 12, (25,) 1914.

With Bulgaria not one of the Balkan States can come to any understanding. The neighboring Balkan peoples, at least the Christians, cannot agree with them—not because they are lacking good intentions, but because the Bulgarians in their demands are unreasonable, unjust, insatiable, monstrous, and treacherous; because the Bulgarians always demand the impossible; because they are pursuing profits at the expense of third parties, whom they invite to cede rights obtained by sacrifices and based on the right of war; because, while they can demand compensations at the expense of a non-Christian neighbor—to which no one would object—they turn on their co-religionists, struggling to take away from them what they lawfully and with sacrifices have acquired.

On account of this policy of the Bulgarians, not one of the Christian peoples of the Balkan Peninsula believes in the possibility of an understanding with them. That, also, is Rumania's position. Accordingly it should be unnecessary to deny the news from Sofia announcing the attainment of an alleged Rumano-Bulgarian rapprochement. In order to reach this understanding, the Bulgarians would not confine themselves to the rules of present Rumano-Bulgarian practice, which in itself is a question of secondary importance.

The Bulgarians turn eager eyes to the whole of Dobrondja, which might perhaps be the dowry of the royal Rumano-Bulgarian match so impudently heralded in Sofia, although the whole thing was a monstrous lie, without any appearance of respect for the family affairs of the royal throne of Rumania.

But, as in our own case, neither the Servians can cede even an acre of land to Bulgaria nor Rumania give back Dobrudja, because all of these territories belong to their present owners by right of war. For the same reason the Serbo-Bulgarian relations failed a month ago; likewise no ground was found for an understanding between Bulgaria and Greece; and for the same reason the negotiations between Rumania and Bulgaria are failing today.

The Bulgarians have turned from one to another of the peoples of the Balkans in order to cheat them. But this attempt, made once too often, at length has failed. But will this final failure bring to reason the hotheads of Sofia? After the cruel disappointment they received at the hands of Rumania, the Bulgarian politicians must understand that whatever is won by war by war only is given back. No one is so stupid as to give them willingly his dominions.

Do they wish to take them? Let them come. Let them declare war. Because so long as they are not doing this, and so long as they persist in their present methods, they are offering the spectacle of a childish if not a demented people.

GRECO-RUMANIAN FRIENDSHIP.

The Rumanian Minister, Mr. Filidor, presented his new credentials to King Constantine on Dec. 14. His speech appears below.

Your Majesty! I have the honor to deliver to your Majesty the letters with which his Majesty, my august sovereign, has deigned to confirm my quality as Envoy Extraordinary and Minister Plenipotentiary to your Majesty, a mission which I had already the honor of filling under the glorious reign of the great King Carol I., the founder of the Rumanian dynasty.

I happened to be a witness of the most brilliant period of the history of new Greece, during which your Majesty at the head of his Government has succeeded, by his military talents, in bringing into realization the great achievements of ancient Greece, whose majestic relics are serving still as an inimitable example to the whole of mankind.

The military effort of your Majesty has been crowned by the Treaty of Bucharest, which was a common pacifying work of Greece and Rumania, and which was so instrumental in strengthening the bonds of friendship and interests which so happily unite the two peoples.

Deeply impressed by the conviction that my mission consists in working for this latter end, I dare pray your Majesty to grant me his august favor, as in the past, and I assure you that I will employ all my energy for the fulfillment of this effort, so necessary for the future fortunes of both countries.

Where Rumania Stands in the Crisis Declaration of Neutrality

BUCHAREST, Aug. 5, 1914.

THE Council of the Crown has decided on the neutrality of Rumania—Agence Roumaine.

THE SITUATION IN RUMANIA.

[From the Paris Temps of Aug. 23, 1914.]

From an occasional correspondent we receive the following letter:

The departure of the mobilized French soldiers who were in Bucharest has been the occasion for sympathetic manifestations toward France.

Among the population and in the streets there was not a single voice which was not heartily and enthusiastically for the Triple Entente in general and France in particular.

Certain personages, such as the General Pilot who in 1870 fought on the side of France, and certain newspaper editors who, yielding to national aspirations, have carried on since the first day of the war a violent campaign against Austria, are enthusiastically cheered by the public in the cafés and by the majority of the army officers who assisted in uniform at these scenes.

More than that, there were imposing manifestations in the streets; other meetings, still more effective, were held in secret, at which Generals and superior officers assisted. But notwithstanding this public sentiment the police are on the lookout; the orders they have received are particularly severe, as entire regiments are kept in readiness in the public parks and Government buildings. All those functionaries who are suspected of being openly hostile to Austria are closely followed and watched.

What is the reason of this? One may put the question to himself, as really this sentiment of the nations corresponds too well with a secular and inevitable policy. Despite all contrary reasoning, one fact remains, and this is summed up in Transylvania and Bukowina and the five million Rumanians who are under Austro-Hungarian rule. There is for the Rumanians of the kingdom the unforgettable series of persecutions of every kind to which their brethren on the other side of the mountains are subjected—persecutions dating from yesterday and which are continued today. Only the day before the Austrian mobilization fifty students from the Rumanian Kingdom who happened to be in Brassow (Hungary) on an excursion were arrested and brought before the police authorities, and actually thrown into prison, because they dared display badges with Rumanian colors in their buttonholes.

"If I were to march into Moldavia," a Rumanian was telling me, "against the enemies of Austria, I would have to begin by sabring all the Moldavian peasants, who are crying, 'Down with Austria!' Of course, I never could do this!"

Under such conditions, if the waverings of the Government were to be explained, the task would be a hard one. In our opinion, they may be ascribed to different causes, the more important factor being the opinion of the King himself; but this alone would not suffice.

The King (Carol) is first of all bound to Emperor Francis Joseph by an old friendship. King Carol has never admitted that the diminution of his kingdom after Plevna was a right thing, and the toasts in Constanza (during the Czar's visit to Rumania early in the Summer of 1914) have demonstrated, for those who could read between the lines, in both the politeness of the Czar and the reserved tone of King Carol, that this sentiment had not yet disappeared.

In the face of this disposition, so firmly expressed, the Ministers and the party leaders of Rumania felt rather uncomfortable. It must be borne in mind that a parliamentary régime, properly speaking, does not exist; the Ministries do not fall by vote of the chambers of Parliament. When the King estimates that a Ministry has been too long in power, when he hears distinctly the murmur of the Opposition, then he calls a new President of the Council, who has Parliament prorogued and a new one formed—this is the exact procedure—according to his liking. By reason of this process, and also by reason of a special attraction which the Court exercises over a small, refined, and elegant society, the counsels of the King are inspired by the advices of his counselors.

But there are also other reasons that plead for this uncertain attitude, and by which it is attempted to justify a policy of indifference.

The successes of last year—of which the Rumanians have not understood the causes, because they never tried to understand them—have troubled them in a certain way.

Their statesmen persist perhaps a little too much in playing Machiavelli, and in exalting abstention to a system. Their fondest desire at the present moment is not, we are persuaded, to march on Austria, but, on the contrary, not to march at all, and not to intervene in the war up to the day of the final liquidation.

What is this policy worth? The chances are that it may not always be good, particularly in the present state of things. Rumania is still a small country by reason of its area. In addition to this, her neighbors, on which she was wont to exercise a moderating influence, are bound to change in density of population. And it is very likely that Rumania, on the next day after the war, might find herself suddenly surrounded by homogeneous peoples, who in the meantime would become distinctly more important than she is, and that these people might have against her certain slight grievances which they would make her feel. Moreover, even if Austria by chance is victorious, and even if the Government at Bucharest helped her, is it not clear that her (Rumania's) Hungarian neighbor, becoming stronger, would make her (Rumania) suffer the same as she made the Servians suffer when they were feeble?

Rumania may well protest her friendship, but this will not prevent her, if only by her presence, from being a danger to the tranquillity of the Hungarian subjects in Transylvania. And then who is going to defend her?

Here is what the good sense of the people says, and it is this common sense which will triumph in the end over all vacillation, and will, in spite of everything, assert its way of seeing things.

THE ATTITUDE OF RUMANIA.

[From the Paris Temps of Sept. 25, 1914.]

Mr. Diamandy, Rumanian Minister at Petrograd and an ardent advocate of Rumanian intervention, has returned to the Russian capital after a voyage to Bucharest, where he went in order to explain his views to his Government.

The return of Mr. Diamandy to Petrograd is regarded as a favorable omen, as this diplomat had expressed previous to his departure that he would not come back to his post if he were not successful in placing Rumania on the side of the Triple Entente.

On the other hand, l'Agence de Balkans is in receipt of the following dispatch from Bucharest, Sept. 19, 1914:

"The semi-official papers of the Rumanian Government have published the following statement with regard to the Treaty of Bucharest: The viewpoint of Rumania on the subject of the Treaty of Bucharest, and of its connection with the European war, has been discussed and established in a council of the Crown, held on the 21st of July, (Aug. 3, N.S.) In the Treaty of Bucharest the Rumanian interest was not bound to fixed frontier lines, except so long as these assured an equilibrium necessary to Rumania. Rumania was not obliged to protect this equilibrium in its actual form any longer than in her mind this could be possibly maintained.

"If the European war, in its future consequences, should bring about certain modifications in the actual frontiers of one or the other of the Balkan States, the interest of Rumania requires that the Balkan equilibrium be established in accordance with the changes made to correspond with the purpose of maintaining the real equilibrium in its new form, no matter what the frontier lines will be in their final re-establishment. In connection with the attitude of Rumania in the presence of the European war no new decision has been taken. All the political parties are subjecting their attitude to the action of the Government. Mr. von Busch, the new Minister of Germany, has arrived and was received yesterday in confidence by King Charles."

DEATH OF KING CHARLES.

[From The London Times, Oct. 12, 1914.]

King Charles of Rumania died of heart failure early on Saturday morning at the Castle of Pelesh, Sinäia.

Yesterday Parliament was convoked, and the new King took the oath of allegiance. Subsequently the Government issued a proclamation stating that the new King would follow in the footsteps of his predecessor and realize the ideals of the Rumanian race.

Both in itself and as an episode of the present European conflagration, the death of the King of Rumania is an event of singular importance. The late King was in many respects the maker of his adopted country. When, in March, 1866, he accepted the crown the condition of the Danubian principalities, Moldavia and Wallachia, was little better than that of a misgoverned Turkish province. They still owned Ottoman suzerainty, their army was non-existent, their financial resources were precarious, the condition of their people was wretched, their means of communication were primitive, and their public affairs were in a condition bordering on anarchy. With the support of the French Emperor, to whom he was distantly related, Prince Charles of Hohenzollern-Sigmaringen faced one of the most difficult tasks ever allotted to an inexperienced ruler, and carried it to triumphal completion.

He created an army, introduced railways, won independence for his realm and for himself. He evolved order out of chaos, secured military renown at Plevna as commander of the joint Russo-Rumanian forces in the Russo-Turkish war, established national finance on a sound basis, built up a considerable export trade, extended the frontiers of the principality and raised it to the rank of a kingdom, and watched with untiring vigilance over every aspect of national development. Not only as the first recognized and independent sovereign of modern Rumania, but as her creator, King Charles will ever hold a foremost place in Rumanian history.

In this great work the late ruler derived advantage, not only from his eminent personal qualities, but from his foreign origin. As a German Prince, powerfully connected, he stood outside and above Rumanian party factions, and succeeded gradually in imposing his will on them all. Born on April 20, 1839, at Sigmaringen, near the source of the Danube, he was barely 27 when he accepted the call to rule an unknown country with which his only connection was that, like the estates of his family, it, too, was watered by the Danube. Of middle height, well built, pronounced features, and clear, gray eyes, his personality expressed quiet energy. His statecraft he learned by experience and from the excellent counsel of his father, Prince Charles Anthony of Hohenzollern, head of the senior and Roman Catholic branch of the Hohenzollerns. Only once did he falter. In March, 1871, when the French sympathizers of his subjects exposed him as a German Prince and a Hohenzollern to great unpopularity, while the bankruptcy of the Jewish speculator to whom his railway schemes had been intrusted threw discredit upon his ideas of economic development, he summoned the members of the Provisional Government from whom he had accepted the crown and announced to them his decision to abdicate. Fortunately for Rumania, they succeeded in dissuading him from his purpose. The famous Conservative statesman, Lascar Catargi, formed a Ministry which held office for five years and enabled the ruler to turn the most dangerous corner of his reign. Thenceforward the path was comparatively clear, though by no means easy. It led to Rumanian participation in the Russo-Turkish war, to the conquest of national independence, and eventually, on May 22, 1881, to his coronation as King of Rumania, with a crown made of steel from a Turkish gun captured by Rumanian troops at Plevna.

Yet the Rumanian triumph was not unalloyed. Russia injudiciously and ungratefully insisted on depriving Rumania of the portion of Rumanian Bessarabia of which Russia had been deprived after the Crimean war, and allotted the Dobrudja, a swampy region south of the Danube, to the principality as compensation. The indignation in Rumania was indescribable and has never entirely subsided. The Senate in the Chamber declared the resolve of the country to defend its integrity by force. The Czar threatened to disarm the Rumanian Army—a threat which drew from Prince Charles the proud reply: "The Rumanian Army, which fought so gallantly before Plevna under the eyes of the Czar, may be annihilated, but will never be disarmed." But he nevertheless recognized the futility of resistance to the Russian demand, and exerted himself to calm the national excitement. In later years the breach was partially if not wholly healed.

Of the more material achievements of his reign there is little space to speak. The best record of his life is to be found in the present condition of the country—*si monumentum requiris circumspice*. His furtherance of the petroleum industry, of the export of grain, timber and other agricultural produce, the building of the great bridge over the Danube at Tchernavoda, and the extensive harbor at Constanza, the network of railways, the immense system of fortifications defending the capital, and the line Fokshani-Galatz—all these and much more are mainly his work.

Little is yet known of the action of King Charles in the last crisis of his life. It is a strange coincidence that just as the Franco-German war of 1870-71 brought him into conflict with the Francophil tendencies of his subjects and led to his offer of abdication, so the present war should again have engendered rumors of his abdication on account of his alleged antagonism to the national desire for the acquisition of Transylvania and the Southern Bukovina, which are peopled by more than 3,000,000 Hungarian and Austrian Rumanes. The Rumanian people felt that the hour for the liberation of their kindred had struck. Russia is understood to have invited Rumania to occupy the desired territory. But King Charles, who brought and kept Rumania within the orbit of the Triple Alliance, was, as a Hohenzollern and a German Prince, averse to hostile action against the German Emperor and the Emperor Francis Joseph. It is, moreover, stated that he was bound by his word of honor never to take the field against a Hohenzollern cause.

The late King Charles married, in November, 1869, Princess Elizabeth of Wied, the gifted "Carmen Sylva," whose brilliant literary and artistic talents have gained her a worldwide reputation. The only child of the marriage, the infant Princess Marie, died in 1874—a bereavement that ever left a note of sadness in the lives of her parents.

THE NEW KING.

King Ferdinand, who now succeeds his uncle on the throne of Rumania, was born in August, 1865, and, like his predecessor, is a Hohenzollern and a Roman Catholic.

Among his near relatives are the King of the Belgians and his namesake, Tsar Ferdinand of the Bulgarians, who are both first cousins, and his niece, Queen Augustina Victoria, the consort of Dom Manoel. Through his mother, the Princess Antonia, who was born an Infanta of Portugal, King Ferdinand is kin with all the house of Saxe-Coburg and Gotha, to which his consort, the new Queen Mary, belongs as daughter of the late Duke of Edinburgh.

Her Majesty is thus first cousin to King George and to the Czar, as also to Princess Nicholas of Greece. Her three sisters are married respectively to the Grand Duke Cyril of Russia, Prince Ernest, the eldest son of the mediatized Prince of Hohenlohe-Langenburg, and to the Infante Alfonso d'Orléans of Spain.

Their Majesties have six children, of whom the Crown Prince Carol, who celebrates his 21st birthday this week, and the Princess Elizabeth, born in 1894, are of marriageable age. The youngest, Prince Mircea, who bears a historic Rumanian name closely connected with Silistria, was born during the Balkan war at the beginning of 1913. King Ferdinand's family is a remarkable example of religious differences—his Majesty is a Roman Catholic, the Queen is a Lutheran, and their children are members of the Orthodox Church of Rumania.

The Rumanian Minister has received a copy of a proclamation published in The Official Gazette stating that the new King will follow in the footsteps of the late monarch and will accomplish the ideals of the Rumanian race.

IN RUMANIA'S PARLIAMENT.

[From The Messaggero of Rome.]

BUCHAREST, Dec. 17.

The intention of the Government to avoid in Parliament any discussion of the political action of the Ministry was reaffirmed yesterday by Premier Braliano, who, in a brief declaration in the Chamber, prayed the parties to waive any discussion whatever upon the answer of Parliament to the speech from the throne, and to have confidence in those governing the country.

The independent Deputies, however, have shown themselves determined to provoke a discussion. Among the others, Mr. Couza, a Nationalist, demanded permission to express his personal admiration for the valor of the Servians, and insisted on ample measures being taken for preventing the exportation of articles of which in due time there will be an absolute deficiency in the country.

Constantin Mille, an independent, and proprietor of the newspaper Adeverul, delivered a long speech in which he declared himself dissatisfied with the policy of the Government, which ought to have taken a decisive stand at the beginning of the conflict. Instead of doing this, the Government has put us in the position of not knowing to which side we must turn, as long as our only intention is to turn first to this side and then to that, without having the necessary guarantees.

After paying high tribute to the valor of the Servian Army and the heroism of Belgium, the speaker demonstrated that Rumania, since the beginning of the conflict, ought to enter the war on the side of the Triple Entente.

He afterward protested against certain facts that the expressed neutrality of the country cannot tolerate; such as the passage through Rumanian territory of guns and ammunition from Germany for Turkey; the taking over by Germany of certain medical supplies originally intended for the Rumanian Army, and exchanging the same for grain.

He then assailed the propaganda carried out by German emissaries through certain news agencies, and the corruption of certain papers of the Rumanian press.

And during all this time, concluded Mr. Mille, our brethren in Transylvania are being exterminated by war while expecting our intervention. The Government must break its silence, which is becoming more and more suspicious, and frankly affirm its intention.

RUMANIA'S POLICY.

[From The London Daily Telegraph of Dec. 29, 1914.]

BUCHAREST, Dec. 28.

Today, in the debate on the address in reply to the message from the throne, the Prime Minister repeated the declaration made in the Chamber asking the majority to waive discussion and the Opposition to leave the Government full liberty of action to fulfill its great duty.

The Conservative Party, by the mouth of its chief, expressed its willingness to do this. M. Disesco, on behalf of the Conservative Democrats, repeated the declaration made by M. Take Jonesco, in the Chamber, according to which Rumania ought to abandon her neutral position and make an immediate alliance with the Triple Entente.

M. Disesco added that the Rumano-Austro-German alliance ceased to exist from the day when the Crown Council was held at Sinäia; that council settled the matter of Rumania's neutrality. The speaker laid stress on the ingratitude of Austria toward Rumania in 1913, and alluded to the statements made recently by M. Take Jonesco concerning the threat of Austria against Rumania in 1913 should that country attack Bulgaria.

He concluded by observing that the two sections of the Opposition, Conservative and Conservative-Democrat, had declared for abandonment of neutrality and an alliance with the Triple Entente, and expressed the hope that presently this policy will be adopted officially. The address was afterward agreed to unanimously.

A large number of Senators telegraphed to the President of the Italo-Rumanian League at Rome expressing their happiness at witnessing the realization of the league's initiative, and requesting the President to consider them members of the Rumanian section of the league, which, being convinced of the profound significance and great usefulness of closer relations between the two countries, they joined with enthusiasm.

"LEAGUE OF UNITY."

BUCHAREST, Dec. 27.

At a special session today the League for the National Unity of All Rumanians acclaimed with grand enthusiasm the new committee, which has as President the Rev. Father Lucaci, the great propagandist of and martyr for the Rumanian cause in Transylvania and a member of the Rumanian National Committee of Hungary. There were also elected MM. Take Jonesco, Nicolas Filipescu, and Delavrance Gradischteano, all former Ministers. The committee is charged with the hastening of action by Rumania for the conquest of the Rumanian provinces of Austria-Hungary.

RUMANIAN STATISTICS.

[From Le Messager d'Athenes, Nov. 28, 1914.]

According to statistics published in a Rumanian paper, when the foreign press speaks of Rumanian aspirations it sums up the whole question in the word Transylvania.

It is not unnecessary perhaps to remark that this word has in this case a significance rather political and ethnological than purely geographical. This word comprises all the Austro-Hungarian territories occupied by Rumanians, with the understanding that Transylvania is the most important as regards area and Rumanian popularity.

Actually the Rumanian claims on the Austro-Hungarian territories are the following:

Transylvania—57,250 square kilometers, 2,850,000 inhabitants, of whom 1,750,000 are Rumanians.

Banat—28,510 square kilometers area, and 1,730,000 inhabitants, of whom 700,000 are Rumanians.

Chrishana—Area, 41,338 square kilometers, and 2,920,000 inhabitants, of whom 1,100,000 are Rumanians.

Mamoaresh—Area, 9,720 square kilometers, and 360,000 inhabitants, of whom 120,000 are Rumanians.

Bukowina—Area, 10,471 square kilometers, and 900,000 inhabitants, of whom 300,000 are Rumanians.

Total area, 147,280 square kilometers, and 8,760,000 inhabitants, of whom 3,970,000 are Rumanians.

In consequence, of 8,760,000 inhabitants of trans-Carpathian Rumania, nearly 4,000,000 are Rumanians, 2,200,000 Hungarians, 1,000,000 Serbo-Croatians, 730,000 Germans, and so on.

RUMANIA'S CLAIMS.

[From The London Times, Nov. 25, 1914.]

SOFIA, Nov. 23.

The efforts made by Germany and Austria-Hungary to win over Rumania, or at least to induce her to refrain from prosecuting her claims to Transylvania, are being pursued with indefatigable energy and perseverance. The same methods are being employed in Bucharest as here, but on an even larger scale. The issues involved seem to be more fully realized by the Central European powers than by their opponents, and no pains are being spared to draw Rumania and Bulgaria within the orbit of their influence.

The campaign in Bucharest was at first attended by a certain measure of success, owing to the attitude of M. Bratiano, the Premier; of M. Carp, a former Prime Minister, and of M. Marghiloman, the present leader of the Conservative Opposition. But many influential Liberals have already associated themselves with the programme of the action advocated by M. Take Jonesco, the chief of the Conservative-Democratic Party, and of M. Filipescu, a former Conservative Minister, whose advocacy of a forward policy threatens to cause a split in the Conservative camp. The great bulk of the political world desires to profit by the European crisis to secure Transylvania, the only difference of opinion being with regard to the advisability of immediate action. The consultative committee of the Conservative Party has passed a resolution demanding the abandonment of neutrality.

The concessions offered by Count Tisza, the Hungarian Premier, in the hope of averting the coming storm, make no impression on the Rumanians either within or without the monarchy. He promises to allow the teaching of Rumanian in the schools, the use of the language in the public services, and increased Rumanian representation in the Hungarian Parliament. But the time for concessions has gone by. The Austrian advance into Servia threatens to cut off Rumania from Southern and Western Europe and to prevent the arrival from the United States of the large supplies of stores and medicaments ordered there.

It is evident that neither Rumania nor Bulgaria can long maintain their present attitudes. It remains for the powers of the Entente to devise a means for securing the co-operation of both States.

Servia recently inquired in Bucharest whether Rumania would oppose territorial concessions to a neighboring State, evidently indicating Bulgaria. Rumania replied that she would be happy to see all the quarrels of her neighbors arranged. The Government at Nish, appreciating the necessities of the situation, is now disposed toward a policy of concession. Servia's only hope of maintaining an independent existence lies in the success of the Entente powers. She is, therefore, bound to consent to any course they may deem necessary at the present juncture.

UTTERANCES OF STATESMEN.

The New York Daily Greek Atlantis, in its issue of Nov. 21, 1914, reports as follows the statement of three Rumanian leaders to a Greek paper in Constantinople. The Rumanian Foreign Minister, Mr. Purumbaru, said:

Rumania is inspired by a sincere desire not to displease either of the two European Georges. Having adopted a policy of neutrality, she will maintain it to the end. Russia has expressed her satisfaction with the present attitude of Rumania, while Austria, since the beginning of the war, has avoided taking any oppressive measures against the Rumanians of Transylvania. As regards Italy, the Rumanian people harbor the friendliest intentions toward her. The Italo-Rumanian relations are most cordial. In Rumania the policy of Italy is followed with much attention. The relations of Rumania toward the other Balkan States, and especially toward Servia and Greece, are good. It is true that the Bulgarian intentions are not very clear. It appears, however, that the desire for peace is strong in Sofia, where it is felt that the interest of Bulgaria lies in adapting rather the country to the present situation than in throwing it into a struggle whose results would be unknown beforehand.

As for Servia, Rumania has not intervened on her behalf in this war, as it had not its origin in the Treaty of Bucharest.

In accordance with the common understanding of all the Balkan States, Rumania is always in favor of a union of them all, but opposes any combination between two or more Balkan States to the detriment of another.

M. Jonesco, leader of the Opposition, spoke on the Balkan situation as follows:

I always believed and still believe that the Balkan States cannot secure their future otherwise than by a close understanding among themselves, whether this understanding shall or shall not take the form of a federation. No one of the Balkan States is strong enough to resist the pressure from one or another of the European powers.

For this reason I am deeply grieved to see in the Balkan coalition of 1912 Rumania not invited. If Rumania had taken part in the first one, we should not have had the second. I did all that was in my power and succeeded in preventing the war between Rumania and the Balkan League in the Winter of 1912-1913.

I risked my popularity, and I do not feel sorry for it. I employed all my efforts to prevent the second Balkan war, which, as is well known, was profitable to us. I repeatedly told the Bulgarians that they ought not to enter it because in that case we would enter it too. But I was not successful in my efforts.

During the second Balkan war I did all in my power to end it as quickly as possible. At the conference of Bucharest I made efforts, as Mr. Pashich and Mr. Venizelos know very well, to secure for beaten Bulgaria the best terms. My object was to obtain a new coalition of all the Balkan States, including Rumania. Had I succeeded in this the situation would be much better. No reasonable man will deny that the Balkan States are neutralizing each other at the present time, which in itself makes the whole situation all the more miserable.

In October, 1913, when I succeeded in facilitating the conclusion of peace between Greece and Turkey, I was pursuing the same object of the Balkan coalition. On my return from Athens I endeavored, though without success, to put the Greco-Turkish relations on a basis of friendship, being convinced that the well understood interest of both countries lies not only in friendly relations, but even in an alliance between them.

The dissensions that exist between the Balkan States can be settled in a friendly way without war. The best moment for this would be after the general war, when the map of Europe will be remade. The Balkan country which would start war against another Balkan country would commit, not only a crime against her own future, but an act of folly as well.

The destiny and the future of the Balkan States, and of all the small European peoples as well, will not be regulated by fratricidal wars, but, with this great European struggle, the real object of which is to settle the question whether Europe shall enter an era of justice, and therefore happiness for the small peoples, or whether we will face a period of oppression more or less gilt edged. And as I always believed that wisdom and truth will triumph in the end, I want to believe, too, that, in spite of the pessimistic news reaching me from the different sides of the Balkan countries, there will be no war among them in order to justify those who do not believe in the vitality of the small peoples.

RUMANIANS IN HUNGARY.

N. Filipescu, ex-Minister of War, said:

The position of the Rumanians in Hungary is not so bad after all. Since the beginning of the general war the Rumanians of Hungary gave proofs of their faith and devotion to Hungary.

We hoped to see this country appreciating the fact. Our belief is strengthened every day. I am convinced that if from this war Hungary should emerge victorious she would show less good-will toward the Rumanians of Transylvania. It is the first time that I have expressed in this way my opinion as a seeming threat. I hoped that the Hungarians would in the end take to the right path. But I see that we have nothing to hope from that side, and I only regret our former amicable relations with Germany.

Two Balkan States—Servia and Greece—are nearer to us on account of the recent past. But in saying this I do not mean that our relations in the future will be less friendly. With the other States, and especially Bulgaria, our relations might become better. This is our sincerest desire. As for Turkey, we never ceased to be on good terms with her, and I hope the same will hold good in the future.

Exit Albania?
Departure of Prince William of Wied—
After the
Revolution of July, 1914.

[From Il Corriere della Sera of Milan, Italy, of Sept. 3, 1914.]

DURAZZO, Sept. 3.

AN hour ago the Italian yacht Misurata, flying the Albanian ensign on the foremast and the Italian colors aft, weighed anchor and proceeded to Venice. Aboard the Misurata were Prince William of Wied, Princess Sophie, Tourkhan Pasha, (the Albanian Premier,) Akis Pasha, and other members of the Court.

Princess Sophie, coming aboard the launch which took them to the Misurata, was weeping. Prince William looked calm. The Italian marines and the Rumanian volunteers cheered, and the cruiser Libia saluted the Prince with the regular number of salvos. The square near the seashore was by that time full of refugees.

Prince William bade Durazzo good-bye, but every one is convinced that he will never come back.

Last Monday (Aug. 31) the Ministers of the powers met in the Italian Legation to consider the taking of certain measures, in case of trouble, which was already brewing on account of the non-payment of the apportionments to the men of the garrison.

On the morning of the next day the Minister of Rumania brought to the palace a letter from the insurgents addressed to the representatives of the powers and announcing that the patience of the insurgents was exhausted, and that they were resolved to enter Durazzo by any means. An identical letter was addressed to the inhabitants of the city.

It was then that the Prince decided to abandon Durazzo.

The Ministers, having received the message of the insurgents and having been notified of the intention of the Prince to leave the place, met again in the palace in order to find a way of settlement of the vexing financial problem. At the same time the International Commission of Control decided to call on the insurgent camp at Shiak, (outside of Durazzo,) give them the news of the imminent departure of the Prince, and invite them to the city.

The insurgents replied assuring the commission of their good intentions toward the city and the foreigners. They added that they had not taken any decision regarding the new form of government, because some of their chiefs were at that time in Avlona, and they promised to make their decision known after the departure of the Prince from Durazzo. On the other hand, they left it to be understood that there was already established in Albania a mutual national confidence between all the Musselman Albanians.

On its return to Durazzo the International Commission of Control found itself face to face with another surprise. The gendarmerie had mutinied. The men belonging to this corps were opposing the departure of the Prince before he had paid their wages, and threatened to make use of their weapons.

The commission sent the French delegate to the gendarmerie barracks, and it was with great trouble that the men were dissuaded from their original designs. Yesterday the Prince distributed decorations freely. Today at 7 A.M. he left the palace, and, saluted by the Diplomatic Corps, he repaired to the waterfront.

After the Prince and Princess embarked, the adjoining square was filled with great crowds of people. Malissor and Kotsovessi tribesmen and all those who were yet in Durazzo as protectors of the Prince went to the waterfront in order to embark on an Italian mail steamer bound for San Giovanni di Medua.

These people looked desperate and gave the impression of being in the last degree of poverty. Each one had from two to three pistols, and no one was unarmed. There might have been nearly 2,000 men there, all eager to leave, but this proved impossible, as their chiefs, Issa Boletinotz and Baïram Zouri, had not provided them with the necessary tickets.

At last, with the help of the Almighty, order was re-established, and, after two hours of trouble impossible to describe, these 2,000 refugees embarked on the steamer Citta di Bori.

The Italian marines re-embarked on the cruiser Libia, and the International Commission took charge of the Government.

LAST PROCLAMATION OF PRINCE OF WIED.

Before leaving Durazzo, the Prince of Wied addressed the following proclamation to the Albanian people:

Albanians, when your delegates came to offer me the crown of Albania, I answered with confidence to the appeal of this noble and chivalrous people who were asking me to aid them in the work of their national regeneration. I came to you animated by the most ardent desire to help you in this patriotic task.

You have seen me, from the beginning, devoting all my efforts for the reorganization of the country, and desirous of giving you a good administration and justice for all. But ill-omened events occurred to destroy our common labors. In fact, certain souls, blinded by passion, have misunderstood the scope of our reforms and have not given credit to a Government just born. On the other hand, the war which broke out in Europe has all the more complicated our position.

I therefore thought that, in order not to leave unfinished the work to which I wish to consecrate my forces and my life, I must just for a little while go to the Occident.

But know that, from afar as from near, I will have but one thought—to work for the prosperity of our noble and chivalrous Albanian fatherland. During my absence the International Commission of Control, deriving its powers from Europe, which created our country, will assume the Government.

ESSAD PASHA PRESIDENT.

[From Le Temps, Paris.]

DURAZZO, Oct. 4.

Essad Pasha was today named President of the temporary Government. The time limit for taking possession of the Government expired at 2 P.M. A short time before this hour Essad Pasha occupied the strategic points of the city with his forces of 10,000 Ottomans.

The members of the Albanian Senate elected him President, and expressed to him their congratulations for the confidence the nation has in him.

ALBANIA UNDER MANY RULERS.

[From The Times of London, Oct. 30.]

BUCHAREST, Oct. 27.

There are now six Italian warships at Avlona, where a sanitary station will be established for the relief of Albanian refugees driven from Epirus by the Greek "sacred bands." The duty of maintaining the decisions of the conference in London will apparently be intrusted to Italy as the only neutral power among the signatories to the Albanian settlement. The consent of Austria to this arrangement would seem to have been secured.

At present Albania is under six different régimes. Scutari and its neighborhood is governed by a local commission composed of Moslems and Christians. Avlona is also administered by a commission. The Mirdites form a separate State under Prenk Bib Doda. The Malissors remain isolated under their patriarchal institutions. The southern districts have been appropriated by the Greek invaders. Durazzo and the central regions obey Essad Pasha, who enjoys the title of Prime Minister and is recognized by the International Commission. That shadowy body, now reduced to four members, personates the ghost of the European concert. Except in the south the country is remarkably tranquil under its indigenous institutions.

After he had left Albania Prince William of Wied received a telegram from the King of Italy assuring him of support in the future. His subsequent inclusion, however, in the German General Staff is regarded as seriously compromising to his prospects as sovereign of Albania.

ITALY'S SANITARY MISSION.

[From The London Morning Post, Oct. 28, 1914.]

ROME, Oct. 27.

The dispatch of the battleship Dandolo, the Climene and other Italian warships to Valona is due to the Government's knowledge of a scheme for starting an agitation tending to infringe the decision of the London Conference, which declared Albania neutral. Ismail Kemal Bey, whom I have just seen, expressed his satisfaction at Italy's action at Valona on both political and humanitarian grounds. He did not think that the step would lead to complications, and described the condition of the people at Valona as very miserable.

The Tribuna, commenting on the Government announcement, declares that Italy's aim is for the present solely humanitarian, since the miserable conditions of Valona necessitate sanitary aid. A few companies of marines will land from the Dandolo to protect the Sanitary Mission. With regard to coast surveillance, the British and French Governments have warned Italy of a suspicious Moslem movement in the harbor of Smyrna, whence a thousand rabid young Turks have started or are starting on two steamers hired by the committee for Albania, with the intention of hoisting the Turkish flag and reannexing Albania to Turkey. Italy, in perfect accord with all the signatories of the London Conference, proposes to thwart the attempt.

The Giornale d'Italia considers that what has been done at Valona is sufficient affirmation of Italian interests. Italy never meditated expeditions into the interior or a protectorate over Albania. The Government's intention is to show that whoever touches Valona touches Italian interests, which are that no power shall establish a naval base there.

SASENO OCCUPIED.

[From The London Times, Oct. 30, 1914.]

ROME, Oct. 30.

The Italian occupation of the rocky and desolate islet of Saseno which, from a strategic point of view, completely dominates the sea approaches to Avlona, is a logical consequence of the occupation of that town for the purpose of establishing a hospital and maintaining order. The islet itself was for some months in 1913 and 1914 a bone of contention between the Italians, who insisted on obtaining it for the Principality of Albania, and the Greeks, who were equally anxious to retain it in their own possession. With Saseno under the control of a foreign power, the possessor of Avlona could never make the town into a place of arms.

Saseno, as one of the Ionian Islands, became a British protectorate in virtue of the Treaty of Paris of Nov. 5, 1815, but was given to Greece by the Treaty of London of March 29, 1864. The Ambassadors' Conference decided in the Autumn of last year that it was illogical to allow the chief harbor of Albania to be dominated by the territory of a foreign power, and by the Protocol of Florence, Dec. 19, 1913, it was definitely included in Albania. This decision was ratified by legislative enactment in Greece, to which effect was given by King Constantine's proclamation of June 13, 1914, shortly after which the Hellenic garrison was withdrawn. During the

Greek régime, the island, being neutralized by the Treaty of 1864, was quite unimportant, and at one time the Turks by arrangement with the Hellenic Government, maintained a lighthouse there.

GREEK TROOPS IN EPIRUS.

[From The Morning Post, London, Oct. 28, 1914.]

ATHENS, Oct. 26.

In view of the continuous Albanian attacks and the growing insecurity in Northern Epirus the Greek Government today ordered Greek troops to occupy the districts of Argyrocastro and Premeti. The official communiqué just issued declares this to be an entirely provisional measure to restore order and security in a country already exhausted by prolonged sanguinary conflicts, and Greece proposes to continue to adhere to the international arrangements regarding Epirus. It goes without saying that this reoccupation coincides entirely with public opinion, which has long been exercised over the sufferings of the Epirotes.

ASSENT OF THE POWERS.

[From The London Morning Post, Oct. 30, 1914.]

Following are the replies of the great powers (states Reuter's Agency) to the Greek note announcing the intention of Greece to reoccupy Epirus:

France declared that she saw no objection to the course proposed by M. Venizelos's note.

Russia intimated that she would gladly accept whatever decision in the matter was reached by Great Britain and France.

The British Government accepted M. Venizelos's note.

Germany and Austria-Hungary replied that they accepted the declaration of the Greek Government that the occupation would not be contrary to the decisions of the London Conference.

Italy declared that she, for the same purpose as set forth in the Greek note, namely, the maintenance of order and security, was taking similar steps at Valona, and that she had adopted this course while fully respecting the decisions of the powers. She raised no objection to M. Venizelos's proposal.

ITALIAN OCCUPATION OF AVLONA.

[From the Messaggero of Rome, Dec. 28, 1914.]

AVLONA, Dec. 26.

The following proclamation addressed to the population was posted here:

The grave disorders that become apparent from time to time in this country have paralyzed commerce, work, and initiative, and are endangering the life and property of the inhabitants.

The Italian Government, a watchful guardian of Albanian fortunes, desires that your tranquillity, so cruelly tried, shall be assured. Invoked by your wishes the marines of Italy are disembarking from the ships to establish order and defend you.

(Signed) ADMIRAL PATRIS.

THE LAST WORD.

[From the Messaggero of Rome, Jan. 6, 1915.]

DURAZZO, Jan. 4.

Yesterday the rebels by a letter signed "The Mussulman Committee" demanded that the Ministers of Servia and France be consigned to them.

At 6:30 o'clock the attack against the city began.

Essad Pasha visited the trenches, notified the Italian Legation that there was great danger, and demanded all possible assistance.

At 2:30 a few cannon shots from the Misurata and the Sardegna made themselves heard, defending the city, silencing in this way the rebel musket fire.

The Italian colony and the legations of Italy, France, and Servia are embarked on the ships Sardegna and Misurata.

TO BELGIUM

By EDEN PHILLPOTTS.

[From King Albert's Book.]

CHAMPION of human honor, let us lave
Your feet and bind your wounds on bended knee,
Though coward hands have nailed you to the tree
And shed your innocent blood and dug your grave,
Rejoice and live! Your oriflamme shall wave
While man has power to perish and be free—
A golden flame of holiest liberty,
Proud as the dawn and as the sunset brave.

Belgium, where dwelleth reverence for right
Enthroned above all ideals; where your fate
And your supernal patience and your might
Most sacred grow in human estimate,
You shine a star above this stormy night,
Little no more, but infinitely great.

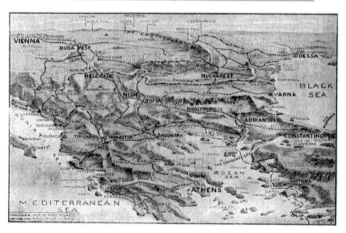

The Balkan States, After the Second Balkan War.

[Enlarge]

The War in the Balkans
General Aspect of the Near East on Aug. 1, 1914.

By Adamantios Th. Polyzoides, Editor The Atlantis.

THE opening of the great European war found the Balkan Peninsula in the political shape given to it by the Treaty of Bucharest, Aug. 10, (old style, July 28,) 1913.

This treaty was signed in the Rumanian capital immediately after the second Balkan war by Greece, Rumania, Bulgaria, Servia, and Montenegro, and, considered in its essential points, was the handiwork of European diplomacy, at whose instance Rumania had entered the war, with the avowed purpose to re-establish the destroyed Balkan equilibrium. Europe had two reasons for interfering in what was then considered as the final settlement of the Balkan question. In the first place, she wanted to reaffirm her authority and predominance over the Balkan States, and, in the second, she considered it as an indispensable part of her Near Eastern policy never to allow much freedom of movement on the part of these same States, which in two successive wars had proved their ability to safeguard and promote their vital interests in spite of all European opposition. To explain this course of European diplomacy one must bear in mind that the Balkan States, since their constitution as such, have always been considered as protégés of Europe, or, to put it more plainly, as not being of age, and therefore deprived of the right and privilege to deal directly with their ancient master, Turkey, in all serious matters in which their most vital interests were involved.

In the Treaty of Berlin after the Russo-Turkish war of 1877 a congress, in which all of the Great European powers participated, most emphatically affirmed that Turkey was responsible to Europe for any complaints that the Balkan States might have against the Ottoman Government regarding the treatment of their connationals, still left under the Sultan. At the same time the Balkan States received due warning regarding their dealings with Turkey, and were made to take a pledge that whenever they had troubles with the Porte the powers and not themselves were to be the arbiters. All the world knows how Turkey, by constant wire-pulling, secured immunity from Europe for not fulfilling the obligations incumbent on her by the Treaty of Berlin, and how one of the Balkan States, namely, Greece, was left alone and unprotected, to be chastised by Turkey in 1897 for not leaving to the powers the settlement of the Cretan question which had brought about the war.

The European powers, having done practically nothing during thirty-five years for the betterment of the conditions under which the non-Moslem populations had to live in Turkey, were overwhelmed to hear in the Autumn of 1912 the news of a series of alliances concluded at Sofia on June 12 between Bulgaria and Servia, and between Bulgaria and Greece, for the purpose of settling once for all the perennial Balkan question. European diplomacy was slow, as usual, in grasping the meaning of the new alliance, and when, on Oct. 5, 1912, Montenegro suddenly declared war on Turkey, with Servia, Bulgaria, and Greece following suit on the 18th, there was consternation in London, Paris, Berlin, Vienna, Rome, and, to a certain degree, in Petrograd.

An idea of the unpreparedness of European diplomacy in the face of the sudden Balkan war can be had by simply glancing at the records of the British House of Commons of the first weeks after the war was declared.

Sir Edward Grey, then and now Foreign Secretary of State for Great Britain, making the first announcement of the rupture between Turkey and the Balkan States, said—exposing the views not only of his Government but of the European concert as well—that Europe, being taken unawares, would not permit any alteration of the Balkan frontiers as the result of the war. After the first victories of the Balkan allies we see Great Britain changing her policy. "The Balkan victors shall not be deprived of the fruits of their victories," Premier Asquith was declaring in Parliament less than a fortnight after Sir Edward spoke. In both these instances the British statesmen were voicing the policy of the European concert taken as a whole. In the first place, the Foreign Secretary was led into believing that Turkey might prove victorious against the Balkan coalition, and the warning about the immutability of the Balkan frontiers was only for Turkey, in case her victorious armies were to cross the boundaries into Bulgaria, Servia, Montenegro, and Greece.

When events marked the utter collapse of the Turkish campaign, Premier Asquith came out with the declaration that Europe had agreed on a policy safeguarding the interests of the victorious Balkan allies. This policy was maintained as long as the Balkan victories were confined in their first progress toward Ottoman territory, at the same time leaving the great European interests unharmed. But when Servian troops arrived at Durazzo, and Montenegro entered Scutari while Greece kept pushing on to Avlona and Bulgaria stood before Tchataldja, the European concert was no longer unanimous in safeguarding the interests of the victors.

Austria, seeing her secular dream of a descent on Saloniki definitely destroyed, and feeling at the same time the imperative need of making impossible a Servian occupation of the Adriatic littoral, raised her voice in favor of the creation of an autonomous Albania at the expense of Servia, Montenegro, and Greece.

Italy, and then Germany, joined their ally in support of Albania. Russia, at the same time not wishing to give any greater impetus to the Bulgarian campaign, dexterously manipulated Rumania, which raised at that time her first claims on Dobrudja. France, who for the last twenty-five years has subjected her Near Eastern policy to the exigencies of the Petrograd statesmen, agreed to the Albanian proposals of the four powers, and finally Great Britain, fearing complications, declared abruptly through Sir Edward Grey that the Balkan war was one of conquest, and for that reason subject to European intervention. In this way European diplomacy stepped into the Balkan conflict and took charge of the final settlement of the first war.

The resolution to interfere in the war once taken, the European powers lost no time in finding a way to end the conflict, and with this object in mind they forced on the belligerents two successive armistices, culminating in the two peace conferences of London. These armistices served two purposes from the diplomatic point of view; first, they exhausted financially the little Balkan countries; and, secondly, they prepared public opinion for the acceptance of any peace terms. The second conference in London succeeded in forcing a peace treaty on the Balkan States. With the exception of Bulgaria, who hoped to retain most of the Turkish territory won by the Balkan coalition, every one was dissatisfied with the way the London conference ended.

Turkey, on one hand, was losing more territory than at first imagined, as the result of her defeat, and the loss of Adrianople was especially hard for every Turk.

Greece was obliged to sign a peace treaty giving her vague and indefinite boundaries and leaving out the question of the Aegean Islands and Epirus, to be settled at a later date by another conference of the Ambassadors of the six great powers in London.

Servia also had to wait for the realization of her fondest hope, which was to obtain a free commercial access to the Adriatic by way of Durazzo or San Giovanni di Medua. That question also was to be decided by the Ambassadorial conference. Montenegro was to lose Scutari, for which she had shed her heart's blood, without getting at the same time any adequate compensation. Such was the Peace of London, from the strictly Balkan point of view, and its conclusion in May, 1913, was the signal for the disruption of the Balkan League and the forerunner of the second war. One month later Bulgaria, having fallen under Austrian influences, quarreled with Servia and Greece over the division of certain Macedonian territories, and on June 16 (29, new style) all of a sudden attacked her erstwhile allies, thereby bringing about the second Balkan conflict, with Greece, Servia, and Montenegro united against her. The outcome of this war, the entry of Rumania and Turkey into the field against Bulgaria, the tearing up of the London Treaty, and the settlement of Bucharest are too well known to need an extensive mention here.

The Treaty of London once torn to pieces by the second Balkan war, it remained for the great powers to find a new way of forcing their terms on the recalcitrant Balkan States, and this they succeeded in doing by adroitly using Rumania as the representative of European diplomacy. Thus the Rumanian Army, without any provocation from Bulgaria, took the field against her neighbor, and acted as a mediator and arbiter of the second Balkan conflict.

The Greek, Servian, Montenegrin, and Bulgarian delegates who went to Bucharest at the close of the war knew beforehand that behind the actions of the Rumanian Government stood united the whole of European diplomacy, again striving to put down once for all these insolent little States who thought themselves emancipated from European guardianship. These delegates knew quite well that there was no escape, but they went, trying and hoping for the best. The Rumanian "Green Papers," published a short time after the Treaty of Bucharest and covering a period between Sept. 20, 1912, and Aug. 1, 1913, give a vivid and true story of the whole proceedings, showing once more what a powerful instrument diplomacy is in the hands of the strong for cheating the weak.

On Aug. 1, 1914, we see the Balkan Peninsula presenting the following aspect:

From the erstwhile European Turkey, of six vilayets, or departments, namely, those of Adrianople, Saloniki, Monastir, Uskub, Jannina, and Scutari, only one, and that mutilated, remains, the Vilayet of Adrianople. Greece, Bulgaria, Servia, Montenegro, and Albania appropriated the rest. Gone is Crete, and gone are the twenty-six Aegean Islands, twelve of them permanently united to their Hellenic motherland, while Italy temporarily occupies fourteen as a result of the Tripolitan war of 1911. Thus Turkey, from an area of 168,500 square kilometers, and 5,000,000 to 6,000,000 inhabitants, forming her European dominions, was reduced to about 30,000 square kilometers and nearly 3,000,000 inhabitants, including the population of Constantinople, amounting, according to the only available foreign statistics, to 1,203,000 inhabitants. Of course Turkey has in Asia an area of more than 2,000,000 square kilometers, with a population approximating 20,000,000, but that, properly speaking, does not enter into Balkan considerations.

Greece, after her two victorious wars, approximates 120,000 square kilometers in territory, with more than 5,000,000 population.

Rumania has 139,690 square kilometers of area and 7,601,660 of population.

Servia has an area of 87,300 square kilometers and a population of 4,256,000.

Bulgaria's area is 114,000 square kilometers, with 4,766,900 of population.

Montenegro has an area of 14,180 square kilometers and half a million in population, and, lastly, Albania, the newborn State, with its scant hope of future political life, has an area of about 17,600 square kilometers, with an approximate population of 800,000 inhabitants.

Were the Balkan States satisfied with the above arrangement when the great European war broke? To this question we have the following answer from those concerned:

Turkey never forgave the European powers the treatment accorded to her in the London peace conference, and proved her dissatisfaction by entering Thrace and occupying Adrianople immediately she saw Bulgaria engaged in the second war. But Turkey desired also the Aegean islands occupied by Greece, and these, all but two at the entrance to the Dardanelles, the powers allotted to Greece, not securing thereby an increase of Turkish sympathies.

Greece was disappointed in two instances by the European powers; first, because they did not make their decision regarding the islands binding upon Turkey, thus creating a series of unending controversies between the Porte and the Government of Athens, one result of which was the wholesale expulsions and persecutions of the Greek element in Turkey, and especially in the Vilayets of Adrianople and Smyrna. The question of settling in a friendly way the Greco-Turkish differences was to be discussed between the Grand Vizier, Prince Said Halim, and the Premier of Greece, E.K. Venizelos, in a meeting of the two statesmen in Brussels, when the great European war broke.

Bulgaria, who for a moment saw her most cherished dream of Balkan hegemony realized and had all her fondest hopes shattered by the second war and the Treaty of Bucharest, cannot help regarding her neighbors as the robbers of what she considers her national patrimony, and at the same time she does not forget that in all their proceedings against her, Greek,

Servian, Rumanian, and Montenegrin acted with the tacit approval of the great powers.

Servia for years had struggled to get an outlet on the Adriatic, and when, after a glorious war, she attained her goal, she found Austria opposing her, and behind Austria the whole of the European concert.

Montenegro in the same way cannot forget the disappointment of being cast out of Scutari after one of the most strenuous and glorious campaigns of her history, and lastly Albania, poor and helpless, without any support from her creators, feels all that a weak and wretched foundling has to feel toward those responsible for its misfortunes and miseries. In contrast with these feelings, Rumania was the only Balkan State perfectly satisfied with the new arrangement. In fact, Rumania, having played in the war the part of a great power, came out of it not only with increased prestige but also with the richest of all the Bulgarian provinces, Dobrudja, as a sort of deserved payment for serving the ends of European diplomacy.

From this general dissatisfaction of the Balkan States with European diplomacy and European intrigue sprang Gavrilo Prinzip and the murder at Serajevo that plunged Europe and the world into the greatest and most disastrous war of all time.

In fairness, however, to the Balkan States it must be said at this juncture that war, in whatever form and character, was far from the Balkan mind on June 28, 1914, when the Austrian Archduke and heir to the throne, Franz Ferdinand, and his consort were assassinated by the Servian youth Prinzip in the capital of Bosnia.

The years 1912 and 1913 had been too costly for the whole of the Balkan Peninsula, and the necessity of a continued peace for a good number of years was universally recognized, with the exception of Constantinople, in Athens, Bucharest, Sofia, Belgrade, Cettinge, and even Durazzo. To prove this we have the opinions of all the Balkan leaders and the views expressed in the Balkan press up to Aug. 1, 1914.

A single point yet calls for a few remarks, and this covers the mutual relations of the Balkan States just before the European war.

We have seen in what a degree the question of the ownership of the Aegean Islands had divided the Governments of Athens and Constantinople. In fact, if any war in the Near East were to be feared, this was one between the two secular enemies, Greek and Turk, and when in May, 1913, the anti-Greek agitation in the Ottoman Empire reached its climax it was only through the tremendous influence of the Greek Premier on Hellenic public opinion and his extreme moderation that a new diplomatic rupture between the two countries was averted.

In anticipation of this eventuality Turkey secured two battleships of the dreadnought type, the Brazilian Rio de Janeiro (then Sultan Osman I. and afterward H.M.S. Erin, England having taken over the ship on Aug. 5, 1914) and the Reshadieh, (likewise taken over by England and renamed H.M.S. Agincourt,) and was preparing for war in such haste that Greece did not hesitate to buy at the original cost price the two old American battleships Idaho and Mississippi, (now Limnos and Kilkis.)

This was in July, 1914, just a few weeks before the European war. Since that time Greco-Turkish relations have been neither better nor worse. It must be said here that these relations had their origin, not in the obsolete London Treaty of May, 1913, but in the Treaty of Athens, signed in December, 1913, between the two countries, and covering in a general way the more essential points of the outstanding questions between the two parties, excluding, however, the Aegean Islands controversy.

After signing the Treaty of Bucharest Bulgaria turned her attention exclusively to Turkey, and, letting bygones be bygones, concluded the Peace Treaty of Constantinople in October, 1913, and inaugurated the most friendly relations with her erstwhile opponent. Since that time the report has spread that an alliance, both offensive and defensive, had been signed by the two countries, but this has been repeatedly denied both from Constantinople and Sofia.

The diplomatic relations between Servia and Turkey and Montenegro and Turkey were re-established a short time before the European war, but these countries, being now in no direct contact with Turkish territory, their relations with the Porte are of little importance.

Between Bulgaria on one hand and Rumania, Greece, Servia, and Montenegro on the other, the diplomatic relations have been re-established, but gone is the old friendship, for reasons already explained. Greece, Servia, and Montenegro are the best of friends, and, according to unofficial and confidential reports, a defensive and offensive alliance for the maintenance of the Balkan status quo, exists between the three countries. Between Rumania and Greece friendly relations exist, and for some time it was said that a marriage was to be arranged between the Greek Crown Prince, George, and the Princess Elizabeth, daughter of the Rumanian King, Ferdinand I., who succeeded to the throne after the death of his uncle, King Charles. This match, however, seems to have been abandoned, perhaps for political reasons, and more so because Greco-Rumanian relations have not as yet reached that firmness which only might justify such a rapprochement of the two royal families.

Between Servia and Rumania there is some courtesy but scarcely any friendship, and this is not surprising, especially now, when each side is aiming to an aggrandizement (at the expense of Austria) in a way injurious to the other. Montenegro naturally follows Servia's course, and as for Albania, what we said previously of her applies now, with this particular observation, that the only neighborly interest shown her is from Italy, trying to play the game of Tripoli at the expense of the Skipetars, while all the other European powers are busily engaged in the great war.

In conclusion we may note that of all the Balkan States only Rumania and, to a certain degree, Greece have any money to run their affairs. This, however, has nothing to do with the matter of their entrance in the war, as in that case there will be one or the other European combination to pay the freight.

Such was the aspect of the Balkan Peninsula at the beginning of the great European war.

(*From The Bystander, London.*)

How the Famous Bernhardi Wrote the Eulogy of Germany's Culture.

THE EUROPEAN WAR AS SEEN BY CARTOONISTS

A SELECTION OF NOTABLE CARTOONS FROM
LEADING ENGLISH, FRENCH, ITALIAN, AND
GERMAN PUBLICATIONS, SHOWING HOW
THE KNIGHTS OF THE PEN AND BRUSH ARE
WAGING THE WAR OF CARICATURE AGAINST
THE FOES OF THEIR RESPECTIVE ALLIANCES

Still Not Letting Go—and Still Breathing!

(From The Sketch, London.)

THE PRUSSIAN EAGLE: "This is no good to me. That pup's growing every minute. I've half a mind to fly away."

Going! Going! ——?

(*From The Tatler, London.*)

The Barbarian Finds His "Place in the Sun" Too Hot for Him.

The God in the Cart

(AN UNREHEARSED EFFECT.)

(*From Punch, London.*)

TURKEY: "I'm getting a bit fed up with this. I shall kick soon."

AUSTRIA: "Well, I was thinking of lying down."

The Great Illusion

(*From Punch, London.*)

KAISER: "My poor bird, what *has* happened to your tail feathers?"

GERMAN EAGLE: "Can you bear the truth, Sire?"

KAISER: "If it's not for publication."

GERMAN EAGLE: "It's like this, then. You told me the British lion was contemptible. Well—he wasn't!"

What Punch Thinks Is Awaiting the Kaiser

(*From Punch, London.*)

The Man Behind the Kaiser

(From the Bystander, London.)

Nothing Doing

(From Punch, London.)

IMPERIAL DACHSHUND: "Here I've been sitting up and doing tricks for the best part of seven weeks, and you take no more notice of me than if—"

UNCLE SAM: "Cut it out!"

As Between Friends

(From Punch, London.)

BRITISH LION: "Please don't look at me like that, Sam. *You*'re not the eagle I'm up against."

Kultur

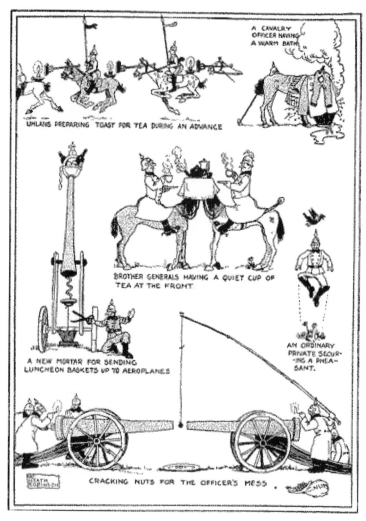

(*From The Sketch, London.*)

Making the German Officers' Mess a Success.

[Enlarge]

Homers

(From The Sketch, London.)

THE POLICEMAN: "What have you got there? Pigeons?"

THE ENGLISHMAN (*naturalized*): "No; they vos singing-birds."

THE POLICEMAN: "What song do they sing?"

THE ENGLISHMAN (*naturalized*): "Home, sveet home."

The New Year's Present That We Are Wishing For

(From La Vie Parisienne, Paris.)

A Million English Soldiers to Help Us Drive the Germans from France and Belgium.

"His" Christmas Sabots

(From La Vie Parisienne, Paris.)

(The conspicuous place taken by children's stockings at Christmas time in English-speaking countries is usurped by the youngsters' shoes in France.)

"Sire, Your Soup's Getting Cold"

(From La Vie Parisienne, Paris.)

How about that famous dinner that the Kaiser ordered in one of the big Paris hotels! Isn't the bill of fare a trifle out of season by this time?

Chaffing the French Censor

(*From La Vie Parisienne, Paris.*)

"At the same instant, happily, a furious gallop resounded along the road from ——, and, full of joy, our Colonel cried: 'They are the ——.' They were, as a matter of fact, the ——."

"Despite this reinforcement, it was hot work. Capt. —— of the —— Company of the —— Regiment especially distinguished himself, leading his men in an irresistible charge. We lost —— men, but the enemy left —— dead in the ruins of the village of ——."

"At the end of the —— —— victory ——
—— —— important strategic point —— —
— —— —— —— ——. 'I am very pleased
with you,' said our General to us."

The Under-Study

(From Numero, Turin.)

The Triple Alliance Revised and Corrected.

A Substitute for Belgian Blocks

(*From Numero, Turin.*)

A New Form of Paving for French and Belgian Cities.

What Italy Thinks of "Guglielmo"

(A SERIES OF ITALIAN POSTCARDS.)

HIMSELF TO GOD: "If I were not afraid of Thee I would declare war upon Thee also!"

GUGLIELMO'S DREAM. The map bears the inscription, "The Great German Empire."

"Isn't there somebody else to declare war upon?"

"There's the Republic of San Marino, your Majesty."

GUGLIELMO (bearing the European war): "Heavens! It's beginning to get heavy."

You Can't Bluff the Turk

(From Simplicissimus, Munich.)

"Will you restore the capitulations
immediately?"

"No."

"Will you give up the Goeben
and the
Breslau immediately?"

"No."

"In respect to the Dardanelles,
will you
immediately——?"

"No. And now suppose you just
put
up that revolver."

"With pleasure! The thing wasn't
loaded
at all!"

The Mistress of the Sea

(From Lustige Blaetter, Berlin.)

Behold, O World, How I Stand Here! Look Out, Britannia!

The "Prize-Taker"

(*From Lustige Blaetter, Berlin.*)

"How long will you allow this brute to tread on your corns?"

[The allusion is to England's attitude toward neutral shipping.]

The Face at the Window

(From Lustige Blaetter, Berlin.)

Novel Coastwise Scenery

(From Jugend, Munich.)

Since it was given out that the German barbarians were refusing to fire on cathedrals, England has worked out a jolly little plan for coast defense.

The Dancers

(*From Lustige Blaetter, Berlin.*)

How the Germans Conduct the English Ballet.

The English Spider

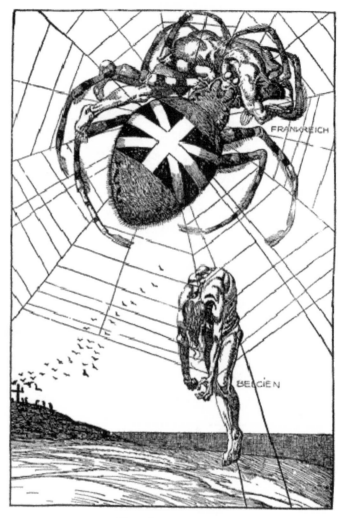

(*From Jugend, Munich.*)

The Jap-Infested British Lion

(From Simplicissimus, Munich.)

"Goddam! What kind of fleas have I got in my mane anyway!"

The Englishman and His Globe

(From Simplicissimus, Munich.)

"Curses! Blood is more slippery than water!"

[The original was in black and red and vividly represented a dripping globe.]

The German Watch in Kiao-Chau

(*From Simplicissimus, Munich.*)

[A superb cartoon published before the fall of the German stronghold in China.]

GERMANY vs. BELGIUM

Case of the Secret Military Documents Presented by Both Sides

[The Belgo-British plot alleged by Germany is thoroughly aired in the following communications. The text of the secret documents, which, according to the German contention, prove that the Allies did not intend to respect Belgian neutrality—that Belgium herself conspired with England to break it—was discovered in the archives of the Belgian Government after the German occupation of Brussels, and is embodied on Pages 1105 to 1109 in the subjoined article, published in behalf of Germany by Dr. Bernhard Dernburg.

The article, called by Dr. Dernburg "The Case of Belgium," as reproduced below, and published between gray covers like the Belgian "Gray Book," prompted publications in rejoinder by the Belgian Legation at Washington. The first of these, entitled "The Innocence of Belgium," appears on Page 1110; it states that the secret documents show in their own statements the "clearest proof of the innocence of Belgium." The second Belgian article, headed "Why Belgium Was Devastated," and appearing on Page 1115, embodies the German proclamations establishing military rule in the violated territory.—EDITOR.]

"THE CASE OF BELGIUM"

"In the Light of Official Reports Found in the Secret Archives of the Belgian Government after the Occupation of Brussels"

Remarks Introductory to the Secret Documents

By Dr. Bernhard Dernburg

HEREWITH are published facsimiles of papers found among the documents of the Belgian General Staff at Brussels, referring to arrangements between the English Military Attaché and the Belgian Minister of War regarding British intervention in Belgium.

It will be remembered from the British "White Book" that in November, 1912, a correspondence passed between Sir Edward Grey and the French Minister in London, in which it was stated that British and French military and naval experts had consulted together from time to time as to plans to be followed in case of war, and it was stated in this correspondence that in accordance with such prearranged plans the French fleet would stay in the Mediterranean to safeguard the joint interests there, whereas the British fleet would safeguard their interests in the north. Of this correspondence the members of the British Cabinet remained ignorant until the Cabinet meeting immediately preceding the written statement by Great Britain on Aug. 2 that in case a German fleet attacked the French coast or passed into the Channel, England would give all the assistance in her power, (British "White Papers," No. 148,) and it was also, of course, concealed from the British public until the speech of Sir Edward Grey on Aug. 3. It will be remembered that in consequence of this revelation the British Minister of Commerce, Mr. John Burns, and two other members, Lord Morley and Mr. Trevelyan, left the British Cabinet under protest; that the leader of the British Labor Party, Mr. Ramsey Macdonald, resigned from the leadership and that Mr. Arthur Ponsonby in his famous letter denounced Sir Edward Grey's practices.

Mr. Ponsonby said that time and again they had been assured that there were no obligations whatsoever on the part of Great Britain to come to France's assistance and yet they found themselves now so hopelessly entangled that as a matter of fact the British Government could not back out.

The fact of these consultations, by which, of course, all the plans of mobilization of both the British and French armies were disclosed to the two allies and which include the landing of English troops in France, is now fully established by the annexed documents. They show that these conversations were also held with Belgium, that plans had been concerted to invade Belgium with an army of 100,000 men by way of three French ports—viz., Dunkirk, Calais, and Boulogne—and that the British plans even considered a landing by way of the Scheldt, thus violating also Dutch neutrality.

The documents, giving all the details as translated and showing that Belgian railway cars were to be sent to the named French ports in order to transport the British troops into Belgium, are dated from 1906.

The Belgian Minister at Berlin, Baron Greindl, a well-known Belgian patriot, protested to his Government. The heading of his protest is also given in facsimile. In it he said that it was not quite safe to trust to the British and French to keep the Belgian neutrality, that it was not wise to take all measures only against a German infraction of Belgian neutrality and that the British spirit was clearly shown by the words of Col. Barnardiston that the Scheldt might be used for transporting troops into Belgium.

Furthermore, it will be remembered that the British and French Governments violently protested when the plans were made public that the Dutch Government intended to fortify the mouth of the Scheldt in 1906. But in 1912, when the Balkan crisis became acute, the British went one step further. When Col. Bridges, in a conversation with Gen. Jungbluth, the Chief of the Belgian General Staff, said that England was ready to strike, that 160,000 men were ready to be landed and that they would land them as soon as any European conflict should break out, Gen. Jungbluth protested that for such a step the permission of Belgium was necessary. The cool reply was that the English knew it, but thought that, as Belgium was not strong enough alone to protect herself, England would land troops anyway. Gen. Jungbluth answered that Belgium felt strong enough to protect herself, which is in keeping with her declaration to France, when she offered to protect Belgium by five army corps, as reported in the British "White Book." The position of England was therefore that, while in 1906 they had already concerted plans for a joint action, in 1912 England intended action in any case, should a European conflagration break out.

Now, it must be recollected that as early as July 28, 1914, Sir Edward Grey said to Prince Lichnowsky, as mentioned in his communication to Sir E. Goschen: "The situation was very grave. While it was restricted to the issues at present actually involved, we had not thought of interfering in it. But if Germany became involved in it and then France, the issue might be so great that it would involve all European interests, and I did not wish him to be misled by the friendly tone of our conversation—which I hoped would continue—into thinking that we should stand aside." (British "White Papers," No. 89.)

This was at a time when the Belgian issue had not been raised at all. It only came about by Sir Edward Grey's notes written on July 31. Thus the British entanglement with France, as evidenced by the British "White Book," prevented England taking the same attitude in 1914 which she had taken in 1870, when she made a treaty with France as against the German invasion of Belgium and with Germany as against the French invasion of Belgium. A similar agreement was suggested by Prince Lichnowsky to Sir Edward Grey on Aug. 1, 1914, as reported in the English "White Book," No. 123, when the former asked Sir Edward Grey whether if Germany gave a promise not to violate Belgian neutrality England would engage to remain neutral, upon which Grey replied that he could not say that.

It is therefore perfectly evident, in the first place, that in case of a German war, that was sure to be brought about by Russia's mobilization against Germany, England would go to war against Germany, and it has been proved that the English assurance to that effect has strengthened the hands of the Russian war party, which thereupon got the upper hand and forced the Russian Czar into the war, (see report of Belgian Chargé d'Affaires at St. Petersburg to the Minister of Foreign Affairs at Brussels, July 30.)

In the second place, it is shown that England meant, with or without Belgium's will, to land her troops, in violation of Belgium's neutrality, in Belgium, irrespective of whether German troops were marching through Belgium or not, because no such declaration had been made in 1912 or any time thereafter until Aug. 4 in the German Reichstag. It is further evident that as soon as Russia mobilized, Germany would have to fight Russia as well as France and England, and that in such a fight she was forced to draw quickly when she saw her enemies reaching for their hip pockets. And only the prompt action at Liége that put this important railway centre commanding the railway connections to France and Germany into German hands prevented the English landing and invading Belgium.

The guilt of the Belgian Government in this matter consists, in the first place, in making and concerting plans with the English and French Governments as to what steps to take in case of war. A plan of the French mobilization was found in the same docket, and it cannot be presumed that the conference between British and French experts was unknown to the

British Military Attaché in Brussels. It is furthermore impossible to believe that the French railway for the shipping of British troops from Calais, Dunkirk, and Boulogne into Belgium in Belgian cars could have been used without the knowledge of the French authorities. Secondly, that Belgium did not heed the advice of Baron Greindl and did not try to insure her independence in the same way by approaching Germany and making a similar contract with her. This disposes of the contention that the Belgian conversation had a purely defensive character as against all comers. It shows the one-sidedness of the inclination, which is evidenced also by the placing of all Belgium's fortresses on the eastern frontier.

The Belgian people had been told at the beginning of the war that Germany demanded that the Belgian forces should fight with the Germans against the French and the English, and the truth had become known only three full months later, when the Belgian "Gray Book" was published. Then Belgium was practically occupied territory. While Belgium pretended neutrality and friendship toward Germany, it was secretly planning for her defeat in a war which was considered unavoidable. The poor Belgian people, however, must suffer because of the large ambitions of King Leopold of Congo fame and of a broken-down diplomacy.

The Imperial Chancellor has declared that there was irrefutable proof that if Germany did not march through Belgium, her enemies would. This proof, as now being produced, is of the strongest character. So the Chancellor was right in appealing to the law of necessity, although he had no regret that it violated international law. This law of necessity has been recognized as paramount by nearly every prominent statesman, including Gladstone, and by all teachers of international law, even by the United States Supreme Court's decision, Vol. 130, Page 601, stating in regard to the treaty with China concerning Chinese immigration into the United States: "It will not be presumed that the legislative department of the Government will lightly pass laws which are in conflict with the treaties of the country, but that circumstances may arise which would not only justify the Government in disregarding their stipulations, but demand in the interests of the country that it should do so, there can be no question. Unexpected events may call for a change in the policy of the country." And to strengthen this opinion another decision by Justice Curtis, rendered in 1908, may be cited, stating that, "while it would be a matter of the utmost gravity and delicacy to refuse to execute a treaty, the power to do so was a prerogative of which no country could be deprived without deeply affecting its independence."

We now let these Belgian documents speak for themselves.

Summary of the Secret Documents

I. The first document is a report of the Chief of the Belgian General Staff, Major Gen. Ducarme, to the Minister of War, reporting a series of conversations which he had had with the Military Attaché of the British Legation, Lieut. Col. Barnardiston, in Brussels. It discloses that, as early as January, 1906, the Belgian Government was in consultation with the British Government over steps to be taken by Belgium, Great Britain, and France against Germany. A plan had been fully elaborated for the landing of two British army corps in French ports to be transferred to the point in Belgium necessary for operations against the Germans. Throughout the conversation the British and Belgian forces were spoken of as "allied armies"; the British Military Attaché insisted on discussing the question of the chief command; and he urged the establishment, in the meantime, of a Belgian spy system in Germany.

II. When in the year 1912 Lieut. Col. Barnardiston had been succeeded by Lieut. Col. Bridges as British Military Attaché in Brussels, and the Chief of the Belgian General Staff, Major Gen. Ducarme, had been succeeded by Gen. Jungbluth as Chief of the Belgian General Staff, the conversations proceeded between the two latter officials. That is to say, these were not casual conversations between individuals, but a series of official conversations between representatives of their respective Governments, in pursuance of a well-considered policy on the part of both Governments.

III. The above documents are given additional significance by a report made in 1911 by Baron Greindl, Belgian Minister in Berlin, to the Belgian Minister for Foreign Affairs, from which it appears that this representative of the Belgian Government in Berlin was familiar with the plans above set forth and protested against them, asking why like preparations had not been made with Germany to repel invasion by the French and English.

Taken together, these documents show that *the British Government had the intention, in case of a Franco-German war, of sending troops into Belgium immediately—that is, of doing the very thing which, done by Germany, was used by England as a pretext for declaring war on Germany.*

They show also that the Belgian Government took, in agreement with the English General Staff, military precautions against a hypothetical German invasion of Belgium. On the other hand, the Belgian Government never made the slightest attempt to take, in agreement with the German Government, military precautions against an Anglo-French invasion of Belgium, though fully informed that it was the purpose of the British Government to land and dispatch, across French territory into Belgium, 160,000 troops, without asking Belgium's permission, on the first outbreak of the European war. *This clearly demonstrates that the Belgian Government was determined from the outset to join Germany's enemies.*

MR. AND MRS. WINSTON SPENCER CHURCHILL
A Recent Photograph of the Head of the British Admiralty.

QUARTERMASTER GENERAL VON STEIN

Germany's Official War News Is Issued Through the Office of the
Quartermaster General.

(*Photo from Brown Bros.*)

DOCUMENT NO. 1

Report of Gen. Ducarme, Chief of the Belgian General Staff, to the Belgian Minister of War

"*Confidential*
Letter to the Minister
Concerning the Confidential Conversations.

"BRUSSELS, April 10, 1906.

"Mr. Minister:

"I have the honor to report to you briefly about the conversations which I had with Lieut. Col. Barnardiston and which have already been the subject of my oral communications.

"The first visit took place in the middle of January. Mr. Barnardiston referred to the anxieties of the General Staff of his country with regard to the general political situation, and because of the possibility that war may soon break out. In case Belgium should be attacked, the sending of about 100,000 troops was provided for.

"The Lieutenant Colonel asked me how such a measure would be regarded by us. I answered him, that from a military point of view it could not be but favorable, but that this question of intervention was just as much a matter for the political authorities, and that, therefore, it was my duty to inform the Minister of War about it.

"Mr. Barnardiston answered that his Minister in Brussels would speak about it with our Minister of Foreign Affairs.

"He proceeded in the following sense: The landing of the English troops would take place at the French coast in the vicinity of Dunkirk and Calais, so as to hasten their movements as much as possible. The entry of the English into Belgium would take place only after the violation of our neutrality by Germany. A landing in Antwerp would take much more time, because larger transports would be needed, and because, on the other hand, the safety would be less complete.

"This admitted, there would be several other points to consider, such as railway transportation, the question of requisitions which the English army could make, the question concerning the chief command of the allied forces.

"He inquired whether our preparations were sufficient to secure the defense of the country during the crossing and the transportation of the English troops—which he estimated to last about ten days.

"I answered him that the places Namur and Liége were protected from a coup de main and that our field army of 100,000 men would be capable of intervention within four days.

"After having expressed his full satisfaction with my explanations, my visitor laid emphasis on the following facts: (1) That our conversation was entirely confidential; (2) that it was not binding on his Government; (3) that his Minister, the English General Staff, he and I were, up to the present, the only ones[1] informed about the matter; (4) that he did not know whether the opinion of his sovereign had been consulted....

"In a following discussion Lieut. Col. Barnardiston assured me that he had never received confidential reports of the other Military Attachés about our army. He then gave the exact numerical data of the English forces; we could depend on it, that in twelve or thirteen days two army corps, four cavalry brigades, and two brigades of horse infantry would be landed.

"He asked me to study the question of the transport of these forces to that part of the country where they would be useful, and he promised to give me for this purpose details about the composition of the landing army.

"He reverted to the question concerning the effective strength of our field army, and he emphasized that no detachments should be sent from this army to Namur and Liége, because these places were provided with garrisons of sufficient strength.

"He asked me to direct my attention to the necessity of granting the English Army the advantages which the regulations concerning the military requisitions provided for. Finally he insisted upon the question of the chief command.

"I answered him that I could say nothing with reference to this last point and promised him that I would study the other questions carefully....

"Later on the English Military Attaché confirmed his former calculations: twelve days would at least be necessary to carry out the landing at the French coast. It would take a considerably longer time (1 to 2-1/2 months) to land 100,000 men in Antwerp.

"Upon my objection that it would be unnecessary to await the end of the landing in order to begin with the railway transportations, and that it would be better to proceed with these when the troops arrived at the coast, Lieut. Col. Barnardiston promised to give me exact data as to the number of troops that could be landed daily.

"As regards the military requisitions, I told my visitor that this question could be easily regulated....

"The further the plans of the English General Staff progressed, the clearer became the details of the problem. The Colonel assured me that one-half of the English Army could be landed within eight days; the rest at the conclusion of the twelfth or thirteenth day, with the exception of the horse infantry, which could not be counted upon until later.

"In spite of this I thought I had to insist again upon the necessity of knowing the exact number of the daily shipments, in order to regulate the railway transportation for every day.

"The English Military Attaché conversed with me about several other questions, namely:

"(1) The necessity of keeping the operations secret and of demanding strict secrecy from the press;

"(2) The advantages which would accrue from giving one Belgian officer to each English General Staff, one interpreter to each commanding officer, and gendarmes to each unit of troops, in order to assist the British police troops....

"In the course of another interview Lieut. Col. Barnardiston and I studied the combined operations to take place in the event of a German offensive with Antwerp as its object and under the hypothesis of the German troops marching through our country in order to reach the French Ardennes.

"In this question, the Colonel said he quite agreed with the plan which I had submitted to him, and he assured me also of the approval of Gen. Grierson, Chief of the English General Staff.

"Other secondary questions which were likewise settled had particular reference to intermediary officers, interpreters, gendarmes, maps, photographs of the uniforms, special copies, translated into English, of some Belgian regulations, the regulations concerning the import duties on English provisions, to the accommodation of the wounded of the allied armies, &c. Nothing was resolved on as regards the activity which the Government or the military authorities might exert on the press....

"During the final meetings which I had with the British Attaché, he informed me about the numbers of troops which would be daily disembarked at Boulogne, Calais, and Cherbourg. The distance of the last place, which is necessary for technical considerations, will involve a certain delay. The first corps would be disembarked on the tenth day, and the second on the fifteenth day. Our railways would carry out the transportation so that the arrival of the first corps, either in the direction of

Brussels-Louvain or of Namur-Dinant, would be assured on the eleventh day, and that of the second on the sixteenth day.

"I again, for a last time, and as emphatically as I could, insisted on the necessity of hastening the sea transports so that the English troops could be with us between the eleventh and twelfth day. The happiest and most favorable results can be reached by a convergent and simultaneous action of the allied forces. But if that co-operation should not take place, the failure would be most serious. Col. Barnardiston assured me that everything serving to this end would be done....

"In the course of our conversations, I had occasion to convince the British Military Attaché that we were willing, so far as possible, to thwart the movements of the enemy and not to take refuge in Antwerp from the beginning.

"Lieut. Col. Barnardiston on his part told me that, at the time, he had little hope for any support or intervention on the part of Holland. At the same time he informed me that his Government intended to transfer the basis of the British commissariat from the French coast to Antwerp as soon as all German ships were swept off the North Sea....

"In all our conversations the Colonel regularly informed me about the secret news which he had concerning the military circumstances and the situation of our eastern neighbors, &c. At the same time he emphasized that Belgium was under the imperative necessity to keep herself constantly informed of the happenings in the adjoining Rhinelands. I had to admit that with us the surveillance service abroad was, in times of peace, not directly in the hands of the General Staff, as our legations had no Military Attachés. But I was careful not to admit that I did not know whether the espionage service which is prescribed in our regulations was in working order or not. But I consider it my duty to point out this position which places us in a state of evident inferiority to our neighbors, our presumable enemies.

"Major General, Chief of the General Staff. (Initials of Gen. Ducarme.)

"Note.—When I met Gen. Grierson at Compiègne, during the manoeuvres of 1906, he assured me the result of the reorganization of the English Army would be that the landing of 150,000 would be assured and, that, moreover, they would stand ready for action in a shorter time than has been assumed above.

"Concluded September, 1906."
(Initials of Gen. Ducarme.)

DOCUMENT NO. 2

Minutes of a Conference Between the Belgian Chief of the General Staff, Gen. Jungbluth, and the British Military Attaché Lieut. Col. Bridges

(Lieut. Col. Barnardiston, British Military Attaché in Brussels, was succeeded in his office by Lieut. Col. Bridges. Likewise, Gen. Ducarme was succeeded, as Chief of the Belgian Staff, by Gen. Jungbluth. A conversation between Col. Bridges and Gen. Jungbluth was committed to writing, and that writing was also found at the Belgian Foreign Office. The document, which is dated April 23 and is presumed to belong to the year 1912, is marked "confidentielle" in the handwriting of Graf v.d. Straaten, the Belgian Foreign Secretary. This is the translation:)

"Confidential.

"The British Military Attaché asked to see Gen. Jungbluth. The two gentlemen met on April 23.

"Lieut. Col. Bridges told the General that England had at her disposal an army which could be sent to the Continent, composed of six divisions of infantry and eight brigades of cavalry—together 160,000 troops. She has also everything which is necessary for her to defend her insular territory. Everything is ready.

"At the time of the recent events the British Government would have immediately effected a disembarkment in Belgium (chez nous) even if we had not asked for assistance.

"The General objected that for that our consent was necessary.

"The Military Attaché answered that he knew this, but that—since we were not able to prevent the Germans from passing through our country—England would have landed her troops in Belgium under all circumstances (en tout état de cause).

"As for the place of landing, the Military Attaché did not make a precise statement; he said that the coast was rather long, but the General knows that Mr. Bridges, during Easter, has paid daily visits to Zeebrugge from Ostend.

"The General added that we were, besides, perfectly able to prevent the Germans from passing through."

DOCUMENT NO. 3

Report of Baron Greindl, Belgian Minister in Berlin, to the Belgian Minister of Foreign Affairs

[On the 23d of December, 1911, Baron Greindl, then and for many years Belgian Minister in Berlin, made a report to the Belgian Minister of Foreign Affairs. There was found in Brussels a copy of this report. Although a copy, the official character of this third document found in Brussels is evident from the official imprint on the paper on which the copy stands. The first page reads:]

.... SECTION

No. ....

..... ENCLOSURE   COPY

Reply to No.

General department

Office of ....

BERLIN, Dec. 23, 1911.

Belgian Legation,
No. 3,022—1,626.

Strictly Confidential.

What is Belgium to do in case of war?

Mr. Minister:

I have had the honor to receive the dispatch of the 27th November last, P without docket number, registration number 1,108....

[Baron Greindl's report is an extremely long one. Extracts from it were published in The North German Gazette of Oct. 13. A facsimile has been made of the first page only of the document, because of its great length.

The writer reveals with great astuteness the ulterior motives underlying the English proposal and draws attention to the danger of the situation in which Belgium had become involved by a one-sided partisanship in favor of the powers of the Entente. In this very detailed report, dated Dec. 23, 1911, Baron Greindl explains that the plan of the General Army Staff for the defense of Belgian neutrality in a Franco-German war as communicated to him only concerned the question as to what military measures should be adopted in case Germany violated Belgian neutrality. The hypothesis of a French attack on Germany through Belgium had, however, just as much probability in itself. The diplomat then goes on in the following manner:]

"From the French side danger threatens not only in the south of Luxemburg, it threatens us on our entire joint frontier. We are not reduced to conjectures for this assertion. We have positive evidence of it.

"Evidently the project of an outflanking movement from the north forms part of the scheme of the entente cordiale. If that were not the case, then the plan of fortifying Flushing would not have called forth such an outburst in Paris and London. The reason why they wished that the Scheldt should remain unfortified was hardly concealed by them. Their aim was to be able to transport an English garrison, unhindered, to Antwerp, which means to establish in our country a basis of operation for an offensive in the direction of the Lower Rhine and Westphalia, and then to make us throw our lot in with them, which would not be difficult, for, after the surrender of our national centre of refuge, we would, through our own fault, renounce every possibility of opposing the demands of our doubtful protectors after having been so unwise as to permit their entrance into our country. Col. Barnardiston's announcements at the time of the conclusion of the entente cordiale, which were just as perfidious as they were naïve, have shown us plainly the true meaning of things. When it became evident that we would not allow ourselves to be frightened by the pretended danger of the closing of the Scheldt, the plan was not entirely abandoned, but modified in so far as the British Army was not to land on the Belgian coast, but at the nearest French harbors.

"The revelations of Capt. Faber, which were denied as little as the newspaper reports by which they were confirmed or completed in several respects, also testify to this. This British Army, at Calais and Dunkirk, would by no means march along our frontier to Longwy in order to reach Germany. It would directly invade Belgium from the northwest. That would give it the advantage of being able to begin operations immediately, to encounter the Belgian Army in a region where we could not depend on any fortress, in case we wanted to risk a battle. Moreover, that would make it possible for it to occupy provinces rich in all kinds of resources and, at any rate, to prevent our mobilization or only to permit it after we had formally pledged ourselves to carry on our mobilization to the exclusive advantage of England and her allies.

"It is therefore of necessity to prepare a plan of battle for the Belgian Army also for that possibility. This is necessary in the interest of our military defense as well as for the sake of the direction of our foreign policy, in case of war between Germany and France."

[The text of the documents presented above is not disputed by the Belgian Government. Instead it is made the basis of the Belgian reply, beginning on the next page.]

THE BELGIAN BATTLEGROUND

By the HON. WILLIAM H. TAFT.

[From King Albert's Book.]

THE heart of the world should go out to the poor people of Belgium. Without being in any respect a party to the controversies of the war, their country has been made the battleground of the greatest and in some respects the most destructive war in history. Any movement to relieve their distress has my profound sympathy.

[The following letter from the Belgian Legation at Washington certifies the official character of the documents presented below.—EDITOR.]

LEGATION DE BELGIQUE,
WASHINGTON, D.C.

Jan. 25, 1915.

To the Editor of The New York Times Current History:

In accordance with the request, in your letter of December 10th addressed to the Belgian Minister, for official documents published by the Legation, I have the pleasure of sending you, herewith, by the Minister's instructions, a copy of a pamphlet entitled "The Innocence of Belgium," dealing with the Military Documents published recently in THE NEW YORK TIMES.

I also take this opportunity to transmit you a copy of a pamphlet entitled "Why Belgium Was Devastated," containing translations of the German Proclamations issued in Belgium.

I have the honor to be, Sir,

Your obedient servant,

JAMES GUSTAVUS WHITELEY.

[BELGIAN LEGATION ARTICLE NO. 1.]

"INNOCENCE OF BELGIUM"

"Reply to Publication of Military Documents by Germany"

THE German Government has at last decided to publish the documents which it says were found in Brussels, and which it claims prove that Belgium violated her neutrality.

As a matter of fact these documents are the clearest proof of the innocence of Belgium.

Document No. 1 refers to a conversation between Major Gen. Ducarme and the English Military Attaché, Lieut. Col. Barnardiston.

The English Military Attaché *went to call* on the Belgian General and told him of the anxiety on the part of the English General Staff in regard to the general political situation and the possibility of war. "*In case Belgium should be attacked,* the sending of about 100,000 troops was provided for."

He (the British Military Attaché) proceeded in the following terms:

"The landing of the British troops would take place on the French coast.... The entry of the English into Belgium would take place only *after the violation of our (Belgian) neutrality by Germany.*"

It almost seems as if Col. Barnardiston had foreseen the future.

The document continues as follows: "My visitor laid emphasis on the following fact: that it (the conversation) was not binding on his Government ... and that he did not know whether the opinion of his Sovereign had been consulted." It was thus clearly shown by the British Military Attaché that his communication was simply a conversation; it is, moreover, perfectly well known that Military Attachés have no power to make conventional agreements.

The document further continues: "In the course of another interview, Lieut. Col. Barnardiston and I studied the combined operations to take place in the event of a *German offensive,* with Antwerp as its object, *and under the hypothesis of the German troops marching through our (Belgian) country,* in order to reach the French Ardennes"—an additional proof that the object of the conversation was solely to prevent a violation of Belgian neutrality.

Document No. 2 refers to a conversation between the British Military Attaché and Gen. Jungbluth, in which the former said that the British troops would effect a landing "even if we (the Belgians) did not ask for assistance." This is an additional proof that no agreement or convention had been made.

To this the Belgian General replied that "our (Belgium's) consent was necessary," and he added that "we (the Belgians) were, moreover, perfectly able to prevent the Germans from passing through Belgium," thus showing his anxiety to preserve the neutrality of Belgium.

Dr. B. Dernburg claims that England would have sent troops into Belgium in any event, even if Germany had not invaded Belgium. Affirmations which are not based upon any evidence cannot destroy the text itself of the documents.

In a letter of Sir Edward Grey, Secretary for Foreign Affairs of England, addressed to the British Minister to Belgium, on the 7th of April, 1913, the British statesman declares in the most formal way, that: "As long as Belgium's neutrality was not violated by any other power, we (the British) should certainly not send troops ourselves into their territory."

The full text of this important letter is as follows:

In speaking to the Belgian Minister today I said, speaking unofficially, that it had been brought to my knowledge that there was apprehension in Belgium lest we should be the first to violate Belgian neutrality. I did not think that apprehension could have come from a British source.

The Belgian Minister informed me that there had been talk, from a British source which he could not name, of the landing of troops in Belgium by Great Britain, in order to anticipate a possible dispatch of German troops through Belgium to France.

I said that I was sure that this Government would not be the first to violate the neutrality of Belgium, and I did not believe that any British Government would be the first to do so, nor would public opinion here ever approve of it. What we had to consider, and it was a somewhat embarrassing question, was what it would be desirable and necessary for us, as one of the guarantors of Belgian neutrality, to do if Belgian neutrality was violated by any power. For us to be the first to violate it and to send troops into Belgium would be to give Germany, for instance, justification for sending troops into Belgium also. What we desired in the case of Belgium, as in that of other neutral countries, was that their neutrality should be respected, and, as long as it was not violated by any other power, we would certainly not send troops ourselves into their territory. I am, &c.,

(Signed) E. GREY.

Document No. 3 contains, according to Dr. B. Dernburg, the personal views of the Belgian Minister in Berlin, but it does not, in any way, indicate the existence of an agreement between Belgium and England against Germany.

It is impossible to say that these documents constitute a proof of an agreement between England and Belgium against Germany, unless one accepts the idea that Germany had a right to violate Belgium's neutrality and that all measures taken as a precaution against violation of neutrality must therefore have been taken against Germany.

The documents contain merely conversations between military officers in regard to a possible future co-operation of their armies in the event of violation of Belgian territory by Germany. They never even resulted in an agreement between those Governments; Military Attachés have no authority to make such agreements.

The events that happened last August and the sudden invasion of Belgium by Germany show that the British Government was fully justified in fearing the violation of Belgian territory by Germany. It seems incredible, after what has passed, that the German Government should denounce the British Government for approaching Belgian military officers and taking precautions against the very thing which eventually happened.

If further proof should be necessary, the documents published in the "Gray Book" show as clearly as possible that, when the war broke out, Belgium had no such agreement with any of the powers.

On July 24 the following letter was sent by the Belgian Minister for Foreign Affairs to the various Belgian Legations concerned, with instructions to communicate the same to the powers as soon as said Legations should have received telegraphic orders to do so:

Mr. Minister:

The international situation is serious; the eventuality of a conflict between several powers cannot be set aside from the anxieties of the Government of the King.

Belgium has observed with the most scrupulous exactness the duties of a neutral State which are imposed on her by the Treaties of April 19, 1839. These duties, whatever the circumstances may be, *will be resolutely fulfilled by her.*

The friendly disposition of the powers toward her has been so often affirmed that Belgium has the confidence that her territory will be untouched by any attack if hostilities should break out on her frontiers.

All the necessary measures have nevertheless been taken, in order to assure the observance of her neutrality.... It is scarcely necessary to insist upon their character.... These measures *are not and can not have been inspired by a design to participate in an armed struggle of the powers, nor by any sentiment of defiance toward any one of them.*

Belgium declared that she would not fail to fulfill all of her duties, that she had not a single agreement of alliance with any one, and that she wanted to remain absolutely neutral.

Seven days later the Belgian Minister for Foreign Affairs communicated to the Belgian Legations his answer to the question which Sir Edward Grey had asked Belgium in the name of England:

"Mr. Minister:

"The British Minister requested to see me very urgently and communicated to me the following:

"'Sir Edward Grey has asked the French and German Governments, separately, whether each of them was prepared to respect the neutrality of Belgium.

"'In view of the existing treaties, I am also instructed to inform the Minister for Foreign Affairs of Belgium that *Sir Edward Grey presumes that Belgium will do her utmost to maintain her neutrality.*'

"I immediately thanked Sir Francis Villiers for this communication, which the Belgian Government appreciates very highly, and I added that Great Britain and the other nations, guarantors of our independence, might be sure that we would neglect no effort to maintain our neutrality, and that we were convinced that the other powers, in view of the excellent relations of friendship and confidence which we have always enjoyed with them, would observe and maintain this neutrality."

At the decisive moment, the attitude of Belgium was thus irreproachable. She was not bound to any other nation; she had her hands free. She declared that she was ready to make the necessary sacrifices to defend her neutrality and to resist any aggression from whatever source, and she added that, trusting in her friendly relations with the powers, she was unwilling to believe that any of them would violate her neutrality.

On Aug. 3, at 7 A.M., after having received the ultimatum from Germany, Belgium declared that she refused to repudiate her engagements.

The next day, the 4th of August, at 3 P.M., the Belgian Minister for Foreign Affairs received from Sir F. Villiers, Minister of England in Brussels, the following note:

BRUSSELS, Aug. 4, 1914.

I am instructed to inform the Belgian Government that if Germany exercises pressure for the purpose of compelling Belgium to abandon her position of a neutral country, the Government of his Britannic Majesty expects Belgium to resist by every possible means. The Government of his Britannic Majesty is ready, in that event, to join with Russia and France, *if desired by Belgium*, to offer to the Belgian Government, at once, common action for the purpose of resisting the use of force by Germany against Belgium, and at the same time to offer a guarantee to maintain the independence and the integrity of Belgium in the future.

England offered her help *but did not impose it*. She did not intend to send troops into Belgian territory as a preventive measure. She expressly subordinated her assistance *to the desire of Belgium.*

It was only on the 4th of August, during the evening, after having vainly hoped and waited for a change in the attitude of Germany, that Belgium called England, France, and Russia to co-operate, as guarantor powers, in the defense of her territory.

In the preface published by Dr. B. Dernburg, with the documents, it is said that "only the prompt action at Liége that put this important railway centre, commanding the railway connections to France and Germany, into German hands, prevented the English landing and invading Belgium."

It is impossible to conceive how the taking of Liége prevented the English from landing and invading Belgium. That statement is hardly a compliment to the intelligence or the geographical knowledge of the American people. The fact is that Liége was taken a long time before the British troops landed at Calais, and it is still today in the hands of the Germans without in the least interfering with the arrival of British reinforcements in France and in the territory still left in the possession of Belgium. The fact is that Liége was not taken to prevent the British from entering Belgium, but because it was part of the plan of the German General Staff to invade Belgium at once, to march across her territory, to crush the army of France as soon as possible, and then to turn and attack the Russians on the east.

It is interesting to recall here the famous conversation held between the British Ambassador in Berlin, on one side, and the Chancellor of the Empire, Mr. Bethmann-Hollweg, and the German Secretary for Foreign Affairs, Mr. von Jagow, on the other side, at the time of the invasion of Belgium by the German troops. These conversations prove, indisputably, the premeditated intention of Germany to violate Belgium's neutrality:

To the request of Sir Edward Goschen, the English Ambassador in Berlin, to be allowed to know if Germany would pledge herself to respect the neutrality of Belgium, the German Secretary of State replied that "this neutrality had already been violated by Germany." Herr von Jagow went again into the "reasons why the Imperial Government had been obliged to take this step, namely, that they had to advance into France by the quickest and easiest way so as to be able to get well ahead with their operations and endeavor to strike some decisive blow as early as possible. It was a matter of life and death to them, for, if they had gone by the more southern route, they could not have hoped, in view of the paucity of the roads and the strength of the fortresses, to have got through without formidable opposition entailing great loss of time. This loss of time would mean time gained by the Russians for the bringing up of their troops to the German frontier. Rapidity of action was the great German asset, while that of Russia was the inexhaustible supply of troops." (Official report of the British Ambassador in Berlin to the British Government.)

This conversation preceded by a few minutes that in which the German Chancellor, giddy at the sight of the abyss into which Germany was falling, uttered these celebrated words: "Just for a word, NEUTRALITY, a word which in war times has been so often disregarded; just for A SCRAP OF PAPER, Great Britain is going to make war on a kindred nation. At what price would that compact (neutrality) have been kept? Has the British Government thought of that?" Sir Edward Goschen replied that fear of consequences would hardly be regarded as an excuse for breaking a solemn engagement. (Official report of the British Ambassador in Berlin to his Government.)

Finally, the solemn avowal of the German Chancellor, during the sitting of the Reichstag on Aug. 4, 1914, settles this question definitely: "We are in a state of legitimate defense. NECESSITY KNOWS NO LAW. Our troops have occupied Luxemburg and have perhaps already penetrated into Belgium. This is against the law of nations."

The truth is that every step taken by Germany was a clear indication of her intentions against Belgium. Her strategic railroads are concentrated on the Belgian frontier, and her military writers, von Bernhardi, von Schliefenbach, and von der Goltz, made no secret of her plan to carry on her war by means of an invasion of Belgium's neutral country. Events have shown how, long before the war, preparations had been made to carry this plan into effect.

Dr. B. Dernburg says that the one-sidedness of the Belgian inclination is indicated by the placing of all Belgian fortresses on the eastern frontier. The distinguished statesman (apparently confused by the ardor of discussion) has already in another article, published in The Independent of Dec. 7, 1914, placed Antwerp at the mouth of the Rhine; today he places Namur on the German frontier, whereas that fortress is situated near the frontier of France. There are three fortresses in Belgium—Antwerp, Liége, and Namur. Antwerp is in the north, Liége in the east, and Namur in the south. Namur, being near the French frontier, could menace Germany only in case the Germans should have penetrated about one-third of Belgium. It is, in fact, a fortress against France.

Nothing has been brought forward to show that, if Germany had not invaded Belgium, France or England would have done so. The exact contrary is clearly indicated by the documents.

Dr. B. Dernburg cites a decision of the Supreme Court of the United States and attempts to apply it to the case of Germany's violation of Belgian neutrality and to justify Germany by the law of necessity. The example chosen (the Chinese question) does not involve massacres, bombardments, nor the burning of towns. It is not an analogous case. The following would be a closer analogy to Germany's action in regard to Belgium: A man pretending that he has been attacked in the street by a powerful enemy, claims that he is justified in killing an innocent person, if by doing so he can gain an advantage over his adversary.

It would be difficult for any one to produce a decision of the Supreme Court justifying a crime on the plea that the perpetration of the crime was advantageous to the culprit who committed it.

When a nation has to resort to such arguments to defend its actions it must realize that its case is desperate.

Germany has converted smiling and peaceful Belgium into a land of sorrow, of mourning, and of ruins. There is not a family that does not mourn one of its dear ones. In the face of the indignation which has aroused the world, Germany, today, endeavors to refute the accusation which rises against her from so many tombs, and she endeavors to throw upon the innocent the terrible responsibility of her own crimes.

It is not probable that this course of action will win back to Germany the sympathy which she has lost throughout the world.

The foregoing documents show clearly that Belgium had made no agreement with England for attacking Germany, nor even an agreement for British military defense of Belgian neutrality.

[Having replied to the representations made in the German indictment drawn by Dr. Dernburg, the Belgian authorities proceeded to compile a pamphlet, the contents of which are reproduced on the following pages, purporting to show from original documents the manner of the German violation of Belgium's neutralized territory.]

THE BIG AND THE GREAT

By WILLIAM ARCHER.

[From King Albert's Book.]

THE Big and the Great
When they to History's judgment seat shall come,
Which will shine glorious in the eyes of men,
Huge Germany or heroic BELGIUM?
Which will be hailed Great, Wilhelm or ALBERT, then?

[The following title and article are reproduced from the second pamphlet referred to in the letter from the Belgian Legation at Washington to THE NEW YORK TIMES CURRENT HISTORY, appearing on Page 1110.—EDITOR.]

[BELGIAN LEGATION ARTICLE NO. 2.]

"Why Belgium Was Devastated"

"As Recorded in Proclamations of the German Commanders in Belgium"

"Necessity knows no law."
—BETHMANN-HOLLWEG.

"The wrong that we are committing we will endeavor to repair as soon as our military goal has been reached."
—BETHMANN-HOLLWEG.

EXTRACT FROM A PROCLAMATION TO THE MUNICIPAL AUTHORITIES OF THE CITY OF LIÉGE.

Aug. 22, 1914.

The inhabitants of the town of Andenne, after having declared their peaceful intentions, have made a surprise attack on our troops.

It is with my consent that the Commander in Chief has ordered the whole town to be burned and that about one hundred people have been shot.

I bring this fact to the knowledge of the City of Liége, so that citizens of Liége may realize the fate with which they are menaced if they adopt a similar attitude.

The General Commanding in Chief.
(Signed) VON BUELOW.

NOTICE POSTED AT NAMUR, AUGUST THE 25TH, 1914.

(1) French and Belgian soldiers must be surrendered as prisoners of war at the prison before 4 o'clock. *Citizens who do not obey will be condemned to enforced labor for life in Germany.*

A rigorous inspection of houses will begin at 4 o'clock. Every soldier found will be immediately shot.

(2) Arms, powder, dynamite, must be surrendered at 4 o'clock. Penalty: death by shooting.

The citizens who know where a store of arms is located must inform the Burgomaster, *under penalty of enforced labor for life.*

(3) Each street will be occupied by a German guard who will take ten hostages in each street, whom they will keep in custody.

If any outrage is committed in the street, *the ten hostages will be shot.*

(4) Doors must not be locked, and at night after 8 o'clock three windows must be lighted in each house.

(5) It is forbidden to remain in the street after 8 o'clock. The people of Namur must understand that there is no greater nor more horrible crime than to endanger the existence of the city and the life of its inhabitants by attacks upon the German Army.

The Commandant of the City.
(Signed) VON BUELOW.

Namur, 25th of August, 1914. (Imprimerie Chantraine.)

LETTER ADDRESSED ON AUG. 27, 1914, BY LIEUT. GEN. VON NIEBER TO THE BURGOMASTER OF WAVRE.

On Aug. 22, 1914, the General commanding the Second Army, Herr von Bülow, imposed upon the City of Wavre a war levy of three million francs, to be paid before Sept. 1, as expiation for its unqualifiable behavior (contrary to the law of nations and the usages of war) in making a surprise attack on the German troops.

The General in command of the Second Army has just given to the General commanding this station of the Second Army the order to send in without delay, this contribution which it should pay on account of its conduct.

I order and command you to give to the bearer of the present letter the two first installments, that is to say, two million francs in gold.

Furthermore, I require that you give the bearer a letter, duly sealed with the seal of the city, stating that the balance, that is to say, one million francs, will be paid, without fail, on the 1st of September.

I draw the attention of the city to the fact that in no case can it count on further delay, as the civil population of the city has put itself outside the law of nations by firing on the German soldiers.

The City of Wavre will be burned and destroyed if the levy is not paid in due time, without regard for any one; the innocent will suffer with the guilty.

PROCLAMATION POSTED AT GRIVEGNEE, Sept. 8, 1914.

Commune of Grivegnee.
Very Important Notice.

The Major Commandant Dieckmann, at the Château des Bruyeres, requests me to bring the following statement to the knowledge of the inhabitants:

Dieckmann   Battalion,
Château des Bruyeres, Sept. 6, 1914.

Present at the discussion:

(1) The Curé Fryns of Bois de Breux.
(2) The Curé Franssen of Beyne.
(3) The Curé Lepropres of Heusay.
(4) The Curé Paquay of Grivegnee.
(5) The Burgomaster Dejardin of Beyne.
(6) The Burgomaster Hodeige of Grivegnee.
(7) Major Dieckmann.
(8) Lieut. R. Reil.

Major Dieckmann brought to the knowledge of the persons present the following orders:

"(1) Before the 6th of September, 1914, at 4 o'clock in the afternoon, all arms, munitions, explosives, and fireworks which are still in the hands of the citizens must be surrendered at the Château des Bruyeres. *Those who do not obey will render themselves liable to the death penalty. They will be shot on the spot, or given military execution, unless they can prove their innocence.*

"(2) All inhabitants of houses in Beyne-Heusay, Grivegnee, Bois de Greux, and Fleron must remain at home after sunset, (at present 7 o'clock P.M., German time.) The aforesaid houses must be lighted as long as any one remains up. The entrance door must be shut. Those who do not conform to the regulations expose themselves to severe penalties. Any resistance to these orders will be followed by sentence of death.

"(3) The Commandant should meet no opposition whatever in these domiciliary visits. Each inhabitant must open all the rooms of his house without even a summons. Whoever makes any opposition will be severely punished.

"(4) Beginning Sept. 7, at 9 o'clock in the morning, I will permit the houses of Beyne-Heusay, Grivegnee, Bois de Breux, to be occupied by persons formerly dwelling in them as long as no formal prohibition to frequent these places shall have been issued against the inhabitants above referred to.

"(5) In order to be sure that this permission is not abused, the Burgomasters of Beyne-Heusay and of Grivegnee shall immediately draw up a list of persons who shall be held as hostages, at the fort of Fleron, in twenty-four-hour shifts; on Sept. 6, for the first time, from 6 o'clock in the evening until midday, Sept. 7.

"*The life of these hostages will depend upon the population of the aforesaid communes remaining pacific under all circumstances.*

"During the night it is strictly prohibited to make any luminous signal whatever. The circulation of bicycles is only allowed from 7 A.M. until 5 P.M., German time.

"(6) I will designate from the lists submitted to me the persons who will be detained as hostages from noon of one day to noon of the next day. If the substitute does not arrive in time, the hostage will remain another twenty-four hours. *After this second period of twenty-four hours, the hostage incurs the penalty of death if the substitution is not made.*

"(7) Hostages will be chosen, primarily, from among priests, Burgomasters, and other members of the civic administration.

"(8) I demand that all civilians living in the vicinity, especially in Beyne-Heusay, Fleron, Bois de Breux, and Grivegnee, shall show deference toward the German officers by taking off their hats and by carrying the hand to the head in military salute. In case of doubt, every German soldier must be saluted. If any one refuses to do so, he must expect the German soldiers to make themselves respected by any means they may select.

"(9) The German soldiers have the right to visit any wagon or package belonging to the inhabitants of the surrounding country. Any opposition will be severely punished.

"(10) *Any one knowing of the location of a store of more than one hundred litres of petroleum, benzine, benzol, or other similar liquids in the aforesaid communes, and who does not report same to the military commander on the spot, incurs the penalty of death, provided there is no doubt about the quantity and the location of the store. Quantities of 100 litres are alone referred to.*

"(11) Any one who does not instantly obey the command of 'hands up' becomes guilty (sic) of the death penalty.

"(12) *The entrance to the Château des Bruyeres* and to the park *is prohibited under the penalty of death* from dark till dawn, (6 P.M. to 6 A.M., German time,) to all who are not soldiers of the German Army.

"(13) During daytime entrance to the Château des Bruyeres is allowed only by the northeast entrance, where there is a guard, and only to the people to whom cards of admission have been given. Any gathering near the guard is prohibited in the interest of the population.

"(14) Any one who by spreading false news prejudicial to the morale of the German troops or who by any means tries to take measures against the German Army renders himself a suspect and incurs the risk of being shot immediately.

"(15) Whereas by the above regulations the inhabitants in the vicinity of the fortress are threatened with severe penalties if they violate these regulations in any way, on the other hand these same inhabitants, if they remain peaceful, may rely upon the most benevolent protection and help on all occasions when wrong is done them.

"(16) The requisition of cattle in specified quantities will take place daily from 10 A.M. until noon and from 2 P.M. to 3 P.M. at the Château des Bruyeres before the Cattle Commission.

"(17) Any one who under the protection of the insignia of the Swiss (Red Cross) Convention harms, or even tries to harm, the German Army and is discovered shall be hung."

(Signed) DIECKMANN,
Major in Command.

Grivegnee, Sept. 8, 1914.

For certified copy: The Burgomaster,
(Signed) VICTOR HODEIGE.

SUMMONS TO CAPITULATE.

Sept. 4, 1914.

To the Commander of Termonde and, at the same time, to the Burgomaster of Termonde:

The Germans have taken Termonde. We have placed the heaviest siege artillery all around the town. Still, at the present time, one dares shoot from houses upon German soldiers. The town and the fortress are summoned to hoist immediately the white flag and to stop fighting. If you do not yield to this summons immediately the town will be razed to the ground within a quarter of an hour by a heavy bombardment. All the armed forces of Termonde will immediately lay down their arms at the Porte de Bruxelles (Brussels Gate) at the south exit from Termonde. Arms held by the inhabitants will be deposited at the same time and at the same place.

The General Commanding the German Forces Before Termonde, (Signed) VON BOEHN.

PROCLAMATION POSTED IN BRUSSELS SEPT. 25, 1914.

General Government in Belgium.

It has happened recently in some places which are not at the present time occupied by strong forces of German troops, military convoys or patrolling parties have been attacked by surprise by the inhabitants.

I draw the attention of the public to the fact that *a record* is kept of the towns and villages in the vicinity in which such attacks have taken place and that they must expect their punishment as soon as German troops pass near by.

The Governor General of Belgium,
(Signed) BARON VON DER GOLTZ,
Field Marshal.

Brussels, 25th September.

NOTICE POSTED AT BRUSSELS OCT. 5, 1914, AND PRESUMABLY IN MOST OF THE COMMUNES IN THE COUNTRY.

On the evening of Sept. 25 the railway and telegraph lines were destroyed on the Lovenjoul-Vertryck line.

Consequently the two above-mentioned places on the morning of Sept. 30 had to give an account and to furnish hostages.

In the future the communities in the vicinity of a place where such things happen (*no matter whether or not they are accomplices*) will be punished without mercy.

To this end hostages have been taken from all places in the vicinity of railroad lines menaced by such attacks, and at the first attempt to destroy the railroad tracks or the telegraph or telephone wires they will be immediately shot.

Furthermore, all troops in charge of the protection of the railroad lines have received orders to shoot any person approaching in a suspicious manner the railroad tracks or the telegraph or telephone lines.

The Governor General of Belgium,
(Signed) BARON VON DER GOLTZ,
Field Marshal.

NOTICE POSTED AT BRUSSELS, NOV. 1, 1914.

A legally constituted court-martial has pronounced, the 28th of October, 1914, the following condemnations:

"(1) Upon Policeman de Ryckere for attacking, in the exercise of his legal functions, an agent vested with German authority, for willfully inflicting bodily injury on two occasions in concert with other persons, for facilitating the escape of a prisoner on one occasion, and for attacking a German soldier—*Five years' imprisonment.*

"(2) Upon Policeman Seghers for attacking, in the exercise of his legal functions, an agent vested with German authority, for willfully inflicting bodily injury upon said German agent, and for facilitating the escape of a prisoner (all these offenses constituting a single act)—*Three years' imprisonment.*"

These sentences have been confirmed by Gov. Gen. Baron von der Goltz on Oct. 31, 1914.

The City of Brussels, excluding suburbs, has been punished for the crime committed by its policeman de Ryckere against a German soldier by an additional fine of 5,000,000 francs.

The Governor of Brussels,
(Signed) BARON VON LUETTWITZ,
General.

Brussels, Nov. 1, 1914.

EXTRACT FROM THE SIXTH REPORT OF THE BELGIUM COMMISSION OF INQUIRY.

After such proclamations, who will be surprised at the murders, burnings, pillage, and destruction committed by the German Army wherever they have met with resistance?

If a German corps or patrolling party is received at the entrance to a village by a volley from soldiers of the regular troops who are afterward forced to retire the whole population is held responsible. The civilians are accused of having fired or having co-operated in the defense and, without inquiry, the place is given over to pillage and flames, and a part of the inhabitants are massacred.

The Commission of Inquiry has already mentioned these facts in its report of Sept. 10, (third report.)

The facts which have been gathered since then have confirmed its conclusions.

The odious acts which have been committed in all parts of the country have a general character, throwing the responsibility upon the whole German Army. It is simply the application of a preconceived system—the carrying out of instructions—which has made of the enemy's troops in Belgium "a horde of barbarians and a band of incendiaries."

The reports which the commission has had the honor of submitting to you up to the present, Mr. Minister, concern especially events of which the towns of Aerschot and Louvain and the communes in the Provinces of Antwerp and Brabant have been the theatre. New reports will be sent you shortly which will permit you to take cognizance of the gravity of acts committed by the invaders in other parts of the country, notably in the Provinces of Liége, Namur, Hainault, and Flanders.

The President,
(Signed) COOREMAN.

The Vice President,
(Signed) COUNT GOBLET D'ALVIELLA.

The Secretaries,
(Signed) CHEVALIER ERNEST DE BUNSWYCK,
(Signed) ORTS.

"FROM THE BODY OF THIS DEATH"

By SIDNEY LOW.

[From King Albert's Book.]

SHE is not dead! Although the spoiler's hand
Lies heavy as death upon her; though the smart
Of his accursed steel is at her heart,
And scarred upon her breast his shameful brand;
Though yet the torches of the vandal band
Smoke on her ruined fields, her trampled bones,
Her ravaged homes and desolated fanes,
She is not dead but sleeping, that wronged land.

O little nation, valorous and free,
Thou shalt o'erlive the terror and the pain;
Call back thy scattered children unto thee,
Strong with the memory of their brothers slain,
And rise from out thy charnel-house, to be
Thine own immortal, radiant self again.

H.I.M. AUGUSTA VICTORIA

The Most Recent Photograph of the German Empress.

(*Photo from American Press Association.*)

A WAR-TIME PICTURE OF THE KAISER

The Effects of the Stress of War Are Noticeable in This Photograph
of the War Lord,
Taken in His Winter Campaign Uniform.

(*Photo from Underwood & Underwood.*)

"A Scrap of Paper"
Recent Versions of the German Chancellor's Reference to the Belgian Treaty of Neutrality[2]

By Chancellor von Bethmann-Hollweg and Sir Edward Grey.

I.

GENERAL FIELD HEADQUARTERS OF THE GERMAN ARMIES IN FRANCE, via Berlin and London, Jan. 24.—"I am surprised to learn that my phrase, 'a scrap of paper,' which I used in my last conversation with the British Ambassador in reference to the Belgian neutrality treaty, should have caused such an unfavorable impression in the United States. The expression was used in quite another connection and the meaning implied in Sir Edward Goschen's report and the turn given to it in the biased comment of our enemies are undoubtedly responsible for this impression."

The speaker was Dr. Theobald von Bethmann-Hollweg, the German Imperial Chancellor, and the conversation with a representative of The Associated Press occurred at the German Army Field Headquarters, in a town of Northern France, and in a villa serving as the office and dwelling for the Imperial Chancellor, for the Foreign Minister, Gottlieb von Jagow, and for the members of the diplomatic suite accompanying Emperor William afield.

The Chancellor apparently had not relished the subject until his attention was called to the extent to which the phrase had been used in discussion on the responsibility of the war. He then volunteered to give an explanation of his meaning, which in substance was that he had spoken of the treaty not as "a scrap of paper" for Germany, but as an instrument which had become obsolete through Belgium's forfeiture of its neutrality, and that Great Britain had quite other reasons for entering into the war, compared with which the neutrality treaty appeared to have only the value of a scrap of paper.

"My conversation with Sir Edward Goschen," said the Chancellor, "occurred Aug. 4. I had just declared in the Reichstag that only dire necessity and only the struggle for existence compelled Germany to march through Belgium, but that Germany was ready to make compensation for the wrong committed.

"When I spoke I already had certain indications, but no absolute proof upon which to base a public accusation, that Belgium long before had abandoned its neutrality in its relations with England. Nevertheless, I took Germany's responsibilities toward the neutral State so seriously that I spoke frankly of the wrong committed by Germany.

"What was the British attitude on the same question?" continued the Chancellor. "The day before my conversation with Ambassador Goschen, Sir Edward Grey had delivered his well-known speech in Parliament, in which, while he had not stated expressly that England would take part in the war, he had left the matter in little doubt.

"One needs only to read this speech through carefully to learn the reason for England's intervention in the war. Amid all his beautiful phrases about England's honor and England's obligations we find it over and over again expressed that England's interests—its own interests—call for participation in the war, for it is not in England's interests that a victorious and therefore stronger Germany should emerge from the war.

"This old principle of England policy—to take as the sole criterion of its actions its private interests regardless of right, reason, or considerations of humanity—is expressed in that speech of Gladstone's in 1870 on Belgian neutrality, from which Sir Edward quoted.

"Mr. Gladstone then declared that he was unable to subscribe to the doctrine that the simple fact of the existence of a guarantee is binding on every party thereto, irrespective altogether of the particular position in which it may find itself at a time when the occasion for action on the guarantee arrives; and he referred to such English statesmen as Aberdeen and Palmerston as supporters of his views.

"England drew the sword," continued the Chancellor, "only because it believed its own interests demanded it. Just for Belgian neutrality it would never have entered the war.

"That is what I meant when I told Sir Edward Goschen in that last interview, when we sat down to talk the matter over privately as man to man, that among the reasons which had impelled England to go into the war the Belgian neutrality treaty had for her only the value of a scrap of paper.

"I may have been a bit excited and aroused," said the Chancellor. "Who would not have been at seeing the hopes and the work of the whole period of my Chancellorship going for nought? I recalled to the Ambassador my efforts for years to bring about an understanding between England and Germany; an understanding which, I reminded him, would have made a general European war impossible, and which absolutely would have guaranteed the peace of Europe.

"Such an understanding," the Chancellor interjected parenthetically, "would have formed the basis on which we could have approached the United States as a third partner; but England had not taken up this plan, and through its entry into the war had destroyed forever the hope of its fulfillment.

"In comparison with such momentous consequences was the treaty not a scrap of paper? England ought really to cease harping on this theme of Belgian neutrality," said the Chancellor. "Documents on the Anglo-Belgian military agreement which we have found in the meantime show plainly enough how England regarded this neutrality. As you know, we found in the archives of the Belgian Foreign Office documents which showed that England in 1911 was determined to throw troops into Belgium without the assent of the Belgian Government if war had then broken out—in other words, to do exactly the same thing for which, with all the pathos of virtuous indignation, it now reproaches Germany.

"In some later dispatch Sir Edward Grey, I believe, informed Belgium that he did not believe England would take such a step because he did not think English public opinion would justify that action. And still people in the United States wonder that I characterized as a scrap of paper the treaty whose observance, according to responsible British statesmen, should be dependent on the pleasure of British public opinion—a treaty which England itself had long since undermined with its military agreements with Belgium!

"Remember, too, that Sir Edward Grey expressly refused to assure us of England's neutrality even in the event that Germany respected Belgian neutrality.

"I can understand, therefore, the English displeasure at my characterization of the Treaty of 1839 as a scrap of paper, for this scrap of paper was for England extremely valuable, furnishing an excuse before the world for embarking in the war.

"I hope, however, that in the United States you will see clearly enough that England in this matter, too, acted solely on the principle of 'right or wrong, my interest.'"

The Chancellor during the conversation had twice risen to take a few impatient steps about the room. He spoke calmly enough, but with an undercurrent of deep feeling, particularly when he mentioned his efforts for an understanding with England and the world peace which he had hoped would come from them based on an agreement between Great Britain, Germany, and the United States, and with a note of thorough conviction as to the justice of the German position toward Belgium.

II.

SIR EDWARD GREY'S REPLY.

London, Jan. 26.—Sir Edward Grey, the British Secretary of State for Foreign Affairs, today authorized the following statement in reply to an interview obtained with Dr. von Bethmann-Hollweg, the German Imperial Chancellor, by a representative of The Associated Press and published in London on Jan. 26 and in the United States on Jan. 25:

"The Secretary of State for Foreign Affairs authorizes the publication of the following observations upon the report of an interview recently granted by the German Chancellor to an American correspondent. It is not surprising that the German Chancellor should show anxiety to explain away his now historic phrase about a treaty being a mere 'scrap of paper.'

"The phrase has made a deep impression because the progress of the world largely depends upon the sanctity of agreements between individuals and between nations, and the policy disclosed in Herr von Bethmann-Hollweg's phrase tends to debase the legal and moral currency of civilization.

"What the German Chancellor said was that Great Britain in requiring Germany to respect the neutrality of Belgium 'was going to make war just for a word, just for a scrap of paper'—that is, that Great Britain was making a mountain out of a molehill. He now asks the American public to believe that he meant the exact opposite of what he said; that it was Great Britain who really regarded the neutrality of Belgium as a mere trifle, and that it was Germany who 'took her responsibilities toward the neutral States so seriously.'

"The arguments by which Herr von Bethmann-Hollweg seeks to establish the two sides of this case are in flat contradiction of the plain facts.

"First, the German Chancellor alleges that 'England in 1911 was determined to throw troops into Belgium without the assent of the Belgian Government.' This allegation is absolutely false. It is based upon certain documents found in Brussels which record conversations between British and Belgian officers in 1906, and again in 1911.

"The fact that there is no note of these conversations at the British War Office or the Foreign Office shows that they were of a purely informal character and that no military agreement of any sort was at either time made between the two Governments. Before any conversations took place between the British and the Belgian officers it was expressly laid down on the British side that discussion of the military possibilities was to be addressed to the manner in which, in case of need, British assistance could be most effectually afforded to Belgium for the defense of her neutrality, and on the Belgian side a marginal note upon the record explains that 'the entry of the English into Belgium would only take place after the violation of our (Belgium's) neutrality by Germany.'

"As regards the conversation of 1911, the Belgian officer said to the British officer: 'You could only land in our country with our consent'; and in 1913 Sir Edward Grey gave the Belgian Government a categorical assurance that no British Government would violate the neutrality of Belgium and that 'so long as it was not violated by any other power we should certainly not send troops ourselves into their territory.'

"The Chancellor's method of misusing documents may be illustrated in this connection. He represents Sir Edward Grey as saying, 'he did not believe England would take such a step because he did not think English public opinion would justify such action.'

"What Sir Edward Grey actually wrote was: 'I said that I was sure that this Government would not be the first to violate the neutrality of Belgium, and I did not believe that any British Government would be the first to do so, nor would public opinion here ever approve of it.'

"If the German Chancellor wishes to know why there were conversations on military subjects between British and Belgian officers he may find one reason in a fact well known to him—namely, that Germany was establishing an elaborate network of strategical railways leading from the Rhine to the Belgian frontier through a barren, thinly populated tract. The railways were deliberately constructed to permit of a sudden attack upon Belgium, such as was carried out in August last.

"This fact alone was enough to justify any communications between Belgium and the other powers on the footing that there would be no violation of Belgian neutrality, unless it was previously violated by another power. On no other footing did Belgium ever have any such communications.

"In spite of these facts the German Chancellor speaks of Belgium as having thereby 'abandoned and forfeited' her neutrality, and he implies that he would not have spoken of the German invasion as a 'wrong' had he then known of the conversations of 1906 and 1911.

"It would seem to follow that according to Herr von Bethmann-Hollweg's code wrong becomes right if the party which is to be the subject of the wrong foresees the possibility and makes preparations to resist it.

"Those who are content with older and more generally accepted standards are likely to agree rather with what Cardinal Mercier said in his pastoral letter: 'Belgium was bound in honor to defend her own independence. She kept her oath. The other powers were bound to respect and to protect her neutrality. Germany violated her oath. England kept hers. These are the facts.'

"In the second part of the German Chancellor's thesis, namely, that Germany 'took her responsibilities toward the neutral States seriously,' he alleges nothing except that 'he spoke frankly of the wrong committed by Germany' in invading Belgium.

"That a man knows the right while doing the wrong is not usually accepted as proof of his serious conscientiousness. The real nature of Germany's view of her 'responsibilities toward the neutral States' may, however, be learned on authority which cannot be disputed by reference to the English 'White Paper.'

"If those responsibilities were in truth taken seriously why, when Germany was asked to respect the neutrality of Belgium if it were respected by France, did Germany refuse? France, when asked the corresponding question at the same time, agreed. This would have guaranteed Germany from all danger of attack through Belgium.

"The reason of Germany's refusal was given by Herr von Bethmann-Hollweg's colleague, (the German Foreign Secretary, Herr von Jagow.) It may be paraphrased in the well-known gloss upon Shakespeare: 'Thrice is he armed that hath his quarrel just, but four times he that gets his blow in fust.'

"'They had to advance into France,' said Herr von Jagow, 'by the quickest and easiest way so as to be able to get well ahead with their operations and endeavor to strike some decisive blow as early as possible.'

"Germany's real attitude toward Belgium was thus frankly given by the German Foreign Secretary to the British Ambassador, and the German Chancellor in his speech to the Reichstag claimed the right to commit a wrong in virtue of the military necessity of hacking his way through. The treaty which forbade the wrong was by comparison a mere scrap of paper.

"The truth was spoken in these first statements by the two German Ministers. All the apologies and arguments which have since been forthcoming are afterthoughts to excuse and explain away a flagrant wrong. Moreover, all the attacks upon Great Britain in regard to this matter and all talk about 'responsibilities toward neutral States' come badly from the man who, on July 29, asked Great Britain to enter into a bargain to condone the violation of the neutrality of Belgium.

"The German Chancellor spoke to the American correspondent of his 'efforts for years to bring about an understanding between England and Germany.' An understanding, he added, which would have 'absolutely guaranteed the peace of Europe.'

"He omitted to mention what Mr. Asquith made public in his speech at Cardiff,[3] that Germany required as the price of an understanding an unconditional pledge of England's neutrality. The British Government were ready to bind themselves not to be parties to any aggression against Germany. They were not prepared to pledge their neutrality in case of aggression by Germany.

"An Anglo-German understanding on the latter terms would not have meant an absolute guarantee for the peace of Europe, but it would have meant an absolutely free hand for Germany, so far as England was concerned, for Germany to break the peace of Europe.

"The Chancellor says that in his conversation with the British Ambassador in August last he 'may have been a bit excited at seeing the hopes and work of the whole period of his Chancellorship going for nought.'

"Considering that at the date of the conversation, Aug. 4, Germany had already made war on France, the natural conclusion is that the shipwreck of the Chancellor's hopes consisted not in a European war, but in the fact that England had not agreed to stand out of it.

"The sincerity of the German Chancellor's professions to the American correspondent may be brought to a very simple test, the application of which is more apposite because it serves to recall one of the leading facts which produced the present war.

"Herr von Bethmann-Hollweg refused the proposal which England put forward and in which France, Italy, and Russia concurred, for a conference at which the dispute would have been settled on fair and honorable terms without war. If he really wished to work with England for peace why did he not accept that proposal? He must have known after the Balkan conference in London that England could be trusted to play fair. Herr von Jagow had given testimony in the Reichstag to England's good faith in those negotiations.

"The proposal for the second conference between the powers was made by Sir Edward Grey with the same straightforward desire for peace as in 1912 and 1913. The German Chancellor rejected this means of averting the war. He who does not will the means must not complain if the conclusion is drawn that he did not will the end.

"The second part of the interview with an American newspaper correspondent consists of a discourse upon the ethics of the war. The things which Germany has done in Belgium and France have been placed on record by those who have suffered from them and who know them at first hand. After this it does not lie with the German Chancellor to read to the other belligerents a lecture upon the conduct of the war."

THE KAISER AT DONCHERY.

[By The Associated Press.]

BERLIN, Jan. 29, (via London.)—The Lokalanzeiger has published some further accounts of the visit of Dr. Ludwig Ganghofer, the author, to Emperor William at the German Field Headquarters. It tells of a trip made by the Emperor and Dr. Ganghofer to Donchery, in the region of the Sedan battlefield. Here the Emperor, in speaking of the unity of the German people, is quoted as saying to Dr. Ganghofer: "It is my greatest pleasure that I could live to see it."

The Emperor pointed out to the author where his father had stood at Sedan, where Napoleon and Bismarck met, and other historic spots.

The trip by automobile finally brought the party to the headquarters of Crown Prince Frederick William, where, after luncheon had been eaten, the Emperor turned smiling to his son and said:

"One gets better things to eat at your headquarters than at mine. I shall consider whether I shall not requisition your cook."

The Emperor here had an opportunity to see a thousand French prisoners march by. He was greatly pleased when some of them doffed their caps to him and he returned their salute. During this review he turned to a photographer who was taking pictures, and said:

"Photograph the prisoners and not always me."

The party later climbed a steep ascent to get a view of the surrounding region. When descending, Dr. Ganghofer slipped, but the Emperor quickly grasped him by the arm and saved him from a fall, saying at the same time:

"Soldiers and citizens must help each other all they can."

HAIL!
A HYMN TO BELGIUM

POEM BY

JOHN GALSWORTHY

MUSIC BY

FREDERIC H. COWEN.

(From King Albert's Book.)

[Listen]

N.B.—If it is desired to sing this as a simple Hymn, the Melody of the 3rd verse should be omitted and the words sung to the opening eight bars, as in the 1st and 2nd verses

Holland's Future

By H.G. Wells.

The article which follows was written by H.G. Wells for publication in England. The British censor, however, refused to permit its appearance there, and thus it was printed in the United States for the first time by THE NEW YORK TIMES on Feb. 7, 1915. In the development of his argument Mr. Wells points out that "the Dutch hold a sword at the back of Germany." That Holland has no intention of sheathing this sword, so removing a menace from Germany, is indicated by the recent cable from The Hague telling of the message sent by the Government to the Second Chamber of the Legislature dealing with pending legislation to prolong the term of enlistment in the regular army, in which this language is used: "The position of our country demands today, as it did in August, that our entire military force should be at all times available."

WHAT changes for Holland are likely to result from the present war?

Let me, as an irresponsible journalist, try to estimate them, and try to forecast what Holland is likely to do in the next few months. I do not want for a moment to suggest what Dutchmen ought to do; this preaching to highly intelligent neutrals is not a writer's business, but I want to imagine how things must look in the private mind of a wary patriotic Hollander, and to guess what may be the outcome. Because in many ways Holland does seem to hold the key to the present situation.

It is clear that whatever fears may have been felt for the integrity of Holland at the beginning of the war must now be very much abated. The risk of Germany attacking Holland diminishes with each day of German failure, and the whole case and righteousness of the Allies rests upon their respect for Holland. Holland's position as regards Germany now is extraordinarily strong materially, and as regards the Allies it is overwhelmingly strong morally. She has behaved patiently and sanely through a trying crisis. She has endured much almost inevitable provocation and temptation with dignity and honesty. Were she now subjected to any German outrage she could strike with her excellent army of 400,000 men at Aix-la-Chapelle, and turn repulse into rapid disaster.

That is the interesting thing about the Dutch position now. The Dutch hold a sword at the back of Germany. Were they to come into the war on the German side, they would, no doubt, provide a most effective but certainly not a decisive reinforcement to the German western front, but they would also lay open a convenient way for the Allies to the vital part of Germany, Westphalia. But were they to come in on the side of the Allies they would at once deliver a conclusive blow. They could cut the main communications of the German army in Flanders, they could round up and assist to capture a very large portion of the German western forces, and they could open the road not only to attack but to turn the Rhine defenses. In fact, they could finish Germany.

This situation is already fairly obvious; I betray no strategic secret; it must become manifest to every Dutchman before many more weeks. One has but to look at the map. Every day now diminishes the possibility of Germany being able to make any effective counterattack, any Belgian destruction, in Holland, and every day increases the weight of the blow that Holland may deliver. What are the chances that Holland may not ultimately realize to the full the possibilities of that blow and join the Allies?

Against her doing so is the consideration that she is doing very well as she is. She keeps her freedom. Practically the Allies fight to secure it for her. The dread of Germanization which has hung over Holland for forty years seems to recede.

And, of course, as a secondary restraining force there is the reasonable fear of devastation. The "good German" vindictiveness might make one last supreme effort.

But, on the other hand, is she really doing as well as it seems? Unless she intervenes this war will probably last for another full year. She wants it to end. It is a terrible oppression. Her army must remain mobilized, even if it does not fight. Her trade stagnates. She is incumbered by refugees. What if she struck to end the war and get the tension over? Not now, perhaps, but presently. Simultaneously with the Franco-British counter-stroke that now draws near.

And what if she struck also for a hatred of what has happened to Belgium? Suppose the Dutch are not so much frightened by the horrible example of Belgium as indignant. My impression of the Dutch—and we English know something of the Dutch spirit—is that they are a people not easily cowed. Suppose that they have not only a reasonable fear but a reasonable hatred of "frightfulness." Suppose that an intelligent fellow-feeling for a small nation has filled them with a desire to give Germany a lesson. There, it may be, is a second reason why Holland should come in.

And by coming in, there is something more than the mere termination of a strain and the vindication of international righteousness to consider.

There is the possibility, and not only the possibility but the possible need, that Holland should come out of this world war aggrandized. I want to lay stress upon that, because it may prove a decisive factor in this matter.

The Dutch desire aggrandizement for the sake of aggrandizement as little as any nation in Europe. But what if the path of aggrandizement be also the path of safety?

It is clear that both France and Belgium will demand and receive territorial compensation for these last months of horror. It is ridiculous to suppose that the Germans may fling war in its most atrocious and filthy form over Belgium and some of the sweetest parts of France without paying bitterly and abundantly for the freak.

Quite apart from indemnities, France and Belgium must push forward their boundaries so far that if ever Germany tries another rush she will have to rush for some days through her own lost lands. The only tolerable frontier against Germans is a day's march deep in Germany. Of course, Liége will have to be covered in the future by Belgian annexations in the Aix region and stretching toward Cologne, and France will go to the Rhine. I think Belgium as well as France will be forced to go to the Rhine.

It is no good talking now of buffer States, because the German conscience cannot respect them. Buffer States are just anvil States. At any rate, very considerable annexations of German territory by Belgium and France are now inevitable, and Holland must expect a much larger and stronger Belgium to the south of her, allied firmly to France and England.

And to the north is it very likely that the British will be able to tolerate the continued German possession of the Frisian Islands? These islands, and the coast of East Friesland, have had but one use in German hands, and that use has been the preparation of attacks on England. Clearly the British may decide to have no more of such attacks. Every advance in scientific warfare may make them more dangerous and exasperating. The British intend soberly and sanely to do their utmost to make a repetition of the present war impossible. To secure this they may find it necessary to have Germany out of the North Sea. But they have no desire whatever to take either the Frisian Islands or East Friesland, if Holland will save them that trouble.

Now, suppose the Dutch will not think of this now. Suppose, for the want of their aid, the Allies are unable to press the war to the complete regimentation of Germany, what will be the position of Holland in twenty years' time?

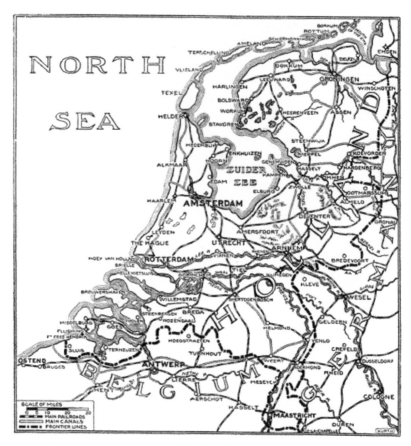

[Enlarge]

She will stand between England and Germany. A Germany incompletely beaten means an Anglophobe Germany. Belgium and France expanded, recuperated, allied, linked by a common literature and language, may be too formidable for another German attack. So that there is the possibility that in twenty years' time or so Germany, recovering and vindictive, may in some way contrive to hold off France and Belgium, and try her luck against England alone. By that time submarine and aeroplane may be so developed as to render a German attack on England much more hopeful than it is at present, especially by way of the Rhine mouth. What, in the light of the Belgian experience and the new doctrine of a "right of way," will be the outlook for a little isolated Holland, as small as she is now, as a buffer State in such a case.

She has always been claimed as a part of the great Pan-German scheme, and at any time she may find the German heel upon her face, vindictively punishing her for her lack of enthusiasm for Teutonic brotherhood. Hadn't she better get herself a little larger and stronger now; hadn't she better help to make the ending of the German threat more conclusive, and link herself definitely with the grand alliance of the Western Powers? Now she could make a very good bargain indeed. If she inquired she would find Britain ready enough to guarantee the integrity and protection of Holland's colonial empire forever by the British fleet. All the four Western Powers, France, Belgium, Holland, Britain, would be willing to make the most binding pledges for such mutual protection. It is the manifest common-sense of the settlement that they should set up such a collective guarantee. And, in addition, there are those Frisian Islands, and East Friesland, and that dangerous wedge that Germany drives into Holland along the Rhine. It is not difficult to map a very much improved Dutch frontier along the Ems, and thence striking down to the Rhine and meeting the iron country on the left bank of the Rhine, whose annexation and exploitation is Belgium's legitimate compensation for her devastation and sufferings. Here are the makings of a safer Greater Holland! Thousands of Dutchmen must be looking on the map at the present time and thinking such things as this. There, clearly and attractively, is the price of alliance.

The price of neutrality is an intact Holland—and a certain isolation in the years ahead. But still, I admit, a not unhappy Holland, Dutch and free. Until a fresh Anglo-German struggle begins. Yet, be it noted, a Holland a little helpless and friendless if some renascent Asiatic Power should presently covet her Eastern possessions.

The price of participation with Germany, on the other hand, is complete envelopment in the warm embrace of the "good German brotherhood"— the gradual substitution of the German language for the Dutch, and a Germanization of such colonies as the Allies may still leave for Holland, frequent State visits from Kaisers, and the subordination of Dutch mercantile interests to those of Hamburg and Altona and (Germanized) Antwerp. And—the everlasting howling everywhere of "Deutschland, Deutschland über Alles."

(No! No! They will never fight for the Germans. No sane people will ever fight for the Germans if they can possibly avoid it. Not even our press censorship, not even the Maximilian Krafts in our silliest weekly papers will provoke Holland to that.)

But I have a sort of feeling, for the reasons I have stated, that even without any serious breach of Dutch neutrality by the Germans, Holland may decide presently to put her troops beside the Belgians. And if, as is always possible, the Germans do make some lumpish onslaught upon

Dutch neutrality, then I am convinced that at once that sturdy little country will up and fight like the very devil. And do remarkably well by it.

And I have a much stronger feeling that presently the Dutch Government will ask the Germans to reconsider their proposed annexation of Belgium. Upon that point Holland has absolutely dictatorial power at the present moment. She could secure the independence of Belgium at the cost of a little paper and ink, she could force Germany to evacuate her sister country by the mere movement of her army.

Copyright in U.S.A.

French Official Report on German Atrocities

Having been instructed to investigate atrocities said to have been committed by the Germans in portions of French territory which had been occupied by them, a commission composed of four representatives of the French Government repaired to these districts in order to make a thorough investigation. The commission was composed of M. Georges Payelle, First President of the Cour des Comptes; Armand Mollard, Minister Plenipotentiary; Georges Maringer, Counselor of State, and Edmond Paillot, Counselor of the Cour de Cassation.

They started on their mission late in September last and visited the Departments of Seine-et-Marne, Marne, Meuse, Meurthe-et-Moselle, Oise, and Aisne. According to the report, they made note only of those accusations against the invaders which were backed up by reliable testimony and discarded everything that might have been occasioned by the exigencies of war.

Presented to the President of the Council by the commission instituted with a view to investigating acts committed by the enemy in violation of international law. Decree of Sept. 23, 1914. MM. Georges Payelle, First President of the Cour des Comptes; Armand Mollard, Minister Plenipotentiary; Georges Maringer, Counselor of State, and Edmond Paillot, Counselor at the Court of Appeal.

To the President of the Council of Ministers:

SIR: Having been appointed by virtue of a decree of the 23d of last September to carry out on the spot an inquiry in relation to acts committed in violation of international law in the portions of French territory occupied by the enemy which have been reconquered by the armies of the republic, we have the honor to lay before you the first results of our mission.

We have already a full harvest of information to submit. It includes, however, a very limited part of the findings at which we should have been able to arrive if we had not submitted all the evidence which was laid before us to severe criticism and rigorous examination. We have indeed believed it to be our duty only to place on record those facts which, being established beyond dispute, constitute with absolute certainty what may be clearly termed crimes, omitting those the proofs of which were, in our view, insufficient, or which, however destructive or cruel they were, might have been the result of acts of war properly so-called, rather than of willful excesses, attributable to the enemy.

Thus we are convinced that none of the incidents which we have investigated could be disputed in good faith. In addition the proof of each of them does not depend only on our personal observations; it is founded chiefly on photographs and on a mass of evidence received in judicial form, with the sanction of an oath.

The lamentable sights which we have had before our eyes have made the task to which we all four addressed ourselves, with a close association of ideas and feelings, a very grievous one. It would indeed have been too painful, if we had not found a powerful support in the sight of the wonderful troops whom we met at the front, in the welcome of the military leaders whose kind assistance has never failed us, and in the sight of the population who bear unprecedented calamities with the most dignified resignation. In the districts which we crossed, and particularly in that country of Lorraine which was so frequently the victim of the scourge of war, not one entreaty for help, not one moan, reached our ears; and yet the terrible misery of which we have been witness surpasses in extent and horror anything which the imagination can conceive. On every side our eyes rested on ruin. Whole villages have been destroyed by bombardment or fire; towns formerly full of life are now nothing but deserts full of ruins; and, in visiting the scenes of desolation where the invader's torch has done its work, one feels continually as though one were walking among the remains of one of those cities of antiquity which have been annihilated by the great cataclysms of nature.

In truth it can be stated that never has a war carried on between civilized nations assumed the savage and ferocious character of the one which at this moment is being waged on our soil by an implacable adversary. Pillage, rape, arson, and murder are the common practice of our enemies; and the facts which have been revealed to us day by day at once constitute definite crimes against common rights, punished by the codes of every country with the most severe and the most dishonoring penalties, and which prove an astonishing degeneration in German habits of thought since 1870.

Crimes against women and young girls have been of appalling frequency. We have proved a great number of them, but they only represent an infinitesimal proportion of those which we could have taken up. Owing to a sense of decency, which is deserving of every respect, the victims of these hateful acts usually refuse to disclose them. Doubtless fewer would have been committed if the leaders of an army whose discipline is most rigorous had taken any trouble to prevent them; yet, strictly speaking, they can only be considered as the individual and spontaneous acts of uncaged beasts. But with regard to arson, theft, and murder the case is very different; the officers, even those of the highest station, will bear before humanity the overwhelming responsibility for these crimes.

In the greater part of the places where we carried on our inquiry we came to the conclusion that the German Army constantly professes the most complete contempt for human life, that its soldiers, and even its officers, do not hesitate to finish off the wounded, that they kill without pity the inoffensive inhabitants of the territories which they have invaded, and they do not spare in their murderous rage women, old men, or children. The wholesale shootings at Lunéville, Gerbéviller, Nomeny, and Senlis are terrible examples of this; and in the course of this report you will read the story of scenes of carnage in which officers themselves have not been ashamed to take part.

The mind refuses to believe that all these butcheries should have taken place without justification. Still, it is so! It is true that the Germans have always advanced the same pretext for them, alleging that civilians had begun by firing upon them. This allegation is a lie, and those who advance it have been unable to give it any probability, even by firing rifle shots in the neighborhood of houses, as they are accustomed to do in order to be able to state that they have been attacked by an innocent population on whose ruin or massacre they have resolved. We have many times ascertained the truth of this; here is one among others:

One evening the Abbé Colin, Curé of Croismare, was standing near an officer when the report of a gun rang out. The latter cried, "Monsieur le Curé, that is enough to cause you to be shot as well as the Burgomaster, and for a farm to be burned; look, there is one on fire." "Sir," replied the priest, "you are too intelligent not to recognize the sharp sound of your German rifle. For my part, I recognize it." The German did not press the point.

Personal liberty, like human life, is the object of complete scorn on the part of the German military authorities. Almost everywhere citizens of every age have been dragged from their homes and led into captivity, many have died or been killed on the way.

Arson, still more than murder, forms the usual procedure of our adversaries. It is employed by them either as a means of systematic devastation or as a means of terrorism. The German Army, in order to provide for it, possesses a complete outfit, which comprises torches, grenades, rockets, petrol pumps, fuse-sticks, and little bags of pastilles made of compressed powder which are very inflammable. The lust for arson is manifested chiefly against churches and against monuments which have some special interest, either artistic or historical.

In the departments through which we have gone thousands of houses have been burned, but we have only investigated in our inquiry fires which have been occasioned by exclusively criminal intention, and we have not believed it our duty to deal with those that have been caused by shells in the course of violent fighting, or due to circumstances which it has not been possible to determine with absolute certainty, such as those at Villotte-devant-Louppy, Rembercourt, Mognéville, Amblaincourt, Pretz, Louppy-le-Château, and other places. The few inhabitants who remained among the ruins furnished us with information in absolute good faith on this subject.

We have constantly found definite evidence of theft, and we do not hesitate to state that where a body of the enemy has passed it has given itself up to a systematically organized pillage, in the presence of its leaders, who have even themselves often taken part in it. Cellars have been emptied to the last bottle, safes have been gutted, considerable sums of money have been stolen or extorted; a great quantity of plate and jewelry, as well as pictures, furniture, objets d'art, linen, bicycles, women's dresses, sewing machines, even down to children's toys, after having been taken away, have been loaded on vehicles to be taken toward the frontier.

The inhabitants have had no redress against all these exactions, any more than they have for the crimes already described; and if some wretched inhabitant dared to beg an officer to be good enough to intervene to spare a life or to protect his goods he received no other reply (when he was not greeted by threats) than the one invariable formula, accompanied by a smile, describing these most abominable cruelties as the inevitable results of war.

As you have already learned from reading the documents of which we have sent you copies, we proceeded first to the Department of Seine-et-Marne. We there collected proofs of numerous abuses of the laws of war, as well as of crimes committed against common rights by the enemy, some of which exhibited features of special gravity.

At Chauconin the Germans set fire to five dwelling houses and to six buildings used for agricultural purposes with the assistance of grenades, which they threw on to the roofs, and with sticks of resin which they placed under the doors. M. Lagrange asked an officer the reason of such acts and the latter merely replied: "It is war." Then he ordered M. Lagrange to point out to him the situation of the property known as the Farm Proffit, and a few moments later the buildings of this farm were in flames.

At Congis a body of the enemy were engaged in burning a score of houses, into which they had thrown straw and poured petrol, when the arrival of a French detachment prevented them from carrying out their design.

At Penchard, where three houses had been burned, Mme. Marius René saw a soldier carrying a torch which, stuck in his belt, appeared to form part of his equipment.

At Barcy an officer and soldier made their way to the Mairie, and, after having taken all the blankets belonging to the schoolmaster, set fire to the muniment room.

At Douy-la-Ramé the Germans set fire to a mill, whose situation they had ascertained by inquiry in the neighborhood. A workman 66 years old had a narrow escape from being thrown into the flames. By struggling violently and clutching on to a wall he was able to avoid the fate with which he was threatened. Finally, at Courtaçon, after having compelled the inhabitants to furnish them with matches and faggots, they sprinkled a great number of houses with petrol and set them ablaze. The village, a great part of which is in ruins, presents a lamentable appearance.

Together with these crimes against property, we have been able to place on record in the Department of Seine-et-Marne many grave offenses against the person.

Early in September a German cavalryman arrived one day at about 5 o'clock in the afternoon at the house of M. Laforest, at May-en-Multien, and asked for a drink. M. Laforest hurried off to draw some wine from the cask, but the German, no doubt annoyed at not being served quickly enough, fired his rifle at the wife of his host, who was seriously wounded. Taken to Livry-sur-Ourcq, Mme. Laforest was there cared for by a German doctor and had her left arm amputated. She died recently in the hospital at Meaux.

On Sept. 8 eighteen inhabitants of Vareddes, among whom was the priest, were arrested without cause and led away by the enemy. Three of them escaped. None of the others had returned up to Sept. 30, the day we were there. From information collected, three of these men were murdered. Anyhow, the death of one of the oldest among them, M. Jourdain, aged 73, is certain.

Dragged as far as the village of Coulombs and being unable to walk further, the unfortunate man received a bayonet wound in the forehead and a revolver bullet through the heart.

At about the same time a man of 66, named Dalissier, living at Congis, was ordered by the Germans to give up his purse to them. When he proved unable to give them any money, he was tied up with a halter and ruthlessly shot. The marks of about fifteen bullets were found on his dead body.

On the 3d of September, at Mary-sur-Marne, M. Mathe, terrified at the arrival of the German troops, attempted to hide himself under the counter of a wine shop. He was found in his hiding place and killed by a thrust of a knife or bayonet in the chest.

At Sancy-les-Provins, on the 6th of September, about 9 o'clock at night, about eighty people were summarily arrested and imprisoned in a sheep pen. On the next day thirty of them were taken by an officer's order some five kilometers from the village to the barn called "Pierrelez," where a German Red Cross ambulance was established. There an army doctor (médecin-major) addressed some words to the wounded under his charge, who at once proceeded to load four rifles and two revolvers, their intention being obvious. Moreover, a French hussar, who had been wounded in the arm and taken prisoner, said to the priest, while asking him for absolution: "I am going to be shot, and it will be your turn next." After having done as the soldier asked him, the priest, unbuttoning his cassock, went and took his place between the Mayor and another of his fellow-citizens, against a wall along which the hostages were lined up; but at this moment two French *chasseurs à cheval* suddenly arrived, and the doctors, with their ambulance staff, surrendered to these soldiers, near whom the hussar had hastened to place himself.

As showing the responsibility of officers of high rank for these proceedings, it is interesting to note that the schoolmaster at Sancy, when he was about to be taken off with the others, was allowed to retain his freedom as a favor by General von Dutag, who was quartered on him.

On the 6th of the same month, after having set on fire some of the houses in Courtaçon, a body of soldiers, believed to belong to the Imperial Guard, took five men and a child of thirteen out into the fields, and exposed them to the French fire so long as the engagement lasted. In the confines of the same commune, Edmond Rousseau, liable to serve in the 1914 class, was arrested for the sole reason that his age marked him out as being on the eve of being called up to the colors, and was murdered under tragic circumstances.

The Mayor, who was one of the hostages, when questioned as to the position of this youth from the military point of view, replied that Rousseau had passed the medical examination, that he had been declared fit for service, but that his class had not yet been called up. The Germans thereupon made the prisoner strip, in order to satisfy themselves of his physical condition, then put his trousers on again, and shot him within fifty meters of his fellow-citizens.

The town of Coulommiers has suffered considerable pillage. Plate, linen, and boots were taken away, principally from empty houses, and a large number of bicycles were loaded on motor wagons. The Germans occupied this place from the 5th to the 7th of September. On this day before they left they arrested, without any pretext, the Mayor and the Procureur de la République, and an officer grossly insulted them. These two officials were kept in custody until the next morning, together with the Secretary of the Mairie. Guards were set over the Procureur during the night, and did their best to persuade him by remarks exchanged between them that his execution was imminent.

It is generally believed at Coulommiers that criminal attempts have been made on many women of that town, but only one crime of this nature has been proved for certain. A charwoman, Mme. X., was the victim. A soldier came to her house on the 6th of September, toward 9:30 in the evening, and sent away her husband to go and search for one of his comrades in the street. Then, in spite of the fact that two small children were present, he tried to rape the young woman. X., when he heard his wife's cries, rushed back, but was driven off with blows of the butt of the man's rifle into a neighboring room, of which the door was left open, and his wife was forced to suffer the consummation of the outrage. The rape took place almost under the eyes of the husband, who, being terrorized, did not dare to intervene, and used his efforts only to calm the terror of his children.

In the same way, Mme. X., at Sancy-les-Provins, and Mme. Z., at Beton-Bazoches, were the victims of similar outrages. The former was forced to submit to the will of a soldier with a revolver at her throat; the second, in spite of her resistance, was thrown upon a bed and outraged in the presence of her little daughter, aged 3. The husbands of these two women have been with the army since the commencement of the war.

On the 6th of September, at Guérard, where two workmen, Maitrier and Didelot, had been killed at the outposts, the enemy took possession of six hostages. One only was able to escape and return to his village.

At Mauperthuis, on the same day, four Germans who had already gone in the morning to the house of M. Roger, presented themselves there again at 2 o'clock in the afternoon. "There were three of you here this morning, and now you are only two. Come out," said one of them. Immediately Roger and a refugee named M. Denet, who was a guest in the house, were seized and led away. The next day, at the end of the village, Mme. Roger found the body of her husband, pierced by two bullets. Denet had also been shot, and his body was discovered some little time afterward in such a state of decomposition as to make it impossible to ascertain the nature of the wounds which the unfortunate man had received.

In a hamlet in the same commune, M. Fournier, caretaker of a farm at Champbrisset, resided with a Swiss named Knell. The Germans took them on a cart as far as Vaudoy and murdered them. An inhabitant of Voinsles, named Cartier, suffered the same fate. As he passed on his bicycle along a road a little way from Vaudoy, he was stopped by the Germans, who searched his bag, in which was a revolver. Cartier, without any resistance, gave up his weapon of his own accord. His eyes were bandaged, and he was shot then and there.

On the 8th of September at Sablonnières, where there were scenes of general pillage, M. Delaitre, who had left his house during the battle to take refuge under a culvert, was discovered in his hiding place by a German soldier, who fired at him five times; he died the same day.

GENERAL CASTELNAU

One of the Most Conspicuous of the French Commanders.

GENERAL DUBAIL

Commanding the French Forces Operating Around Verdun.

(*Photo © International News Service.*)

At the same place, M. Jules Griffaut, 66 years of age, was herding his cows peacefully in a field, when a detachment of the enemy passed 150 meters from him. A soldier who was alone in the rear of the column took aim at him, and shot him in the face. It is proper to add that a German officer took the trouble to have the wounded man attended to by a German army doctor, and that Griffaut recovered fairly soon.

At Rebais, on the 4th of September, at 11 in the evening, the Germans, after pillaging the jeweler's shop of M. Pantereau and loading the goods which they had taken on to a cart, set fire to the house. They also burned three private houses in the Rue de l'Etang by throwing lighted straw into them.

In this little town serious acts of violence were committed. M. Auguste Griffaut, 79 years of age, was treated with horrible brutality. They repeatedly struck him on the head with their fists. A revolver shot grazed his head. His watch and his purse, containing 800 francs, were stolen from his person.

On the same day, some German soldiers grossly ill-treated Mme. X., a wine-shop keeper, aged 29, on the pretense that she was hiding English soldiers. They undressed her and kept her in the middle of them completely naked for one and a half hours; then they tied her to her counter, giving her to understand that they were going to shoot her. They were, however, called out just then, and went away, leaving their victim in charge of an Alsatian soldier, who untied her and restored her to liberty.

Again, on the 4th of September, other soldiers attempted to rape Mme. Z., 34 years of age, after having sacked her grocery shop. Angered by her resistance, they tried to hang her, but she cut the rope with a knife which was open in her pocket. She was then beaten mercilessly until the arrival of an officer, who was fetched by a witness of the scene.

At St. Denis-les-Rebais, on the 7th of September, a Uhlan obliged Mme. X. to undress, threatening her with his rifle; then he threw her on a mattress and raped her while her mother-in-law, powerless to intervene, endeavored to keep her grandson, 8 years old, from this revolting sight.

On the same day, at the hamlet of Marais, in the Commune of Jouv-sur-Morin, the three daughters of Mme. X., aged respectively 18, 15, and 13, were with their sick mother when two German soldiers entered, seized the eldest, dragged her into the next room and raped her in succession; while one committed his crime, the other watched the door and with his weapons kept back the half-maddened mother.

Frightful scenes occurred at the Château de —— in the neighborhood of La Ferté-Gaucher. There lived there an old gentleman, M. X., with his servant, Mlle. Y., 54 years old. On Sept. 5 several Germans, among whom was a non-commissioned officer, were in occupation of this property. After they had been supplied with food, the non-commissioned officer proposed to a refugee, a Mme. Z., that she should sleep with him; she refused. M. X., to save her from the designs of which she was the object, sent her to his farm, which was in the neighborhood. The German ran there to fetch her, dragged her back to the château and led her to the attic; then, having completely undressed her, he tried to violate her. At this moment M. X., wishing to protect her, fired revolver shots on the staircase and was immediately shot.

The non-commissioned officer then made Mme. X. come out of the attic, obliged her to step over the corpse of the old man, and led her to a closet, where he again made two unsuccessful attempts upon her. Leaving her at last, he threw himself upon Mlle. Y., having first handed Mme. Z. over to two soldiers, who, after having violated her, one once and the other twice, in the dead man's room, made her pass the night in a barn near them, where one of them twice more had sexual connection with her.

As for Mlle. Y., she was obliged, by threats of being shot, to strip herself completely naked and lie on a mattress with the non-commissioned officer, who kept her there until morning.

We have also taken note of the fact that, as appears from declarations made by a municipal councilor of Rebais, two English cavalrymen who were surprised and wounded in this commune were finished off with gunshots by the Germans when they were dismounted and when one of them had thrown up his hands, showing thus that he was unarmed.

MARNE.

In the Department of the Marne, as everywhere else, the German troops gave themselves up to general pillage, which was carried out always under similar conditions and with the complicity of their leaders. The Communes of Heiltz-le-Maurupt; Suippes, Marfaux, Fromentières, and Esternay suffered especially in this way. Everything which the invader could carry off from the houses was placed on motor lorries and vehicles. At Suippes, in particular, they carried off in this way a quantity of different objects, among these sewing machines and toys.

A great many villages, as well as important country towns, were burned without any reason whatever. Without doubt these crimes were committed by order, as German detachments arrived in the neighborhood with their torches, their grenades, and their usual outfit for arson.

At Lépine, a laborer named Caqué, in whose house two German cyclists were billeted, asked the latter if the grenades which he saw in their possession were destined for his house. They answered: "No, Lépine is finished with." At that moment nine houses in the village were burned out.

At Marfaux nineteen private houses were burned.

At le Gault-la-Forêt seven or eight houses were burned. Of the Commune of Glannes practically nothing remains. At Somme-Tourbe the entire village has been destroyed, with the exception of the Mairie, the church, and two private buildings.

At Auve nearly the whole town has been destroyed. At Etrepy sixty-three families out of seventy are homeless. At Huiron all the houses, with the exception of five, have been burned. At Sermaize-les-Bains only about forty houses out of 900 remain. At Bignicourt-sur-Saultz thirty houses out of thirty-three are in ruins.

At Suippes, the big market town which has been practically burned out, German soldiers carrying straw and cans of petrol have been seen in the streets. While the Mayor's house was burning, six sentinels with fixed bayonets were under orders to forbid any one to approach and to prevent any help being given.

All this destruction by arson, which only represents a small proportion of the acts of the same kind in the Department of Seine-et-Marne, was accomplished without the least tendency to rebellion or the smallest act of resistance being recorded against the inhabitants of the localities which are today more or less completely destroyed. In some villages the Germans, before setting fire to them, made one of their soldiers fire a shot from his rifle so as to be able to pretend afterward that the civilian population had attacked them, an allegation which is all the more absurd since at the time when the enemy arrived the only inhabitants left were old men, sick persons, or people absolutely without any means of aggression.

Numerous crimes against the person have also been committed. In the majority of the communes hostages have been taken away; many of them have not returned. At Sermaize-les-Bains, the Germans carried off about 150 people, some of whom were decked out with helmets and coats and compelled, thus equipped, to mount guard over the bridges.

At Bignicourt-sur-Saulx thirty men and forty-five women and children were obliged to leave with a detachment. One of the men—a certain Emile Pierre—has not returned nor sent any news of himself. At Corfélix, M. Jacquet, who was carried off on the 7th of September with eleven of his fellow-citizens, was found five hundred meters from the village with a bullet in his head.

At Champuis the curé, his maid-servant, and four other inhabitants, who were taken away the same day as the hostages of Corfélix, had not returned at the time of our visit to the place.

At the same place an old man of 70, named Jacquemin, was tied down in his bed by an officer and left in this state without food for three days. He died a little time after.

At Vert-la-Gravelle a farm-hand was killed. He was struck on the head with a bottle and his chest was run through with a lance.

The garde champêtre Brulefer of le Gault-la-Forêt was murdered at Maclaunay, where he had been taken by the Germans. His body was found with his head shattered and a wound on his chest.

At Champguyon, a commune which has been fired, a certain Verdier was killed in his father-in-law's house. The latter was not present at the execution, but he heard a shot and next day an officer said to him, "Son shot. He is under the ruins." In spite of the search made the body has not been found among them. It must have been consumed in the fire.

At Sermaize, the roadmaker Brocard was placed among a number of hostages. Just at the moment when he was being arrested with his son, his wife and his daughter-in-law in a state of panic rushed to throw themselves into the Saulx. The old man was able to free himself for a moment and ran in all haste after them and made several attempts to save them, but the Germans dragged him away pitilessly, leaving the two wretched women struggling in the river. When Brocard and his son were restored to liberty, four days afterward, and found the bodies, they discovered that their wives had both received bullet wounds in the head.

At Montmirail a scene of real savagery was enacted. On the 5th of September a non-commissioned officer flung himself almost naked on the widow Naudé, on whom he was billeted, and carried her into his room. This woman's father, François Fontaine, rushed up on hearing his daughter's cry. At once fifteen or twenty Germans broke through the door of the house, pushed the old man into the street, and shot him without mercy. Little Juliette Naudé opened the window at this moment and was struck in the stomach by a bullet, which went through her body. The poor child died after twenty-four hours of most dreadful suffering.

On the 6th of September at Champguyon, Mme. Louvet was present at the martyrdom of her husband. She saw him in the hands of ten or fifteen soldiers, who were beating him to death before his own house, and ran up and kissed him through the bars of the gate. She was brutally pushed back and fell, while the murderers dragged along the unhappy man covered with blood, begging them to spare his life and protesting that he had done nothing to be treated thus. He was finished off at the end of the village. When his wife found his body it was horribly disfigured. His head was beaten in, one of his eyes hung from the socket, and one of his wrists was broken.

At Esternay, on the 6th of September, toward 3 in the afternoon, thirty-five or forty Germans were leading away M. Lauranceau, when he made a sharp movement as if to free himself. He was immediately shot down.

In the same town the following facts have been laid before us:

During the night, between Sunday, the 6th of September, and Monday, the 7th, the soldiers who were scattered among the houses pillaging, discovered the widow Bouché, her two daughters, and Mmes. Lhomme and Macé, who had taken refuge under the cellar staircase. They ordered the two young girls to undress, then, as their mother tried to intervene, one of the soldiers, bringing his rifle to his shoulder, fired in the direction of the group of women. The bullet, after having struck Mme. Lhomme near the left elbow, broke the right arm of Mlle. Marcelle Bouché at the armpit. During the following day the young girl died as a result of her wound. According to the declarations made by witnesses, the wound was horrible to behold.

Further, our inquiry in the Department of the Marne established other crimes of which women were the victims.

On the 3rd of September, at Suippes, Mme. X., 72 years of age, was seized by a German soldier, who pushed the barrel of his revolver under her chin and brutally flung her on her bed. Her son-in-law rushed up at the noise, fortunately for her, at the moment when the rape was about to be consummated.

At the same place and time little ———, 11 years old, was for three hours the prey of a licentious soldier, who, having found her with her sick grandmother, dragged her to a deserted house and stopped her mouth with a handkerchief to prevent her crying out.

On the 7th of September, at Vitry-en-Perthois, Mme. X., aged 45, and Mme. Z., aged 89, were both raped; the latter died a fortnight later.

At Jussecourt-Minecourt, on the 8th of September, toward 9 in the evening, Mlle. X. was violated by four soldiers, who broke in the door of her room with the help of a billhook. All four flung themselves on this young girl, who was 21 years old, and ravished her in succession.

As the bombardment of open towns constitutes without doubt a violation of international law, we thought it necessary to go to Rheims, which was for eighty days bombarded by the Germans. We received a sworn statement from the Mayor, from which we learned that about 300 of the civilian population had already been killed; we saw that in different parts of the town numerous buildings had been destroyed, and we took note of the enormous and irreparable damage which had been inflicted on the cathedral. The bombardment has continued since the 7th of October, the day of our visit; the number of the victims, therefore, must now be very considerable. Every one knows how the unhappy town has suffered, and that the attitude of the municipality has been above all praise.

While we were working at the Hôtel de Ville, six shells were fired in the direction of this building. The fifth fell only a short distance from the principal front, and the sixth burst fifteen or twenty meters from the bureau.

Next day we went to the Château of Baye and witnessed the traces of the sack which this building has suffered. On the first floor a door which leads into a room next to a gallery, where the owner had collected valuable works of art, has been broken in; four glass cabinets have been broken and another has been opened. According to the declarations of the caretaker who, in the absence of her masters, was unable to acquaint us of the full extent of the damage, the principal objects stolen were jewels of Russian origin and gold medals. We noticed that the mounts covered with black velvet, which must have been taken out of the cases, were stripped of a part of the jewels which had previously been affixed to them.

Baron de Baye's room was in the greatest disorder. Numerous objects were strewn on the floor from the drawers which remained open. A writing table had been broken open. A Louis XVI. commode and a bureau à cylindre of the same period had been ransacked.

This room must have been occupied by a person of very high rank, for on the door there still remains a chalk inscription, "J.K. Hoheit." No one could give us exact information as to the identity of this "Highness"; however, a General who lodged in the house of M. Houllier, Town Councilor, told his host that the Duke of Brunswick and the staff of the Tenth Corps had occupied the château.

The same day we visited the Château of Beaumont, which is near Montmirail, and belongs to the Comte de la Rochefoucauld-Doudeauville. The wife of the caretaker declared that this house had been sacked by the Germans in the absence of its owners during an occupation which lasted from the 4th to the 6th of September. The invaders left it in an indescribable state of disorder and filth. The writing tables, bureaus, and safes had been broken open. The jewel boxes had been taken from the drawers and emptied.

On the doors of the rooms we could read inscriptions in chalk, among which we took note of the following: "Excellenz," "Major von Ledebur," "Graf Waldersee."

MEUSE.

The Department of the Meuse, a great part of which the German armies still occupy, has suffered cruelly. Important communes there have been destroyed by fires lighted willfully by the Germans in the absence of any kind of military necessity, and without the population's having given any provocation for such atrocities by their attitude. This is the case particularly at Revigny, Sommeilles, Triaucourt, Bulainville, Clermont-en-Argonne, and Villers-aux-Vents.

The Germans having completely sacked the houses of Revigny and carried off their booty on vehicles, burned two-thirds of the town during three consecutive days from the 6th to the 9th of September, sprinkling the walls with petrol by means of hand pumps, and throwing into the houses little bags full of compressed powder in tablets. We have been furnished with specimens of these little bags and these tablets, as well as with fuse sticks of inflammable matter which had been left by the incendiaries.

The church, which was classed as a historical monument, and the Mairie with all its archives, have been destroyed.

Many inhabitants, among whom were children, have been taken away as hostages. They were, however, set at liberty next day, with the exception of M. Wladimir Thomas.

Few localities in the Department of the Meuse have suffered as much as the Commune of Sommeilles. It is nothing but a heap of ruins, having been completely burned on the 6th of September by a regiment of German infantry bearing the number fifty-one. The place was set on fire with help of machinelike bicycle pumps with which many of the soldiers were furnished.

This unhappy village was the scene of a terrible drama. At the commencement of the fire Mme. X., whose husband is with the colors, took refuge in the cellar of M. et Mme. Adnot, together with these latter and their four children, aged respectively 11, 5, 4, and 1-1/2 years. A few days afterward the bodies of all these unfortunate people were discovered in the middle of a pool of blood. Adnot had been shot, Mme. X. had her breast and right arm cut off; the little girl of 11 had a foot severed, the little boy of 5 had his throat cut. The woman X. and the little girl appeared to have been raped.

At Villers-aux-Vents, on the 8th of September, German officers invited the inhabitants who had not yet fled to leave their dwellings, warning them that the village was about to be burned, because, they alleged, three French soldiers had dressed themselves in civilian clothes; others gave the pretext that an installation of wireless telegraphy had been found in a house. The threat was carried out so rigorously that one house alone remains standing.

At Vaubecourt, where six dwelling houses were burned by the Württemburgers, fire was set to a barn with straw piled up by the soldiers.

At Triaucourt the Germans gave themselves up to the worst excesses. Angered doubtless by the remark which an officer had addressed to a soldier, against whom a young girl of 19, Mlle. Hélène Procès, had made complaint on account of the indecent treatment to which she had been subjected, they burned the village and made a systematic massacre of the inhabitants. They began by setting fire to the house of an inoffensive householder, M. Jules Gand, and by shooting this unfortunate man just as he was leaving his house to escape the flames; then they dispersed among the houses in the streets, firing their rifles on every side. A young man of 17, Georges Lecourtier, who tried to escape, was shot. M. Alfred Lallemand suffered the same fate; he was pursued into the kitchen of his fellow-citizen, Tautelier, and murdered there, while Tautelier received three bullets in his hand.

Fearing, not without reason, for their lives, Mlle. Procès, her mother, her grandmother of 71, and her old aunt of 81, Mlle. Laure Mennehand, tried with the help of a ladder to cross the trellis which separates their garden from a neighboring property. The young girl alone was able to reach the other side and to avoid death by hiding in the cabbages. As for the other women, they were struck down by rifle shots. The village curé collected the brains of Mlle. Mennehand on the ground on which they were strewn, and had the bodies carried into Procès's house. During the following night the Germans played the piano near the bodies.

While the carnage raged, the fire rapidly spread and devoured thirty-five houses. An old man of 70, Jean Lecourtier, and a child of two months perished in the flames. M. Igier, who was trying to save his cattle, was pursued for 300 meters by soldiers, who fired at him ceaselessly. By a miracle this man had the good fortune not to be wounded, but five bullets went through his trousers. When the curé, Viller, expressed his indignation at the treatment inflicted upon his parish to the Duke of Württemburg, who was lodged in the village, the latter replied: "What would you have? We have bad soldiers just as you have."

In the same commune an attempt at rape was made which was unsuccessful by reason of the obstinate and courageous resistance of the victim. Three Germans made the attempt on Mme. D., 47 years old. Further, an old woman of 75, Mme. Maupoix, was kicked so violently that she died a few days afterward. While some of the soldiers were ill-treating her others were ransacking her wardrobes.

The little town of Clermont-en-Argonne, on the slope of a picturesque hill in the middle of a pleasant landscape, used to be visited every year by numerous tourists. On the 4th of September, at night, the 121st and 122d Württemburg Regiments entered the place, breaking down the doors of the houses and giving themselves up to unrestrained pillage, which continued during the whole of the next day. Toward midday a soldier set fire to the dwelling of a clockmaker by deliberately upsetting the contents of an oil lamp which he used for making coffee. An inhabitant, M. Monternach, at once ran to fetch the town fire engine, and asked an officer to lend him men to work it. Brutally refused and threatened with a revolver, he renewed his request to several other officers, with no greater success. Meanwhile the Germans continued to burn the town, making use of sticks on the top of which torches were fastened. While the houses blazed the soldiers poured into the church, which stood by itself on the height, and danced there to the sound of the organ. Then, before leaving, they set fire to it with grenades as well as with vessels full of inflammable liquid, containing wicks.

After the burning of Clermont, bodies of the Mayor of Vauquois, M. Poinsignon, (which was completely carbonized,) and that of a young boy of 11, who had been shot at point-blank range, were found.

When the fire was out pillage recommenced in the houses which the flames had spared. Furniture carried off from the house of M. Desforges and stuffs stolen from the shop of M. Nordmann, a draper, were heaped together in motor cars. An army doctor (médicine-major) took possession of all the medical appliances in the hospital, and an officer of superior rank, after having put up a notice forbidding pillage on the entrance door of the house of M. Lebondidier, had a great part of the furniture of this house carried away on a carriage, intending it, as he boasted without any shame, for the adornment of his own villa.

At the time when this happened the town of Clermont-en-Argonne was occupied by the Thirteenth Württemburg Corps, under the command of Gen. von Durach, and by a troop of Uhlans, commanded by Prince von Wittenstein.

On the 7th of September half a score of German cavalrymen entered the farm of Lamermont in the Commune of Lisle-en-Barrois, and, after having milk given to them, went away apparently satisfied. After their departure rifle shots were heard in the distance. A little later a second troop, composed of about thirty men, presented themselves in their turn, and accused the farm people of having killed a German soldier. Immediately the farmer, Elly, and one of his guests, M. Javelot, were seized and taken to a place near, where, in spite of their protestations of innocence, they were mercilessly shot.

At Louppy-le-Château the Germans gave themselves over to immorality and disgusting brutality during the night of the 8th and 9th in a cellar where several women had taken refuge from the bombardment. All these unhappy women were vilely ill-treated. Mlle. X., aged 71; Mme. Y., aged 44, and her two daughters, one aged 13 and the other 8, and Mme. Z. were violated.

Hostages have been taken away from many communes. At the beginning of September, at Laimont, eight persons were obliged to follow the German troops, and on the 27th of October none of them had returned. The curé of Nubécourt, who was carried off on the 5th of September, has not yet reappeared in his parish.

At Saint-André, M. Havette, who was among the number of persons arrested, obtained from an officer permission to watch over the body of his wife, who had been killed on the previous day by a fragment of a shell. In the evening the inhabitants were ordered to collect together in a barn. Havette believed that he was exempt from this order by reason of the authority he had received, and remained at his house until 11 in the evening. When he left his house he was struck down by a rifle bullet.

Of the other villages besides those whose burning we have related, Vassincourt and Brabant-le-Roi were more or less completely burned. Up to now it has not been possible for us to ascertain completely the circumstances of their destruction. Our inquiry so far as it concerns them will be further pursued.

It has been brought to our knowledge that in the Department of the Meuse the enemy has committed acts of cruelty toward the French soldiers who were wounded and prisoners. We will set out the facts of this at the end of the present report.

MEURTHE-ET-MOSELLE.

We arrived in the Department of Meurthe-et-Moselle on the 26th of October, and visited a great number of communes in the arrondissements of Nancy and Lunéville.

Nancy, an open town into which the German Army has not been able to enter, was bombarded without formal warning during the night of the 9th and 10th of September. About sixty shells fell into the middle of the town and in the southern cemetery—that is, in places where there is no military establishment. Three women, a young girl, and a little girl were killed; thirteen people were wounded; the material damage done was considerable.

The enemy's aviators have flown over the town twice. On the 4th of September one of them dropped two bombs, by one of which a man and a little girl were killed and six people wounded, in the Place de la Cathédrale. On the 13th of October three bombs were thrown on the goods station. Four persons employed by the Eastern Railway Company were wounded.

When we reached Pont-à-Mousson, on the morning of the 10th of November, seven shells had just been fired by the German batteries a few hours before. It was the 24th day of the bombardment, which began on the 11th of August. The evening before a young girl of 19 and a child of 4 had been killed in their beds by fragments of shells. On the 14th of August the Germans took as their special objective the hospital, from whose towers floated Red Cross flags, visible from a great distance. No less than seventy shells fell on to this building, and we have witnessed the damage they have caused.

About eighty houses were damaged by the different bombardments, all of which took place without any warning. Fourteen civilians, mainly women and children, were killed. There were about the same number of wounded. Pont-à-Mousson is not fortified. Only the bridge over the Moselle had been put in a state of defense, on the outbreak of hostilities, by the Twenty-sixth Battalion of Chasseurs, who were then quartered in the town.

We experienced real horror when we found ourselves before the lamentable ruins of Nomeny. With the exception of some few houses which still stood near the railway station in a spot separated by the Seille from the principal group of buildings, there remains of this little town only a succession of broken and blackened walls in the midst of ruins, in which may be seen here and there the bones of a few animals partially charred and the carbonized remains of human bodies. The rage of a maddened soldiery has been unloosed there without pity.

Nomeny, on account of its proximity to the frontier, received from the beginning of the war the visits of German troopers from time to time. Skirmishes took place in its neighborhood, and on Aug. 14, in the courtyard of the farm de la Borde, which is a little distance off, a German soldier, without any motive, killed by a rifle shot the young farm servant, Nicholas Michel, aged 17.

On Aug. 20, when the inhabitants sought refuge in the cellars from the bombardment, the Germans came up after having fired upon each other by mistake and entered the town toward midday.

According to the account given by one of the inhabitants, the German officers asserted that the French were torturing the wounded by cutting off their limbs and plucking out their eyes. They were then in a state of terrible excitement. That day and part of the next the German soldiers gave themselves over to the most abominable excesses, sacking, burning and massacring as they went. After they had carried off from the houses everything which seemed worth taking away, and after they had dispatched to Metz the product of their rifling, they set fire to the houses with torches, pastilles of compressed powder and petrol which they carried in receptacles placed on little carts. Rifle shots were fired on every side; the unhappy inhabitants, who had been driven from the cellars before the firing, were shot down like game—some in their dwellings and others in the public streets.

MM. Sanson, Pierson, Lallemand, Adam Jeanpierre, Meunier, Schneider, Raymond, Duponcel, and Hazotte, father and son, were killed by rifle shots in the streets. M. Killian, seeing himself threatened by a sabre stroke, protected his neck with his hand. He had three fingers cut off and his throat gashed. An old man aged 86, M. Petitjean, who was seated in his armchair, had his skull smashed by a German shot. A soldier showed the corpse to Mme. Bertrand, saying: "Do you see that pig there?" M. Chardin, Town Councilor, who was Acting Mayor, was required to furnish a horse and carriage. He had promised to do all he could to obey, when he was killed by a rifle shot. M. Prevot, seeing the Bavarians breaking into a chemist's shop of which he was caretaker, told them that he was the chemist, and that he would give them anything they wanted, but three rifle shots rang out and he fell, heaving a deep sigh. Two women who were with him ran away and were pursued to the neighborhood of the railway station, beaten all the way with the butts of rifles, and they saw many bodies heaped together in the station garden and on the road.

Between 3 and 4 o'clock in the afternoon the Germans entered the butcher shop of Mme. François. She was then coming out of her cellar with her boy Stub, and an employee named Contal. As soon as Stub reached the threshold of the entrance to the door he fell severely wounded by a rifle shot. Then Contal, who rushed into the street, was immediately murdered. Five minutes afterward, as Stub was still groaning, a soldier leaned over him and finished him off with a blow of a hatchet on the back.

The most tragic incident in this horrible scene occurred in the house of M. Vassé, who had collected a number of people in his cellar in the Faubourg de Nancy. Toward 4 o'clock about fifty soldiers rushed into the house, beat in the door and windows, and set it on fire. The refugees then made an effort to flee, but they were struck down one after the other as they came out. M. Mentré was murdered first; then his son Léon fell with his little sister, aged 8, in his arms. As he was not killed outright, the end of a rifle barrel was placed on his head and his brains blown out. Then it was the turn of the Kieffer family. The mother was wounded in the arm and shoulder. The father and little boy aged 10 and little girl aged 3 were shot. The murderers went on firing on them after they had fallen. Kieffer, stretched on the ground, received another bullet in the forehead, and his son had the top of his head blown off by a shot. Last of all M. Strieffert and one of the sons of Vassé were murdered, while Mme. Mentré received three bullets, one in the left leg, another in the arm on the same side, and one on her forehead, which was only grazed. M. Guillaume was dragged into the street and there found dead. Simonin, a young girl of 17, came out last from the cellar, with her sister Jeanne, aged 3. The latter had her elbow almost carried away by a bullet. The elder girl flung herself on the ground and pretended to be dead, remaining for five minutes in terrible anguish. A soldier gave her a kick, crying "Capout."

An officer arrived at the end of this butchery, and ordered the women who were still alive to get up, and shouted to them: "Go to France!"

While all these people were being massacred, others, according to an expression used by an eyewitness, were driven like sheep into the fields under the threat of immediate execution. The curé, in particular, owed his escape from being shot to extraordinary circumstances.

According to the depositions which we have received, all these abominations were committed chiefly by the Second and Fourth Regiments of Bavarian infantry. To explain them, the officers have alleged that civilians had fired on their troops. As our inquiry has established formally, this allegation is a lie, for at the moment when the enemy arrived all arms had been deposited at the Mairie, and the part of the population which had not quitted the country had hidden itself in the cellars, a prey to the greatest terror. Besides, the reason alleged, even were it true, would assuredly be insufficient to excuse the destruction of a whole city, the murder of women, and the massacre of children.

A list of persons who were killed in the course of the burning and the shootings has been drawn up by M. Biévelot, Conseiller d'Arrondissement. The list includes no less than 50 names. We have not quoted all of them. For one thing, among the people whose death has been proved, some died under conditions which are not stated with sufficient precision; on the other hand, the dispersal of the inhabitants of the town which has now been destroyed made our inquiry very difficult. Our efforts will be continued. In any case, what we have already been able to establish beyond dispute is enough to give an idea of what was, on the day of Aug. 20, the martyrdom of Nomeny.

Lunéville was occupied by the Germans from Aug. 27 to Sept. 11. During the first few days they were content to rob the inhabitants without molesting them in any other way. Thus, in particular on Aug. 24, the house of Mme. Jeaumont was plundered. The objects stolen were loaded on to a large vehicle in which were three women, one of them dressed in black and the two others wearing military costumes and appearing, as we were told, to be canteen women.

On Aug. 25 the attitude of the invaders suddenly changed. M. Keller, the Mayor, went to the hospital about 3:30 o'clock in the afternoon and saw soldiers firing in the direction of the attic of a neighboring house, and heard the whistling of the bullets, which appeared to him to come from behind. The Germans declared to him that the inhabitants had fired on them. He protested, and offered to go around the town with them in order to prove the absurdity of this allegation. His proposal was accepted, and as at the beginning of the circuit they came across in the street the body of M. Crombez, the officer commanding the escort said to M. Keller, "You see this body. It is that of a civilian who has been killed by another civilian who was firing on us from a house near the synagogue. Thus, in accordance with our law, we have burned the house and executed the inhabitants." He was speaking of the murder of a man whose timid character was known to all, the Jewish officiating minister, Weill, who had just been killed in his house, together with his 16-year-old daughter. The same officer added, "In the same way we have burned the house at the corner of the Rue Castara and the Rue Girardet, because civilians fired shots from there." It is from this dwelling that the Germans alleged shots had been fired on to the courtyard of the hospital, but the position of the building makes it impossible for such a statement to be true.

While the Mayor and the soldiers who accompanied him were pursuing their investigation the fire broke out on different sides; the Hôtel de Ville was burned as well as the synagogue, and a number of houses in the Rue Castara, and the Faubourg d'Einville was in flames. The massacres, which were continued until the next day, began at the same time. Without counting M. Crombez, the officiating minister, Weill, and his daughter, whose deaths we have already mentioned, the victims were MM. Hamman, Binder, Balastre, (father and son,) Vernier, Dujon, M. Kahn and his mother, M. Steiner and his wife, M. Wingerstmann and his grandson, and, finally, MM. Sibille, Monteils, and Colin.

The murders were committed in the following circumstances:—

On Aug. 25, after having fired two shots into the Worms Tannery to create the belief that they were being attacked from there, the Germans entered a workshop in this factory, in which the workman, Goeury, was working, in company with M. Balastre, father and son. Goeury was dragged into the street, robbed there and brutally ill-treated, while his two companions, who were found trying to hide themselves in a lavatory, were killed by rifle shots.

On the same day soldiers came to summon M. Steiner, who had hidden in his cellar. His wife, fearing some misfortune, tried to keep him back. As she held him in her arms she received a bullet in the neck. A few moments after, Steiner, having obeyed the order which had been given to him, fell mortally wounded in his garden. M. Kahn was also murdered in his garden. His mother, aged 98, whose body was burned in the fire, had first been killed in her bed by a bayonet thrust, according to the account of an individual who acted as interpreter to the enemy. M. Binder, who was coming out to escape the flames, was also struck down. The German by whom he was killed realized that he had shot him without any motive, at the moment when the unfortunate man was standing quietly before a door. M. Vernier suffered the same fate as Binder.

Toward 3 o'clock the Germans broke into a house in which were Mme. Dujon, her daughter aged 3, her two sons, and M. Gaumier, by breaking the windows and firing shots. The little girl was nearly killed; her face was burned by a shot. At this moment, Mme. Dujon, seeing her youngest son, Lucien, 14 years old, stretched on the ground, asked him to get up and escape with her. She then saw that his intestines were protruding from a wound, and that he was holding them in. The house was on fire; the poor boy was burned, as well as M. Gaumier, who had not been able to escape.

M. Wingerstmann and his grandson, aged 12, who had gone to pull potatoes a little way from Lunéville, at the place called Les Mossus, in the District of Chanteheux, were unfortunate enough to meet Germans. The latter placed them both against a wall and shot them.

Finally, toward 5 o'clock in the evening, soldiers entered the house of the woman Sibille, in the same place, and without any reason took possession of her son, led him 200 meters from the house and murdered him there, together with M. Vallon, to whose body they had fastened him. A witness, who had seen the murderers at the moment when they were dragging their victim along, saw them return without him and noticed that their saw bayonets were covered with blood and bits of flesh.

On the same day a hospital attendant named Monteils, who was looking after a wounded enemy officer at the hospital of Lunéville, was struck down by a bullet in the forehead while he was looking through a window at a German soldier who was firing.

The next day, the 26th, M. Hamman and his son, aged 21, were arrested in their own house and dragged out by a band of soldiers who had entered by breaking down the door. The father was beaten unmercifully; as for the young man, as he tried to struggle, a non-commissioned officer blew out his brains with a revolver shot.

At 1 o'clock in the afternoon M. Riklin, a chemist, having been informed that a man had fallen about thirty meters from his shop, went to the spot indicated and recognized in the victim his brother-in-law, M. Colin, aged 68, who had been struck in the stomach by a bullet. The Germans alleged that this old man fired upon them. M. Riklin denied this statement. Colin, we are told, was a harmless person, absolutely incapable of an aggressive act, and completely ignorant of the means of using a firearm.

It appeared to us desirable to deal also at Lunéville with acts which are less grave, but which throw a peculiar light on the habits of thought of the invader. On Aug. 25 M. Lenoir, 67 years of age, together with his wife, were led into the fields with their hands tied behind their backs. After both had been cruelly ill-treated, a non-commissioned officer took possession of 1,800 francs in gold which M. Lenoir carried on him. As we have already stated, the most impudent theft seems to have formed part of the customs of the German Army, who practiced it publicly. The following is an interesting example:

During the burning of a house belonging to Mme. Leclerc, the safes of two inhabitants resisted the flames. One, belonging to M. George, Sub-Inspector of Waters and Forests, had fallen into the ruins; the other safe, belonging to M. Goudchau, general dealer, remained fixed to a wall at the height of the second story. The non-commissioned officer, Weiss, who was well acquainted with the town, where he had often been welcomed when he used to come before the war to carry on his business of hop merchant, went with the soldiers to the place and ordered that the piece of wall which remained standing should be blown up with dynamite, and saw that the two safes were taken to the station, where they were placed on a truck destined for Germany. This Weiss was particularly trusted and esteemed by the persons in command. It was he who, installed at Headquarters, was given the duty of administering the commune in some sense, and was in charge of the requisitioning.

After having committed numerous acts of pillage at Lunéville, after having burned about seventy houses with torches, petrol, and various incendiary machines, and after having massacred peaceful inhabitants, the German military authorities thought it well to put up the following proclamation, in which they formulated ridiculous accusations to justify the extortion of enormous contributions in the form of an indemnity:

NOTICE TO THE POPULATION.

On Aug. 25, 1914, the inhabitants of Lunéville made an attack by ambuscade against the German columns and transports. On the same day the inhabitants fired on hospital buildings marked with the Red Cross. Further, shots were fired on the German wounded and the military hospital containing a German ambulance. On account of these acts of hostility a contribution of 650,000 francs is imposed on the commune of Lunéville. The Mayor is ordered to pay this sum—50,000 francs in silver and the remainder in gold—on Sept. 6, at 9 o'clock in the morning, to the representative of the German military authority. No protest will be considered. No extension of time will be granted. If the commune does not punctually obey the order to pay 650,000 francs all the goods which are available will be seized. In case payment is not made domiciliary searches will take place, and all the inhabitants will be searched. Any one who shall have deliberately hidden money or shall have attempted to hide his goods from the seizure of the military authorities, or who seeks to leave the town, will be shot. The Mayor and hostages taken by the military authorities will be made responsible for the exact execution of the above order. The Mayor is ordered to publish these directions to the commune at once.

Hénaménil, Sept. 3, 1914.

Commander in Chief,
Von FOSBENDER.

On reading this extraordinary document one is justified in asking whether the arson and murders committed at Lunéville on Aug. 25 and 26 by an army which was not acting under the excitement of battle, and which during its preceding days had abstained from killing, were not ordered on purpose to make more plausible the allegation which was to serve as a pretext for the exaction of an indemnity.

The village of Chanteheux, situated quite close to Lunéville, was not spared either. The Bavarians, who occupied it from the 22d of August to the 12th of September, burned there 20 houses in the customary manner and massacred 8 persons on the 25th of August, MM. Lavenne, Toussaint, Parmentier, and Bacheler, who were killed, the first three by rifle shots, the fourth by two shots and a blow with a bayonet; young Schneider, aged 23, who was murdered in a hamlet of the commune; M. Wingerstmann and his grandson, whose death we have recorded above in setting out the crimes committed at Lunéville; lastly, M. Reeb, aged 62, who certainly died as the result of the ill-treatment which he suffered. This man had been taken as hostage with some 42 of his fellow-citizens who were kept for 13 days. After having received terrible blows from the butt of a rifle in his face and a bayonet wound in his side, he continued to follow the column, although he lost much blood and his face was so bruised that he was almost unrecognizable, when a Bavarian, without any reason, gave him a great wound by throwing a wooden pail at his forehead. Between Hénaménil and Bures his companions saw that he was no longer with them; no doubt he fell by the way.

If this unhappy man was to suffer the most cruel martyrdom of all, the hostages taken with him in the commune had also to suffer violence and insult. Before setting fire to the village, the hostages were set with their backs to the parapet of the bridge while the troops passed by ill-treating them. As an officer accused them of firing on the Germans, the schoolmaster gave him his word of honor that it was not so. "Pig of a Frenchman," replied the officer, "do not speak of honor; you have none."

At the moment when her house was burning Mme. Cherrier, who was coming out of the cellar to escape suffocation, was drenched with an inflammable liquid by some soldiers who were sprinkling the walls. One of them told her that it was benzine. She then ran behind a dunghill to hide herself with her parents, but the fire raisers dragged her by force in front of the blaze and she was obliged to witness the destruction of her dwelling.

Like Nomeny, the pretty town of Gerbéviller, on the banks of the Mortagne, fell a victim to the fury of the Germans under terrible circumstances. On the 24th August the enemy's troops hurled themselves against some sixty chasseurs à pied, who offered heroic resistance, and who inflicted heavy loss upon them. They took a drastic vengeance upon the civilian population. Indeed, from the moment of their entrance into the town, the Germans gave themselves up to the worst excesses, entering the houses, with savage yells, burning the buildings, killing or arresting the inhabitants, and sparing neither women nor old men. Out of 475 houses, 20 at most are still habitable. More than 100 persons have disappeared, 50 at least have been massacred. Some were led into the fields to be shot, others were murdered in their houses or struck down in passing through the streets as they were trying to escape from the conflagration. Up to now 36 bodies have been identified. They are those of MM. Barthélemy, Blosse (Senior), Robinet, Chrétien, Rémy, Bourguignon, Perrin, Guillaume, Bernasconi, Gauthier, Menu, Simon, Lingenheld (father and son), Benoit, Calais, Adam, Caille, Lhuillier, Regret, Plaid (aged 14), Leroi, Bazzolo, Gentil, Victor Dehan, Charles Dehan, Dehan the Younger, Brennevald, Parisse, Yong, François, Secretary of the Mairie; Mmes. Perrot, Courtois, Gauthier, and Guillaume, and Mlles. Perrin and Miquel.

Fifteen of these poor people were executed at a place called "La Prèle." They were buried by their fellow-citizens on Sept. 12 or 15. Almost all had their hands tied behind their backs; some were blindfolded; the trousers of the majority were unbuttoned and pushed down to their feet. This fact, as well as the appearance of the bodies, made the witnesses think that the victims had been mutilated. We did not think we ought to adopt this view, the bodies being in such an advanced state of decomposition that a mistake on the subject might be made. Besides, it is possible that the murderers unbuttoned the trousers of the prisoners so as to incumber their legs, and thus make it impossible for them to escape.

On Oct. 16, at a place called Le Haut-de-Vormont, buried under fifteen to twenty centimeters of earth, we found the bodies of ten civilians with the marks of bullets upon them. On one of them was found a laissez passer in the name of Edward Seyer, of Badonviller. The other nine victims are unknown. It is believed that they were inhabitants of Badonviller, who had been taken by the Germans into the neighborhood of Gerbéviller to be shot there.

In the streets and houses, during the day of the sacking, the most tragic scenes took place.

In the morning the enemy entered the house of M. and Mme. Lingenheld, seized the son, 36 years of age, who wore the brassard of the Red Cross, tied his hands behind his back, dragged him into the street, and shot him. They then returned to look for the father, an old man of 70. Mme. Lingenheld then took to flight. On her way she saw her son stretched on the ground, and as the unhappy man was still moving some Germans drenched him with petrol, to which they set fire in the presence of the terrified mother. In the meantime M. Lingenheld was led to La Prèle, where he was executed.

At the same time the soldiers knocked at the door of the house occupied by M. Dehan, his wife, and his mother-in-law, the widow Guillaume, aged 78. The latter, who opened the door, was shot point-blank, and fell into the arms of her son-in-law, who ran up behind her. "They have killed me!" she cried. "Carry me into the garden." Her children obeyed and laid her at the end of the garden with a pillow under her head and a blanket over her legs, and then stretched themselves at the foot of the wall to avoid shells. At the end of an hour the widow Guillaume was dead. Her daughter wrapped her in a blanket and placed a handkerchief over her face. Almost immediately the Germans broke into the garden. They carried off Dehan and shot him at La Prèle, and led his wife away on to the Fraimbois road, where she found about forty people, principally women and children, in the enemy's hands, and heard an officer of high rank say: "We must shoot these women and children. We must make an end of them." However, the threat was not carried into effect. Mme. Dehan was set at liberty next day, and was able to return twenty-one days later to Gerbéviller. She is convinced, and all those who saw the body share her opinion, that her mother's body had been violated. In fact, the body was found stretched on its back with the petticoats pushed up, the legs separated, and the stomach ripped open.

When the Germans arrived M. Perrin and his two daughters, Louise and Eugénie, had taken refuge in a stable. The soldiers entered, and one of them, seeing young Louise, fired a shot point-blank at her head. Eugénie succeeded in escaping, but her father was arrested as he fled, placed among the victims who were being taken to La Prèle and shot with them.

M. Yong, who was going out to exercise his horse, was struck down before his own house. The Germans in their fury killed the horse after the master, and set fire to the house. Some others raised the trap-door of a cellar in which several people were hidden and fired several shots at them. Mme. Denis Bernard and the boy, Parmentier, 7 years of age, were wounded.

At 5 in the evening Mme. Rozier heard an imploring voice crying, "Mercy! Mercy!" These cries came from one of two neighboring barns belonging to MM. Poinsard and Barbier. A man who was acting as interpreter to the Germans declared to a certain Mme. Thiébaut that the Germans boasted that they had burned alive in one of these barns, in spite of his entreaties and appeals to their pity, a man who was the father of five children. This declaration carries all the more conviction, since the remains of a burned human body have been found in the barn belonging to Poinsard.

Side by side with this carnage, innumerable acts of violence were committed. The wife of a soldier, Mme. X., was raped by a German soldier in the passage of the house of her parents, while her mother was obliged to flee at the bayonet's point.

On Aug. 29 Sister Julie, Mother Superior of the hospital, whose devotion has been admirable, went to the parish church with a mobilized priest to examine the state of the interior of the building, and found that an attempt had been made to break through the steel door of the tabernacle. The Germans had fired shots around the lock in order to get possession of the ciborium. The door was broken through in several places, and the bullets had caused almost symmetrical holes, which proved that the shots had been fired point blank. When Sister Julie opened the tabernacle she found the ciborium pierced with bullet holes.

The excesses and crimes which were committed at Gerbéviller were principally the work of the Bavarians. The troops which committed them were under the command of the German General, Clauss, whose brutality has been brought to our notice in other places.

On the 22d of August the Germans burned part of the village of Crévic, using torches and rockets. Seventy-six houses were burned, including in particular that of Gen. Lyautey, which the fire-raisers had entered, led by an officer, crying aloud: "We want Mme. and Mlle. Lyautey in order to cut their throats." A Captain, leveling his revolver at M. Voigin's throat, threatened to shoot him and throw him into the flames, together with one of his fellow-citizens, "whose brains," he said, "we have already blown out." He was alluding to the death of an old gentleman, M. Liégey, 78 years of age, whose body was found in the ruins with a bullet wound under his chin. The officer added, "Come and see the property of Gen. Lyautey, who is in Morocco—it is burning." Meanwhile a workman named Gérard was forced at the bayonet's point to go up to his garret. The Germans set fire to a heap of forage and obliged Gérard to remain near the blaze. When the soldiers were driven out by the intolerable heat, Gérard was able to escape through a little opening, but he had had one cheek already badly burned.

At Deuxville, where the enemy willfully set fire to fifteen houses, the Mayor, Bajole, and the curé, Thiriet, were arrested. L'Abbé Marchal, curé of Crion, saw them both in his parish in the hands of the Germans; he approached his colleague and asked the reason of his arrest. The latter replied, "I made signs." L'Abbé Marchal gave him a little bread and went away; but he had scarcely gone thirty paces when he heard the sound of a volley. The two prisoners had just been executed. The next day an officer who spoke our language perfectly, and said that for eight years he had been attached to the German Embassy in Paris, told L'Abbé Marchal that the curé of Deuxville had made signs and had admitted it. "As for the Mayor," he added, "I do not believe the poor devil had done anything."

At Maixe the Germans burned thirty-six houses and murdered MM. Gauçon, Demange, Jacques, Thomas, Marchal, Chaudre, Grand, Simonin, Vaconet, and Mme. Beurton on the pretext that they had been firing at them. Gauçon was dragged from his own house and thrown on a dunghill where a soldier killed him with a rifle shot in the stomach. Demange, who was wounded in both knees while in his cellar, succeeded in dragging himself as far as the kitchen. The Germans set fire to the house and prevented Mme. Demange from rescuing her husband, and left their victims to be burned in the blazing house.

Mme. Beurton was also in her cellar with her family when two soldiers came down into it; one of them carried a lantern and the other a rifle. The latter fired haphazard on to the group and hit the unhappy woman. Vaconet was struck by a bullet in the side at the foot of M. Rediger's staircase; as for Simonin, he was taken away in the direction of Drouville. A few days afterward a German officer handed to M. Thouvenin, Municipal Councilor of the commune, a note stating that Simonin had been shot and that his last wishes were expressed in a document which was in the hands of the General commanding the Third Bavarian Division. On this document, of which a copy has been sent to us, appears the signature of an officer of the Third Regiment of the Chevauxlégers. The other victims at Maixe met their deaths under conditions which we have been unable to ascertain.

In the same village, Mlle. X., aged 23 years, was raped by nine Germans during the night of Aug. 23-24. An officer was sleeping in the room above that in which this revolting scene was being enacted, but he did not consider it necessary to intervene, though he must certainly have heard the cries of the young girl and the noise made by the German soldiers.

The Château of Beauzemont was broken into on the 22d of August. On the fifteenth day of its occupation, the wives of several German staff officers arrived in motor cars. Everything that had been stolen from the Château, especially plate, hats, and silk dresses, was loaded on the motor cars. On the 21st of October the Lieutenant Colonel commanding the — — French Infantry Regiment took possession of this château. He found it in a state of disorder and revolting filth. The drawers of most of the furniture had been broken into and left open, and the floor of the billiard room was in a filthy condition. There was a disgusting smell in the bedroom occupied by the German General commanding the Seventh Reserve Division. The cupboard at the head of the bed contained body linen and muslin curtains full of excrements.

At Baccarat the enemy did not massacre anybody, but on the 25th of August they carried out a systematic pillage, and in order to be able to do this undisturbed they had ordered the population to assemble at the railway station. The pillage was carried out under the supervision of the officers. Clocks and various articles of furniture and objets d'art were carried off. When the inhabitants returned home they were ordered out again an hour later and informed that the town was to be burned. Indeed, the centre of the town was ablaze. The conflagration, which was started by torches and pastilles, destroyed 112 houses; only four or five were burned by shells. After the fire sentinels were placed, who prevented the owners from approaching the ruins of their houses, and when the blaze had abated the Germans ransacked the ruins themselves in order to gain access to the cellars. After this operation Gen. Fabricius, commanding the artillery of the Fourteenth Baden Corps, said to M. Renaud, the Acting Mayor: "I did not think that Baccaret contained such a quantity of fine wine. We found more than 100,000 bottles." One must, however, add that at the glass works the enemy really displayed comparative honesty, inasmuch as they only exacted, at the revolver's point, a reduction of 60 to 75 per cent. on the goods which they bought.

At Jolivet, on the 22d of August, M. Villemin was leaving M. Cohan's house with the latter and a M. Richard when German soldiers fell upon M. Richard. Struck on the head by the butt of a rifle, Richard fell. Cohan rushed back to his house. Villemin went to look after his cattle, after having followed Richard for a short distance as the latter was being led away by his aggressors. At about 5 o'clock in the evening he went out to see a neighbor, but was immediately arrested and shot. His assassins threw his body over a fence into a garden.

On the 25th of August, in the same commune, Mme. Morin's house was pillaged. The Germans took linen, plate, furs and hats. The next day the house was set on fire by lighting bits of wood found in packing cases.

At Bonvillers, on the 21st, 23d, and 25th of August, twenty-six houses were set on fire by the Germans, who made use of squibs and candles.

At Einville, on the 22d of August, the day the Germans arrived, they shot a Town Councilor, M. Pierson, whom they wrongfully accused of having fired on them. They also executed, without reason, MM. Bouvier and Barbelin, whom they had taken away a short distance from the village. They also massacred a poacher called Pierrat, whom they had found carrying a sack containing a small net and a gun in pieces. The wretched man was terribly tortured by them. Having dragged him beyond the village, they brought him back in front of Mme. Famôse's house. This lady saw him pass by in the midst of the Germans. His nose was nearly cut off. His eyes were haggard and, to quote the witness's remark, he seemed to have aged ten years in a quarter of an hour. At this moment an officer gave an order and eight soldiers went off with the prisoner. When they returned ten minutes later without him one of them said in French, "He was already dead."

On the 12th of September M. Dieudonné, Mayor of Einville, was taken off as a hostage with his assistant and another of his townsmen by the enemy at the time of their retreat. He and his companions were taken to Alsace, then into Germany, where they were kept until the 24th of October. Before his arrest, and during a fight which took place around his commune, M. Dieudonné had been forced, notwithstanding his protests, to commandeer several of his townsmen in order to bury the dead. Three of the inhabitants of Einville thus forcible employed on this duty were wounded by bullets; another, M. Noël, was killed by a fragment of a shell.

The farm of Remonville, situated within the boundaries of the same village, was burned down. The women were able to escape. Four men who were working on this estate must have been all killed. The bodies of two of them, Victor Chaudre and Thomas Prosper, were discovered two months later buried together near the buildings which had been burned. Both had been decapitated, and Thomas's head was smashed to pieces.

At Sommerviller the enemy's course on the 23d of August was marked by the sack of the cafés and grocers' shops and of several private houses, and by the murder of M. Robert, aged 70, and M. Harau, aged 65, who were killed by rifle shots. The latter at the moment when he received his death wound was quietly eating a piece of bread.

At Rehainviller, on the 26th of August, the Germans seized the curé, Barbot, and M. Noircler in the street. The bodies of these two men were found a long time afterward buried in the fields a few hundred meters from the village. Their bodies were in an advanced state of decomposition, and it was therefore impossible to ascertain the wounds which the curé had received; as for Noircler, his head was found in the grave by the side of the rest of his body, in a line with his hip.

AVIATOR-COMMANDANT MARCONNAY

One of the Oldest and Best Known French Military Aviators Killed
During a Reconnoissance.

(*Photo from Underwood & Underwood.*)

GENERAL SIR DOUGLAS HAIG

**Commanding the First British Army, One of the Six Armies
Recently Incorporated.**

(Photo © American Press Association.)

In this commune twenty-seven houses have been burned. No one saw the fire lighted, but after the disaster a certain number of little fuse-sticks which the Germans frequently use for the purpose of fire-raising, and which the peasants call "macaronis," were collected.

At Lamath, on the 24th of August, the Bavarians shot an old man of 70, M. Louis, who had come out of his house to relieve the needs of nature. The unhappy man received at least ten bullets in the chest. His son-in-law, who was in an advanced stage of tuberculosis, was taken and led away. No news has been received of him. Two other inhabitants of the commune who were made prisoners at the same time as this man are still in captivity in Bavaria.

The Abbé Mathieu, curé of Fraimbois, was arrested on the 29th of August on the false allegation that shots had been fired at the Germans in his parish. In the course of his captivity, which lasted sixteen days, he was present at the murder of two of our fellow-countrymen, M. Poissonnier of Gerbéviller and M. Victor-Meyer of Fraimbois; the former, an invalid who could scarcely stand, was accused of having followed the armies as a spy. The latter had been arrested because his little girl had picked up a bit of telephone wire broken by shrapnel. One morning toward 6 o'clock the Bavarian officers went through a travesty of justice, reading documents drawn up in German, collecting the votes of eight or nine young Lieutenants to whom voting papers had been given. The two men were condemned unanimously and warned that they were about to die, and the priest was requested to give them the consolations of religion. They protested their innocence with prayers and tears, but they were compelled to kneel down against the embankment of the road, and a platoon of twenty-four soldiers drawn up in double file fired twice at them.

The village of Fraimbois was pillaged, and the objects stolen were loaded on to vehicles. The Abbé Mathieu complained to Gens. Tanner and Clauss of the burning of his bee-house, and received from the former the simple reply, "What do you expect? It is war!" The latter did not even reply.

At Mont three houses were burned with petrol. At Hériménil, on the 29th of August, the enemy, who had arrived on the 24th, were guilty of monstrous acts. The inhabitants were asked to come to church and were kept there for four days, while their houses were sacked and the French bombarded the village. Twenty-four people were killed inside the church by a shell. As a woman, who had succeeded with great trouble in leaving the church for a moment, was returning with a little milk for the children, a Captain, furious at seeing that this prisoner had been allowed to pass, cried out, "I meant that the door should not be opened! I meant the French to fire on their own people." This same Captain, a short time before, had been guilty of a revolting cruelty. He was present, eyeglass in eye, when Mme. Winger, a young woman of 23, was going to church in obedience to the general order, together with her servants, a girl and two young men, each of them 18 years old, and, considering their progress too slow, with a word he directed the soldiers to fire, and the four victims fell mortally wounded. The Germans left the corpses in the street for two days.

Next day they shot M. Bocquel, who was ignorant of the orders which had been given and had remained in his house. They also killed in his own house M. Florentin, aged 77. This old man, who received several bullets in the chest, was probably killed in consequence of his deafness, which prevented him from understanding what the enemy had ordered.

In this commune twenty-two houses were burned with petrol. Before setting fire to Mme. Combeau's house the soldiers dug up the floor of a cellar and distinterred the sum of 600 francs, which they appropriated.

On the 23d of August young Simonin, aged 15-1/2, living at Hadiviller, was going back from Dombasle when the Germans threatened him with their rifles and took him prisoner. They began by beating him unmercifully. Then on the orders of an officer, he was led away by a soldier. As he went along he saw his father about 50 meters off calling to him. The soldier then tied him to a telegraph pole, and fired on Simonin's father, who fell vomiting blood, and soon after died as he lay. Meanwhile, the young man was able to free himself from his bonds, and succeeded in running the gauntlet of several shots, one of which tore his coat.

At Magnières, where one house only was burned, a German armed with a rifle entered, toward the end of August, the house of M. Laurent and compelled a girl of 12, young ———, who had taken refuge there, to accompany him into a room, where he raped her twice, in spite of her ceaseless cries and groans. The poor girl was absolutely terrorized. In addition, the soldier was so threatening that M. Laurent did not dare to interfere.

At Croismare on the 25th of August, when the Germans were forced to beat a retreat, maddened by their check, they began to fire on everybody they met. A Uhlan officer killed with a rifle shot M. Kriegel, who had gone into the field to pull potatoes. He then saw MM. Matton and Barbier returning from their work. He rode up to them and ordered them to stop and stand up against an embankment. The two peasants thought at first that he was anxious to see them sheltered from the rifle shots that were being fired all round. But their delusion was soon dispelled when they saw him load his revolver. In the course of this operation three cartridges were dropped, and the officer ordered Matton and Barbier to pick them up. Barbier handed him one of the cartridges back with the words, "Do not do us any harm; we have just been working in the fields." "Nicht pardon, cochon de franzose, capout," replied the officer, and fired twice. Matton ducked quickly, and thanks to this movement was only hit in the right shoulder instead of full in the chest. As for Barbier, a bullet went through both his thumbs and ripped open his left forefinger.

At Réméréville on the 7th of September the enemy, alleging falsely that the inhabitants had fired on them from the steeple, set fire to the houses with the assistance of rockets. A few houses only escaped the flames. Before being burned the village had been bombarded by the Germans, who had taken as their objective an ambulance, whose flag they saw perfectly.

The commune of Drouville, which was twice occupied, was absolutely sacked on the 5th of September. The invaders burned thirty-five houses, using torches and doubtless petrol also, for they left on the spot a can which contained twenty-five to thirty liters.

At Courbesseaux arson and pillage were also committed on the 5th of September. Nineteen houses were burned, and M. Alix, who was trying to put out a fire in a stack of luzerne on his property, was shot at several times and obliged to flee.

Finally, on the 23d of August, at Erbéviller, a Saxon Captain found a very practical means of getting money for himself. He collected the men in the village and tried vainly, by threatening to shoot them, to obtain a declaration from them that the sentries had been shot at, although he knew perfectly well that it was untrue. Then he shut them up in a barn. In the evening he had brought before him the wife of M. Jacques, a retired schoolmaster, who was one of the prisoners, and said to her, "I am not certain that these are the men who fired. They will be set at liberty tomorrow morning if you can give me a thousand francs in the next few minutes." Mme. Jacques gave him the amount, and in reply to her request he gave her a receipt for it, and the hostages were set at liberty.

The receipt drawn up by the officer reads as follows:

Erbéviller, 23d August, 1914.

RECEIPT.

As a punishment for being suspected of having fired on German sentries during the night of August 22d and 23d I have received from the Commune of Erbéviller one thousand francs, (1,000 fr.)

BARON —— (illegible).

haupt. reit. regim.

In a commune of the Department of Meurthe-et-Moselle two nuns were for several hours exposed without defense to the lust of a soldier. By terrorizing them he obliged them to undress, and after having compelled the elder to pull off his boots, he committed obscenities on the younger.

We undertook not to publish the names of the victims of this abominable scene, or of that of the village in which it took place, but the facts were laid before us under the sanction of an oath by witnesses who deserve the fullest confidence, and we take the responsibility of pledging ourselves as to their accuracy.

During our stay at Nancy and Lunéville, we had the opportunity of receiving a good deal of evidence with reference to crimes committed by the Germans in districts which were still occupied by their troops, and which the majority of the inhabitants had been forced to evacuate. The most cruel of these acts took place at the village of Emberménil. At the end of October or the beginning of November, an enemy patrol met near this commune a young woman, Mme. Masson, who was obviously pregnant, and questioned her as to whether there were French soldiers at Emberménil. She replied that she did not know, which was true. The Germans then entered the village and were received by our soldiers with rifle fire. On the 5th of November a detachment of the Fourth Bavarian Regiment arrived and collected all the inhabitants in front of the church. An officer then asked which person it was who had betrayed them. Suspecting that he referred to her meeting with the Germans some days before, and realizing the danger that all her fellow-citizens ran, Mme. Masson with great courage stepped forward and repeated what she had said, and declared that in saying it she had acted in good faith. She was immediately seized and forced to sit down on a bench beside young Dime, aged 24, who had been taken haphazard as a second victim. The whole population begged for mercy for the unhappy woman, but the Germans were inflexible. "One woman and one man," they said, "must be shot. Those are the Colonel's orders. What will you? It is war." Eight soldiers drawn up in two ranks fired three times at the two martyrs in the presence of the whole village. The house of Mme. Masson's father-in-law was then set on fire. That of M. Blanchin had been burned a few moments before.

Mme. Millot of Domèvre-sur-Vezouze has described to us the murder of her nephew, Maurice Claude, aged 17, of which she was an eyewitness. On the 24th of August, at the moment when the Germans arrived at Domèvre, this young lad was with his family in his father's house, at the foot of a staircase, when he saw that soldiers were aiming at him from the street. He stepped aside to shield himself, but was not able to find shelter, and was struck by three bullets. Wounded in the stomach, in the buttock, and in the thigh, he died three days later, after having displayed admirable resignation. When he knew that he was dying he said to his disconsolate mother, "I can well die for my country."

The same day MM. Auguste Claude and Adolphe Claude, the latter aged 75, were also killed, and 136 houses in the village were burned by means of incendiary cartridges. Further, two inhabitants, MM. Bretton and Labart, were taken as hostages. It is not known what has become of them since.

M. Véron, retired schoolmaster, at Audun-le-Roman, in the arrondissement of Briey, made a deposition before us which runs as follows:

"On the 21st of August, toward 5 in the evening, the Germans who had occupied for seventeen days the village of Audun-le-Roman, began without any reason to fire upon the houses with rifles and machine guns. Four women, Mlle. Roux, Mlle. Tréfel, Mme. Zapolli, and Mme. Giglio, were wounded. Mlle. Tréfel was struck while she was giving a drink to a German soldier. Three men were killed: M. Martin, an agriculturist, aged 68, whose house was burned, was led out and shot in the street in the presence of his wife and children. M. Chary, aged 55, foreman roadmaker, was escaping from the conflagration, holding his wife by the hand, when he was killed by rifle shots. I have seen his body, which was riddled with wounds. M. Ernest Samen was struck by five revolver bullets at the moment when he was shutting the door of his coach house.

"I saw the enemy set fire to the Café Matte with petrol. Mme. Matte went out with a little bag in her hand containing her savings, about two thousand francs. She was robbed by a German officer, who snatched the bag away."

The witness added that the Mayor must have been carried off by a patrol, but in any case he had disappeared.

At Arracourt, M. Maillard was killed in the fields by a bullet which went right through him; five houses were burned.

The village of Brin-sur-Seille was almost entirely destroyed by fire lighted by cartridges and round fuses. Further, the wife of a man at Raucourt who is with the colors, Mme. X., declared to us that she had been raped in her own house in the presence of her little boy, aged 3-1/2, by a soldier who had placed the point of his bayonet on her breast to overcome the resistance which she opposed to him.

OISE.

In the Department of Oise we have ascertained the following facts:

When on the 31st of August the Germans entered the village of Monchy-Humières a group of about fifteen people were in the street looking at them as they entered. No act of provocation was committed, but an officer believed that he heard some one say the word "Prussian." At once he directed three dragoons to fall out and ordered them to fire. Young Gaston

Dupuis was killed, M. Grandvalet was wounded in the right shoulder by a bullet, and a little girl of 4 who belonged to a family of refugees from Verdun was slightly wounded in the neck.

Next day the commune of Ravenel was sacked, and the stolen objects were taken away in a carriage. A man named Vilette, while bicycling on the road near the village, met a motor car in which were several Germans. They began to fire at him without any reason. He jumped down from his machine and took to flight across country, but a bullet stopped him on his way. He died a few hours afterward, leaving a widow and two children.

On the same day, near Méry, the enemy opened fire on some English guns which were drawn up at the place called Le Bout de la Ville, and an engagement began between the cavalry of the two armies. At this moment the Germans entered the sugar factory, which is situated in a hamlet of the commune. They seized the manager, his family, and all the staff of the factory, and, during the three hours which the engagement lasted, made them walk in a parallel line to themselves in order to protect themselves against the fusillade which was catching them on the flank. Among the twenty-five people who were thus exposed to grave danger were women and children. A work girl, Mme. Jeansenne, was killed, and a foreman, Courtois, had a bullet through his left arm. At 10 in the evening, the enemy returned in force to the village. They left the next day after having burned the houses and carried out a general sack.

On the 2d of September the Germans entered Senlis, where they were greeted by rifle fire from African troops. Alleging that they had been fired on by civilians, they set fire to two quarters of the town. One hundred and five houses were burned in the following manner: The Germans marched along the streets in a column; at a whistle from an officer, some of them fell out, and proceeded to break in the doors of the houses and the shop fronts; then others came along and lit the fire with grenades and rockets; patrols who followed them fired incendiary bullets with their rifles into those houses in which the fire was not taking hold fast enough.

While our soldiers were firing in the outskirts of the town, the hostages who had been taken into the streets by the Germans were forced to walk in the middle of the road, while the Germans prudently kept to the footpaths. M. Levasseur, Mme. Dauchy and her little girl aged 5, MM. Pinchaux, Minouflet, and Leymarie were among the number of the hostages who were thus exposed to death. Near the hospital Levasseur was killed. Soon Leymarie in his turn fell mortally wounded. As he was carrying him to lay him at the foot of a wall, Minouflet was struck by a bullet on the knee. An officer approached him, and told him to show his wound, and then suddenly fired with his revolver into his shoulder. At the same spot a witness saw another officer in the act of torturing a French wounded soldier by beating him in the face with a stick.

Meanwhile several murders were committed. M. Simon was dragged out of his house and killed by a rifle shot in the side. At 2 o'clock the Germans broke in the door of M. Mégret's house. The latter came forward, promised to give them everything they asked for, and brought them ten bottles of wine. He was murdered by a shot full in the chest. MM. Ramu, Vilcoq, Chambellant and Gaudet, drawn by curiosity, went to look at the burning forage store to which the French troops had set fire as they retired. Enemy soldiers fired on them several times. Ramu was wounded, Gaudet was killed on the spot, Chambellant received two bullets, one in his right hand and the other below the groin, and died a week later. MM. Simon, Ecker, Chery, Leblond, Rigauld, Louis, and Momus were also killed in Senlis.

At 3 o'clock the Mayor, M. Odent, was arrested at the Hôtel de Ville on the allegation, against which he protested, that civilians had fired on the German troops. While he was being led away the Secretary of the Mairie joined him near the Hôtel du Grand Cerf, and proposed that he should go and fetch his Deputies. "It is useless," he replied, "one victim is enough." The Magistrate was taken to Chamant, and during the journey was the butt of hateful brutality. His gloves were torn from him and thrown in his face; his stick was taken from him and he was violently beaten with it on the head. Finally, toward 11 o'clock, he was made to appear before three officers. One of them questioned him, persisting in accusing him of having fired or caused others to fire on the Germans, and warned him that he was about to die. M. Odent then went to his fellow-captives, handed them his papers and money, shook hands with them, and with great dignity made his last adieu. He then returned to the officers. On their order, two soldiers dragged him ten meters away and sent two bullets through his head. The murderers made a little hollow in the ground, and flung over the corpse a layer of earth so thin that it did not cover the victim's feet. A few hours before, 200 meters off, six other inhabitants of Senlis, MM. Pommier, Barbier, Aubert, Cottereau, Arthur Rigault, and Dewert, had already been shot and buried.

The same evening M. Jeandin, a baker, who had been arrested at 3 or 4 in the afternoon without any reason, and then taken by the Forty-ninth Pomeranian Regiment of Infantry to Villers-Saint-Frambourg, was fastened to a stake in a field and pierced repeatedly with the point of a bayonet.

It is unnecessary to say that the town of Senlis was pillaged. While the enemy sacked the houses they took pleasure in exciting the worst instincts of the populace by offering part of the booty to women in wretched circumstances.

At Villers-Saint-Frambourg the woman X. was raped by a soldier who got into her house. After the crime she took refuge in a neighboring house. The precaution was a wise one, for numerous comrades of the aggressor broke into her house and, furious at not finding the victim they sought, smashed the windows and seized the chickens, rabbits, and pig which they found in an outhouse.

On Sept. 3 at Creil, under the orders of a Captain who tried to force MM. Guillot and Demonts to show him the houses of the richest inhabitants, the Germans scattered among the houses, breaking in doors and windows, and gave themselves up to pillage with the complicity of their leaders, to whom they came constantly to show the jewelry which they had stolen. Demonts and Guillot were then led into the country, where they found about 100 inhabitants of Creil and Nogent-sur-Oise and the neighborhood. All these persons were forced to suffer the shame and grief of working against the defense of their country by cutting down a field of maize which hindered the firing of the enemy and by digging trenches intended to shelter the Germans. For seven days the enemy kept them there without giving them food. Some women of the neighborhood were, fortunately, able to give them a little.

Meanwhile in the town several people were put to death. M. Parent, who was escaping, was killed in the Rue Victor Hugo by a shot by a Uhlan. As soon as he fell, troopers hurled themselves upon him to search his clothes. M. Alexandre had his head shattered, at the intersection of the Rue Gambetta and the Rue Carnot. Germans entered the shop of M. Brèche, wine seller. Thinking, no doubt, that he was not serving them quickly enough, they dragged him into the courtyard of Mme. Egasse, his neighbor, where an officer accused him of having fired on the soldiers, and ordered, in spite of his denial, that he should be shot at once. Mme. Egasse tried to soften the murderers, but she was brutally ordered off. From the room to which she went she heard the reports, and through the window she saw Brèche's body stretched on the ground. When she came down she could not prevent herself from expressing her grief. The officer then said to her: "A dead man! We see too many to take any notice. Besides, wherever we are fired upon, we kill and burn."

A young man named Odener, carrying a bag of rice, had been taken from Liancourt of Creil. When he reached the Place de l'Eglise, worn out by fatigue and the ill-treatment which he had received, he put down his load and tried to escape. Two soldiers took aim at him, fired, and struck him down. A certain Leboeuf, who had been his fellow-prisoner, died at Creil a few days afterward in consequence of a wound which he had received on the way.

Gen. von Kluck's army arrived at Crépy-en-Valois on the 2d of September, and took four days to march through. The town was completely sacked under the eyes of the officers. In particular the jewelers' shops were ransacked.

Thefts of jewelry and body linen were committed in a house in which lodged a General commanding with some twelve officers of the General Staff. Almost all the safes in Crépy were gutted.

On the 3d of the same month, at Baron, an artist of great talent, Prof. Albéric Magnard, fired two shots from a revolver on a troop which was entering his property. One soldier was killed and another wounded. The Germans, who in so many places have committed the worst cruelties without any motive, here contented themselves with burning the property of their aggressor. The latter committed suicide to avoid falling into their hands. None the less the commune was sacked. M. Robert, notary, was robbed of his jewelry, his linen, and of 1,471 bottles of wine, and forced to open his safe and allow an officer to take 8,300 francs which were locked up there. In the evening he saw another officer who wore on his finger nine women's rings, and whose arms were adorned with six bracelets. Two soldiers told him, besides, that they received a premium of four marks whenever they brought their commanding officers a piece of jewelry.

In this commune, Mme. X., a most respectable young woman, was violated by two soldiers in succession in the absence of her husband, who is with the colors. One of these two men ransacked a chest of drawers while his comrade was committing his crime.

At Mesnil-sur-Bulles on the evening of the 4th of September two Germans arrived in a carriage and one on a bicycle and went to the house of the Deputy Mayor, M. Gustave Queste. As the latter did not understand them, he asked his cousin, M. Queste, Professor at the Lycée of Amiens, to act as interpreter for him. After having fulfilled this office the professor returned home. A few minutes afterward, hearing a shot, he went out to ascertain what was happening. He found himself in the presence of one of the three soldiers to whom he had just spoken in his cousin's house. This man, who was drunk, fired at him and killed him.

The same three soldiers, passing through Nourard-le-Franc, set fire to seven houses with torches which they had brought with them in their carriage. A few hours before their arrival at Mesnil-sur-Bulles a Uhlan patrol had already made a reconnoissance in this commune. Troopers entered the house of M. Amédée Queste, burst open a door, broke the furniture, and stole a quantity of jewelry as well as a sum of 60 francs.

At Choisy-au-Bac the Germans, who had been in the village since the 31st of August, willfully set fire on the 1st and 2d of September to forty-five houses under the grossly false allegation that they had been fired upon, and previously, in the presence of their officers, gave themselves up to a general pillage, the product of which was carried away in vehicles stolen from the inhabitants. Two army doctors, wearing the brassards of the Red Cross, themselves pillaged the house of Mme. Binder.

M. Morel, working carpenter, who was in his garden, was shot in the groin by a soldier who was passing on the road. He died next day. Four young men were taken as hostages and led away on the 8th of September. One of them was able to escape. His comrade, René Leclere, is said to have been shot at Besme, in the Department of the Aisne; as for the other two, no one knows what has become of them.

At Compiègne, which was occupied by the enemy from the 31st of August to the 12th of September, the château suffered comparatively little; the thefts there were not very important. But a great number of houses were pillaged. The house of Comte d'Orsetti, which is situated opposite to the palace, was literally sacked, principally by non-commissioned officers. Plate, jewelry, and valuables were collected in the courtyard of the château, examined, inventoried, and packed up, and were then loaded in two removal vans on which had been placed the Red Cross flag.

Application was made to Capt. Schroeder to put an end to the burglary and the scandalous orgy which was going on in the villa, and at last he went to the place; but after having glanced at the interior of the pillaged houses he went off again, saying, "It is war, and besides I have no time."

On Sept. 4 a soldier, who had gone to pass the night at the house where Mme. X. was concierge, drove the husband with several of the former's relations out of the house, threatening them with his rifle, and then obliged Mme. X. to pass the night with him.

At Trumilly, where they remained from the 2d to the 4th of September, the Germans pillaged the commune and carried off the product of their theft in artillery wagons as well as in carriages. The first day, Mme. Huet, on whom were billeted a part of the staff of the Nineteenth Regiment of Hanover Dragoons and a great number of soldiers, saw a non-commissioned officer take possession of a box containing her jewels to the value of about 10,000 francs. She went to complain to the Colonel, who contented himself with saying, with a smile, "I am sorry, Madame, it is war."

On the 3d of September the advance troops had left, but stragglers remained in the country. One of them, a soldier of the Ninety-first

Regiment of Infantry, on whose medal was engraved the name of "Ahne," stole in Mme. Huet's house 115 francs from the servants, 300 francs from the mistress of the house, and 400 francs from M. Cornillet. This man then went to the house of Mme. X., whose husband was with the colors, and forced this woman to submit to him by threatening her with his revolver.

During the occupation of the commune by the Germans M. Cornillet, the victim of one of the thefts of which we have just spoken, had an officer billeted upon him. After the departure of this guest he discovered that the sum of 150 francs, which had been placed in the wardrobe of the room in which the German had slept, had disappeared. Finally M. Colas, an old man of 70, was searched in the street by a soldier, and robbed of about 30 francs.

One of the most serious acts of which we have been informed in the Department of the Oise was committed near Marquéglise, by an officer of high rank. Two young men of Saint Quentin, named Charlet and Gabet, who had left Paris to return to their native place with the object of obeying the summons to be enrolled for military service, met on the road two Belgian subjects making their way to Jemmapes, where they lived. The latter offered them a lift in their carriage, and the four men journeyed together as far as the village of Ressons, where they were arrested by a German detachment. They were bound, and then taken to the District of Marquéglise, and brought before a superior officer, who questioned them. When he learned that two of them were natives of Belgium this officer declared that the Belgians were "sales gens"; then without any explanation he took his revolver and fired on each of the prisoners in turn. The two Belgians and young Gabet fell dead, struck in the head. As for Charlet, who was wounded in the neck and right shoulder, he pretended to be killed, and after the departure of the murderer, was able to drag himself a certain distance. Before being taken to Compiègne, where he died next day, the unfortunate man was able to describe to the Abbé Boulet, curé of Marquéglise, the cowardly deed of which his companions and himself had been the victims.

AISNE.

In the communes of the Department of the Aisne which we have been able to visit we have everywhere found evidences of acts of pillage and numerous crimes against women.

At Connigis on the 8th of September at about 8 o'clock in the evening Mme. X. was the victim of grievous violence at the hands of two Germans, who had gone to her parents-in-law's house, where she was living in the absence of her husband, who had been mobilized. One of the Germans held M. X., the father, in front of the door while the other, threatening the young woman with his rifle, committed acts of revolting obscenity upon her in the presence of the mother-in-law. When he had accomplished his crime he took the place of his comrade, mounting guard over M. X., while the former in his turn outraged the young woman.

At Brumetz, where the occupation by the enemy lasted from the 3d to the 10th, the village was pillaged. One house, as well as the château of M. de Maleyssie, a Captain on the staff of the Sixth French Army Corps, were burned.

At Chierry, the Château of Varolles was burned with torches with petrol. The Château of Sparre was also set on fire after it had been completely pillaged, pictures taken from their frames, and the tapestries cut up with blows of the sword.

At Jaulgonne, between the 3d and 10th of September, the Prussian Guard emptied the cellars, stole the linen, and did 250,000 francs' worth of damage. In addition, they burned a house on the allegation that the owner had fired on them when in reality he was hiding in terror in his cellar.

Two inhabitants of this commune were killed. One, M. Rempenault, aged 87, was found in the fields killed by a bullet; the other, named Blanchard, aged 61, had been arrested because the Prussians had seen him talking in a street with a French chasseur-à-pied, who, after having delayed in the village, had succeeded in taking to flight on a bicycle and escaped a rifle fusillade which was aimed at him. Blanchard was led into an outlying part of Jaulgonne and wounded with a bayonet by a soldier and then finished off by an officer, who shattered his head with a revolver shot.

At Charmel the Germans, from the moment of their arrival, entered the houses by breaking in the doors. They did not leave a bottle of wine in the cellars and they pillaged chiefly the empty houses, carrying away linen, money, jewelry, and other articles. At the house of the schoolmaster they took the funds of the School Savings Bank, which amounted to 240 francs. On the 3d of September, at 11 o'clock at night, they set fire to the château of Mme. de Rougé, and the same day one of them entered the house of Mme. X., seized her by the throat and violated her.

At Coincy, on the 3d and 4th of September, they emptied the cellars and sacked the empty houses and committed outrages on several women in the village.

At Bezu-St.-Germain, on the 8th of September, two soldier cyclists came to the farm of —— and passed part of the night there. Having obliged the inhabitants to go to bed, and having forbidden them on pain of death to move, whatever sounds they might hear, one of them went into the room of the little servant girl, aged 13, and, putting his hand on her mouth, committed a complete rape upon her. Hearing a loud cry, the farmer's daughter escaped through her window and called some officers who were lodging with a neighbor. One of them came down, had the two cyclists, who at that moment were coming from the farm, arrested, and marched to headquarters. The next day, when the victim was asked to recognize the culprit and point him out, he had disappeared.

On the 3d of September, at Crézancy, the soldiers made young Lesaint, aged 18, come out of his house, and an officer killed him with a revolver shot. One of the murderer's comrades declared later that this murder had been committed because Lesaint was a soldier, and when a man to whom he was speaking denied this, he added, "He was on the way to be one." He said also that the young man had stupidly caused his own death, because, with the intention of escaping, he had put out the candle which was lighted in his room. Now this candle had not been put out by the unfortunate Lesaint, but had been removed by a soldier who wished to visit the house. In any case, the officer reluctantly admitted that his comrade had fired too soon.

In the same locality M. Dupont, "gérant du familistère," was arrested on the 4th of September because he had tried to protect his till against a soldier who was in the act of ransacking it. With a trooper's cap on his head, which they had drawn down to his chin, and both his hands tied behind his back, he was made the butt of the Germans, who amused themselves by forcing him to go on to a very high slope, raining blows upon him and pricking him with bayonets every time he fell down. He was taken on the 6th to Charly-sur-Marne with a convoy of military prisoners, and on the 8th of September, in the morning, his murderers in their retreat forced him to follow the column. As he could not drag himself along in consequence of the violence which he had suffered, the Germans struck him with redoubled vigor and pushed him along, holding him under the arms. A kilometer further on they killed him with a blow from a lance or bayonet through the heart.

At Château-Thierry, where the German troops remained from the 2d to the 9th of September, the pillage was carried out under the eyes of the officers. Later on army doctors who remained in the town after the departure of the army were included in an exchange of prisoners, and their canteens were opened. They contained articles of clothing which were the product of the sack of the shops.

On the 5th of September the girl ——, aged 14, met a soldier as she was coming back from fetching some bread for her parents. She was dragged into the shop of a shoemaker, and from there into a room where two other Germans joined the first. She was threatened with a bayonet, thrown on to a bed, and violated by two of these men. The third was prepared to follow his comrades' example, but allowed himself to be moved by the child's entreaties.

The aunt of this young girl was also the victim of serious crimes at Verdilly, where her family have the farm ———. After having bound her husband four soldiers belonging to the heavy artillery chased her to the house of a neighbor, whom they terrorized with threats, and while one of them held her the others violated her in succession.

At Hartennes-et-Taux, in the Arrondissement of Soissons, the Germans, as everywhere else, pillaged the houses. At the hamlet of Taux they set fire to the straw with which they had stopped up the openings of an isolated cellar in which were three of the inhabitants whom they had taken for soldiers. The three men were suffocated by the smoke.

ACTS OF A MILITARY NATURE.

Acts committed in the violation of the laws of war and affecting combatants, murder of wounded or prisoners, stratagems forbidden by international conventions, attacks on doctors and stretcher bearers, have been innumerable in all the places in which there has been fighting. We have not been able to verify the majority of them because the witnesses are for the most part soldiers, who are obliged to move from place to place continually. Besides, these acts have been set forth in reports addressed by corps leaders to the military authorities, who may add them to the documents of our inquiry if they think fit to do so. Many are also attested by evidence collected by magistrates in hospitals, and we are engaged at this moment in analyzing them with a view to drawing up a supplementary report. A certain number, however, have been laid before us in the course of our investigation.

At Bar-le-Duc M. Ferry, the head surgeon, gave us a report of depositions made to him in the course of his duties. Sergt. Lemerre of the —th Infantry Regiment told him that on the 6th of September, when he was wounded in the leg at Rembercourt by a fragment of a shell, he had been left on the battlefield eight days by the German Red Cross people although they knew quite well that he was there. On the fourth day this non-commissioned officer received a further wound by a soldier, who fired at him on the order of an officer who was going over the scene of action with his revolver in his hand. Moreover, he repeatedly saw near him German stretcher bearers firing on our wounded.

The soldier Dreyfus of the —th Infantry Regiment related the following story to Dr. Ferry:

"On the 10th of September at Somaine, as he was leaving the battlefield, wounded, he met three Germans. He told them in German that he had just been wounded, but these men answered that this was no reason why he should not receive another bullet, and they thereupon shot him point blank in the eye."

At Vaubecourt an infantry sergeant and two soldiers were shot by the enemy. They alleged that one of the latter was found on the church tower in the village, from which he would have been able to exchange signals with our troops.

On the 22d of August a detachment of Germans arrived in the vicinity of Bouvillers in the Department of Meurthe-et-Moselle at the farm of La Petite Rochelle, where the owner, M. Houillon, had lodged some French wounded soldiers. The officer in command ordered four of his men to go and finish off nine wounded who were lying in the barn. Each one was shot in the ear. Mme. Houillon begged mercy for them, and the officer, placing the barrel of his revolver to her breast, told her to be silent.

On the 25th of August the Abbé Denis, curé of Réméréville, tended in the evening Lieut. Toussaint, who last July headed the list of candidates who left the School of Forestry. As he fell wounded on the battlefield this young officer was struck with bayonets by all the Germans who passed near him. His body was covered with wounds from head to foot.

At the hospital at Nancy we saw the soldier Voyer of the —th Infantry Regiment, who still bore traces of German barbarity, having been badly wounded in the backbone outside the Forest of Champenoux on the 24th of August, and paralyzed in both legs as the result of his wound. He was lying on his face when a German soldier turned him over brutally with his gun and hit him three times on the head with the butt of his rifle. Other soldiers passing by kicked him and hit him also with the butts of their guns. Finally one of them with a single blow caused a wound of about three or four centimeters under each eye with what Dr. Weiss, head doctor and Professor of Faculty at Nancy, thinks must have been a pair of scissors.

A hussar who was treated by the same doctor relates that, having fractured his leg falling off his horse, and being unable to extricate himself, he was assaulted by Uhlans, who stole his watch and chain after having taken his carbine and shot him in the eye with it.

Seven French soldiers, also treated by Dr. Weiss, told him that they had seen the enemy finish off the wounded on the battlefield. As they had feigned death to escape massacre, the Germans belabored them with the butts of their guns to see if they were still alive.

In the same hospital a German soldier wounded in the stomach told Dr. Rohmer that his wound had been caused by a revolver shot fired by his own officer because he had refused to finish off a French wounded soldier. Again, another German, wounded in the back, the result of a shot fired point-blank, told Dr. Weiss that a soldier had fired at him by order of an officer to punish him for having carried into a village near the battlefield several French wounded soldiers.

On the 25th of August, at Einvaux, the Germans fired at a distance of 300 yards at Dr. Millet, army doctor, belonging to the —th Colonial Regiment, just as, together with two stretcher bearers, he was attending to a man lying on a stretcher. As his left side was turned toward them, the enemy could perfectly see his brassard. And, furthermore, they could not mistake the nature of the work upon which these three men were engaged.

On the same day Capt. Perraud of the same regiment, having noticed that the soldiers of a section of men upon whom his mitrailleuses were firing were wearing red trousers, ordered the firing to cease. Immediately this section fired on him and on his men. They were Germans in disguise.

Believe us, &c.,

G. PAYELLE, President.
ARMAND MOLLARD.
G. MARINGER.
PAILLOT, Rapporteur.

Paris, Dec. 17, 1914.

A FRENCH MAYOR'S PUNISHMENT.

[By The Associated Press.]

NANCY, (via Paris,) Jan. 30.—The Mayor of a large township in the vicinity of Nancy has been suspended from office for a fortnight for shooting at a German aeroplane as it was flying over his town.

In taking this measure the authorities of Nancy held that a civilian had no right to act as a combatant, as by so doing he only brought upon the heads of the civilian population severe reprisals.

We Will Fight to the End

By Premier Viviani of France.

Premier Viviani recently delivered to Parliament an address upon the war which attracted worldwide attention. Viviani served notice on Germany and Austria that France will not lay down her arms until she and her allies have won such a victory that they can dictate terms. Premier Viviani's speech was delivered by himself in the Chamber of Deputies on Dec. 22, while on the same day the speech was read in the Senate by M. Briand, Minister of Justice. It is as follows:

GENTLEMEN: This is not the usual communication in which a Government presenting itself for the first time before Parliament sets forth its policy. Just now there is only one policy—a relentless fight until we attain definite freedom for Europe by gaining a victory which shall guarantee peace.

Gentlemen, that was the cry uttered by all when, in the sitting of Aug. 4, a sacred union arose, as the President of the Republic has so well said, which will throughout history remain an honor to the country. It is the cry which all Frenchmen will repeat after having put an end to the disagreements that have so often embittered our hearts and which a blind enemy took for irremediable division. It is the cry that rises from the glorious trenches into which France has thrown all her youth, all her manhood.

Before this unexpected uprising of national feeling, Germany has been troubled in the intoxication of her dream of victory. On the first day of the conflict she denied right, appealed to force, flouted history, and, in order to violate the neutrality of Belgium and to invade France, invoked the law of self-interest alone.

Since then her Government, learning that it had to reckon with the opinion of the world, has recently attempted to put her conduct in a better light by trying to throw the responsibility for the war upon the Allies. But through all the gross falsehoods, which fail to deceive even the most credulous, the truth has become apparent.

All the documents published by the nations interested, and the remarkable speech made the other day at Rome by one of the most illustrious representatives of the noble Italian Nation, demonstrate that for a long time our enemy has intended a coup de force. If it were necessary, a single one of these documents would suffice to enlighten the world.

When, on July 31, 1914, at the suggestion of the English Government all the nations concerned were asked to suspend their military preparations and enter into negotiations in London, France and Russia adhered to this proposal. But Germany precipitated matters. She declared war on Russia on Aug. 1, and made an appeal to arms inevitable. And if Germany by her diplomacy killed the germ of peace it is because for more than forty years she had untiringly pursued her aim, which was to crush France in order to achieve the enslavement of the world.

All the revelations are brought before the tribunal of history, where corruption has no place, and as France and her allies, despite their attachment to peace, have been obliged to endure war they will pursue it to the uttermost.

Faithful to the signature which she attached to the treaty of Sept. 4, 1914, and by which she engaged her honor, that is to say, her life, France, in accord with her allies, will not lay down her arms until she has avenged outraged right and regained forever the provinces which were torn from her by force, restored heroic Belgium to the fullness of her material prosperity and political independence, and broken Prussian militarism so that the Allies may eventually reconstruct a regenerated Europe founded upon justice and right.

We are not inspired, gentlemen, in this plan of war and of peace by any presumptuous hope, for we have the certainty of success. We owe this certitude to our army of all ranks and to our sailors, who, joined to the British Navy, secure for us the control of the seas, and to the troops who have repulsed in Morocco incessant aggressions.

We owe it also to the soldiers who defend our flag in those far-off French colonies, who from the very first outbreak of the war hastened back with their tender solicitude for the mother country.

We owe it to our army, whose heroism has been guided by incomparable leaders throughout the victory of the Marne, the victory of Flanders, and in many fights, and we owe it to the nation, which has equaled this heroism by a corresponding demonstration of silence and serenity during the critical hours through which the country has passed.

Thus we have shown to the world that an organized democracy can serve by its vigorous action the ideal of liberty and equality which constitute its greatness. Thus we have shown to the world, to use the words of our Commander in Chief, who is both a great soldier and a noble citizen, that "the republic may well be proud of the army that she has prepared." And thus, this impious war has brought out all the virtues of our race, both those with which we were credited—of initiative, élan, bravery, and fearlessness—and those which we were not supposed to possess—endurance, patience, and stoicism.

Let us do honor to all these heroes. Glory to those who have fallen before the victory, and to those also who through it will avenge them tomorrow! A nation which can arouse such enthusiasm can never perish.

Sheltered by this heroism the nation has lived and labored, accepting all the consequences of the war, and domestic tranquillity has never been troubled.

The Minister of Finance has laid before you in a masterly statement the financial situation and has explained the resources that we have obtained from the issue of Treasury bonds and advances from the Bank of France, which have enabled us to bear the expenditure imposed by the war, so that we have not had any need to resort to a loan. The Bank of France is in a position, thanks to its excellent condition, to furnish resources to the Treasury and to aid in the resumption of the economic life of the country.

Everything serves to demonstrate the vitality of France, the security of her credit, the confidence which she inspires in all, despite the war which is shaking and impoverishing the world. The state of her finances is such that she can continue the war until the day when the necessary reparation has been obtained.

Gentlemen, it is not sufficient for us to salute the victims who have fallen on the field of battle. We must uncover also before the civil non-combatants and innocent victims who up to now have been protected by the laws of war, but whom, in order to terrify a nation which is and will ever remain unshaken, the enemy either captured or massacred. The Government has done its duty toward their families, but the debt of the country is not yet discharged.

Under the force of invasion, departments have been occupied and the ruins in them have accumulated. The Government solemnly undertakes before you—it has already partly carried it out, and has asked for a first credit of $70,000,000—that France will rebuild again those ruins, and the carrying out of this work will certainly be borne in mind in the indemnities which we shall exact.

The day of a definite victory has not yet come. Our task until then will be heavy, and it may be long. Let us bring all our strength to bear in the carrying out of this task. Our allies know that we will do so, as well as the neutral nations, and it is in vain that a wild campaign of false news has been set on foot. If Germany at the outset pretended to have any doubt as to the attitude of France, she no longer doubts.

Let Germany bear witness now that when the French Parliament reopened after over four months of war, it has renewed before the world the spectacle it offered on the day when, in the name of the nation, it took up the challenge.

To conquer, heroism at the frontier will not suffice. It is necessary also to have internal union. Let us continue to preserve this sacred union from any blemish today, as in the past, and in the future. Let us keep before our minds the one cry of victory, the vision of our motherland, and the ideal of right.

That is what we are fighting for and what Belgium is still fighting for, Belgium, who is giving to this ideal all the blood in her veins, and what also unshakable England is fighting for, as also faithful Russia, intrepid Servia, and the audacious Japanese Navy.

Nothing more sublime has ever presented itself before the eyes of men than this struggle against barbarism and despotism, against a system of provocation and continual threats, which Germany called peace, against a system of murders and collective pillage, which Germany called war, against the insolent hegemony of a military caste. France with her allies has let loose the scourge of war against all these. France the emancipator and avenger has sprung up at one bound.

That is the issue at stake. It goes beyond the life of the present generation. Let us continue to have but one soul and one mind, and tomorrow, when peace is restored and when our opinions, now voluntarily enthralled, are again given their liberty, we will recall with pride these tragic days, for they have tended to make us more valiant and better men.

NUITS BLANCHES

By H.S. HASKINS.

The diminishing of lights in Paris houses as a precaution against a raid by the enemy's aeroplanes is the new rule.—Cable Dispatch.

The gaslights cast a saffron glow,
The ghostly tapers sputter low,
The lampwicks smolder, dimly red.
(Beware the gray shapes overhead!)
Lock tight the windows, bar the door!
Have done with laughter, sing no more,
For fear lays hand upon the throat.
(Beneath the stars the airmen float.)
Hush, hush, my babe, lest fiends that fly
Shall come to still your hunger cry.
Let grief not speak its tale aloud!
(Black death is racing with a cloud.)
Through heav'n's eternal window panes,
Far, far above the swift air lanes,
God's starlight shines forever more.
(How restless glide the ships of war!)

Unconquered France
Story of Two Months' Combat with 2,000,000 Invaders.

[From the Bulletin Français.]

Two million men were engaged on the German side in October and November when the Kaiser's forces hammered at the Allies' lines in an attempt to break through to Dunkirk and Calais. Around Ypres alone the invaders' losses were more than 120,000 men. These statements are made in a semi-official account of the fighting in Flanders, which takes up three pages of the Bulletin Français, copies of which reached THE NEW YORK TIMES on Jan. 11, 1915. As translated, the article in the December Bulletin appears below.

THE hour has arrived when the balance of these last weeks can be established and the results clearly seen. The formidable attempt by the Germans, first to turn the left of ourselves and our allies, and then, that having been prevented, to break through, has entirely failed. By the effort the enemy tried to repair the defeats of the Marne, and they have only added another check to the failure of September.

Meanwhile, in order to invade our territory, according to their old plans the Germans have neglected nothing. On the front that extends from Lys to the sea they massed, in the beginning of October, fifteen army corps, including four divisions of cavalry. Their army heads, the Crown Prince of Bavaria, Gen. Deemling, the Duke of Württemburg, have multiplied their exhortations and appeals to the troops in the effort to maintain the morale of their men.

We have found their orders on dead officers and prisoners, and always they are the same. It is a question of "a decisive action against the French left" or a question of "piercing the line at Dupres or Ypres," for, as one of these orders stated, "the decisive coup remains to be struck, and to accomplish this the allied line must be pierced." This, the orders stated, had to be accomplished at any price and in all haste. They wanted a decision in the western theatre of war before turning to the east.

Then the Emperor himself was with his troops, hoping to animate the German soldiers with his presence. He announced to them that he would be at Ypres on Nov. 1, and that was the date fixed for the annexation of

Belgium. In fact, everything had been taken into account, except, of course, the victorious resistance of the allied armies.

To make possible this effective resistance it was necessary for the Allies to oppose the enemy with a force which if not equal to theirs was nevertheless sufficient for the purpose in view.

What was the situation at the beginning of Oct. 1? The Belgian Army came out of Antwerp intact, but too exhausted to participate in the actions then pending. The English Army had left the Aisne to operate in the north. The army of Gen. de Castelnau did not extend on its left south of Arras. The army of Gen. Maudhuy stretched out from that point to the south of Lille. Further on were the territorial cavalry and the marines. This was not a sufficient force to meet the German advance.

Gen. Joffre, the Commander in Chief, ordered Gen. Foch to the command of the armies of the north. Reinforcements were sent him in the ensuing three weeks, and during that period the rail and automobile services operated day and night, hurrying up reinforcements. They arrived on time by divisions and by corps, every man being animated by an admirable spirit.

About Oct. 20 our battle line was from Nieuport to Dixmude, between which places one of our divisions and the marines held the railroad. Meanwhile, just back of them, the Belgian Army was being reorganized. South of Dixmude, and along the canal, our line stretched to the east, forming before Ypres a vast half circle occupied by four French and one British army corps. The line then descended toward the south of Messines to Armientières, forming two sections, the first held by the English and the second by the French.

The German attack had as its object the seizure of Dunkirk, which was necessary if Calais and Boulogne were to be reached. The purpose was to envelop us and cut the British lines of communication to the sea. All the heavy artillery was brought up from Antwerp and made ready for use against the Allies. What happened?

On Nov. 3 the attack was made and repulsed, crushing the enemy, who had managed to gain the left bank of the river. We then pushed the German rear guard into the water, and to this day German cannon and the carcasses of their animals can be seen half buried in the water and mud.

Finding it impossible to turn our left, the enemy tried to break through our lines. This was the battle of Ypres, a furious and savage struggle, with the German commanders hurling their organizations in enormous masses, regardless of the life of their men, sacrificing all for the end they hoped to attain.

This end was not attained. During the following three weeks we suffered and withstood their repeated and frantic attacks. All these attacks were repulsed, and this despite the fact that our front, with its circular form, was not easy to maintain.

In these actions about Ypres the armies of France and England worked in the closest union, and this union, in which co-operation was so splendidly maintained, is worthy to be recorded on the brightest pages of military history.

On Nov. 12 the Germans were successful to the north of Ypres and crossed the canal in two places. A day passed and they were thrown back to the other side. On the 12th also they gained a little ground south of Ypres, but this loss was quickly regained, and by the 15th their attacks had become fewer and our position by then was practically impregnable.

Subsequent actions by the Germans were likewise repulsed, and in these encounters we were brilliantly supported by our Allies. These actions have sealed the fraternity of the allied troops, and the energy of our resistance has likewise encouraged and strengthened the confidence of the Belgians.

The losses of the Germans certainly exceed 120,000 men. In certain trenches of 1,200 meters length as many as 2,000 bodies have been found, and this is impressive when we take into consideration that the Germans take advantage of every opportunity to remove their dead from the fields of battle. These great losses explain the recent formation of new army corps in Germany.

The numerous artillery commands that we have put in action south of Ypres have opened great chasms in the German masses. All this marks the importance of our successes, and significance is added by the fact that the Germans have always regarded the taking of Ypres as one of the decisive features of the campaign.

If Dunkirk, Calais, and Boulogne had been taken, England would have found her lines of communication with her armies in France gravely endangered. In maintaining her lines from the sea to Arras we have obtained at the same time the best guarantee against the return of the enemy to Paris.

To measure the extent of the allied successes we must compare the line occupied by our left and the German right at the beginning of September and since the middle of November. When we consider this, it is plain that our successes were not temporary, but have been a constant progress, rendering vain the attacks of the Germans.

It has been demonstrated by facts that Gen. Joffre has read the plans of the German commanders and is ready for them everywhere and always. As for the allied troops, they have gained the qualities they perhaps lacked most in the beginning, particularly as regards rapid organization for the defensive and the digging of trenches. Today our troops are as expert in trench work as are the soldiers of the enemy.

France remains unconquered. Since Sept. 6 she has registered only successes, in spite of the massing against her of fifty German army corps. These fifty German corps, it must be said, and said again, for such is the truth, are still facing us. Fifteen German army corps and the whole of the Austrian force are facing Russia. Yet the formidable mass which assails us has not made us flinch in any part of our line, and in many cases our enemy has drawn back under the weight of the Allies' efforts.

Four Months of War

[From the Official Bulletin des Armées, Dec. 6, 1914.]

The Bulletin des Armées, the newspaper published by the French Government for the soldiers at the front, in the issue of Dec. 6, 1914, contains an article bearing the title, "Four Months of War," which is a summary account of the events that have taken place since the outbreak of hostilities. This document estimates as fifty-two army corps and ten cavalry divisions the military forces which Germany hurled against France. In a chapter entitled "Our Reverses in August," it sums up the events that preceded the battle of the Marne, as presented below.

OUR concentration had to be flexible enough to enable us to bring our chief effort to bear upon the spot where the enemy would prove most active. The violation of Belgium made us acquainted with the intentions of the German staff—the great conflict would take place in the north.

As we were obliged, before engaging in it, to wait for the coming into line of the English army, which was to take place only on Aug. 20, we at once took measures to retain the greatest possible number of German troops in Alsace and in Lorraine.

In Alsace, our first attack, which was badly conducted, took us to Mülhausen, but we could not hold the city (Aug. 7.)

A second attack, led by General Pau, brought us back there. On Aug. 20 we held the road to Colmar through the Vosges and the plain. The enemy had sustained great losses.

But from that time the unfortunate events in Lorraine and Belgium forced us to limit the field of operations in Alsace as well as the intensity of our efforts (Aug. 20.)

In Lorraine our offensive had first been brilliantly successful. On Aug. 19 we had reached Sarrebourg, Les Etangs, Dieuze, Morhange, Delme, and Château-Salins.

But on the 20th the enemy, strongly intrenched on thoroughly fortified territory, resumed the offensive.

On the 22d, 23d, and 24th we were compelled to fall back on Grand-Courenne de Nancy and south of Lunéville.

On the 25th simultaneous counterattacks from the armies of Gens. Dubail and Castelnau greatly strengthened our positions.

But seven or eight German army corps and four divisions of cavalry had overcome the magnificent resistance of Liége. Every one knows of the conditions under which the French took the offensive in Belgium with the armies of Gens. Ruffey and Langle de Cary.

As soon as the English Army was ready in the region of Mons we took the offensive in Belgian Luxemburg with the armies of Gens. Ruffey and Langle de Cary. This offensive was at once checked, with great losses on our side.

Here again the ground had been strongly fortified by the enemy. There was also, in some of our army corps, a failure to transmit and carry out orders (Aug. 21-23.)

On the left of these two armies and in conjunction with the English army Gen. Lanrezac's army, anxious for its right wing, then fell back (Aug. 24) on the line that stretches between Beaumont and Givet.

On the 25th and 26th the English army, kept in check at Landrecies and Le Cateau, withdrew toward the Marne.

These days were marked by bloody contests. The enemy lost heavily, but constantly gained ground.

At that time we either had to hold the ground under the perilous conditions resulting from the retreat of our left wing or else retreat along the whole front until it were possible to resume the offensive under favorable conditions.

The Commander in Chief decided upon the latter alternative.

The first object to attain was withdrawing in good order while weakening and delaying the enemy by constant attacks. Several of these attacks were brilliantly conducted, especially those of Lanrezac's army at Saint-Quentin and Guise, of Langle's army on the Meuse, and of Ruffey's army further east. They were supported from Nancy to the Vosges by Castelnau's and Dubail's armies. In order to prepare for the offensive a new army had been formed, that of Gen. Maunoury. It was to be concentrated in the last days of August in the vicinity of Amiens.

But the advance of the enemy, by stages of forty-five kilometers a day, was so swift that Gen. Joffre, in order to realize his plan for the offensive, had to order the retreat to be continued.

The army should withdraw to the Aube, and as far as the Seine if necessary; everything should be subordinated to preparing a successful offensive.

On Sept. 5 the conditions which the General in Chief sought to realize were fulfilled—our left wing (Maunoury's army, the English Army, the army of Lanrezac which was now d'Espéray's army) was no longer in danger of being cut off.

On the contrary, the German right, (Gen. von Kluck,) marching to the south toward Meaux and Coulommiers, was exposing its right wing to Maunoury's army.

On the evening of the 5th the General in Chief ordered a general advance, adding: "The hour has come to advance at any cost and to die rather than fall back."

VICTORY OF THE MARNE.

As early as Sept. 8 the menace directed by Gen. Maunoury against the German right was beginning to tell.

The enemy brought back from the south to the north two army corps and wheeled about facing west.

Thus it presented a weak point to the English Army, which, having advanced from the line stretching from Rozoy to Lagny, (on the 6th,) straightened its line toward the north, crossed the Marne on the 9th, thus flanking the German Army already battling with Gen. Maunoury.

On the right of the British d'Espéray's army also crossed the Marne, forcing the enemy to retreat, and at the same time supporting the action of its neighbors, that is to say, the English Army on the left and Foch's army on the right.

Map of Operations in France During First Four Months of the War

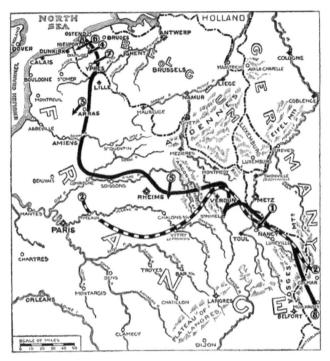

[Enlarge]

(1) Point where Germans failed to hold Nancy, Sept. 12, 1914.

(2) Extreme limits of the dash to Paris, terminating Sept. 8, 1914.

(3) Point to which the first unsuccessful flanking movement against the French left wing extended, Aug. 30, 1914.

(4) Point of extension of similar flanking operations, balked Nov. 12, 1914.

(5) Scene of frustrated efforts to break through French centre, Sept. 26, 1914.

(6) Line of attacks upon Calais and Dunkirk, defeated Oct. 18, 1914.

(7) Ypres, where desperate and fruitless assaults, ending Nov. 15, 1914, were made by the Germans.

(8) Intrenched line of battle, Feb. 1, 1915.

For it was on our centre, made up of Foch's army, which had been constituted on Aug. 20, that the Germans were going to seek revenge for the check of their right wing; if they had succeeded in cutting us off between Sézanne and Mailly, the situation would have been reversed with the advantage on their side.

From Sept. 6 to Sept. 9 Foch's army met with repeated assaults, but on the evening of the 9th the left of his army, shifting from west to east toward Fère-Champenoise, flanked the Prussian Guard and the Saxons who were advancing southeast of this town.

This bold manoeuvre insured success. The Germans withdrew in great haste, and on the 11th in the morning Gen. Foch entered Châlons-sur-Marne.

On his right Langle de Gary's army had also moved forward, and on the 12th, after spirited encounters, it joined, and added to, the line of Gen. Foch's army.

Meanwhile Ruffey's army (now Darrail's) had succeeded in stretching its lines north, and, although meeting with a stubborn resistance, hastened the German retreat, which was accelerated by the offensive taken by Castelnau's and Dubail's armies from Nancy to the Vosges.

Thanks to this strategic offensive, the campaign turned in our favor. We have maintained this advantage over the enemy ever since.

THE RACE FOR THE COAST.

After Sept. 13 the German resistance, strengthened by strong defensive works prepared in advance, checked the French and English pursuit; then began the "race for the sea." During this long battle the German staff never lost the hope of turning the allied left wing, while we hoped to be able to outflank their right wing. The result was a race which at the end of October extended the fronts of the opposing armies as far as the North Sea.

In this race the Germans had an advantage over us, namely, the concentric shape of their front which simplified the problem of carrying troops and supplies.

In spite of this advantage, the turning movement attempted by their right with twelve army corps, six reserve corps, and four corps of cavalry, utterly failed.

This failure confirmed the victory of the Marne.

As early as Sept. 11 Gen. Joffre had directed the effort of Maunoury's army against the German right wing. But this army was not large enough to cope with the situation.

So about Sept. 20 a new army was formed on the left of Maunoury's army and intrusted to Gen. de Castelnau.

This army strongly intrenched itself in the district which stretches over Lassigny, Roye, and Péronne. It was supported on its left by the territorial divisions of Gen. Brugère. (Sept. 21-26.)

But still it was inadequate to achieve our end, and on Sept. 30 further north than the army of Castelnau, Maudhuy's army came to the front, and occupied the region of Arras and Lens, extending toward the north to co-operate with the divisions coming from Dunkirk.

Nevertheless, all these troops, in presence of the strenuous exertions of the enemy, formed too thin a line, a line too extended to allow any breaking.

At that time and at the request of Field Marshal French the transportation of the English Army from the Aisne to the Lys region was decided upon.

The valiant Belgian Army which had left Antwerp on Oct. 9 thanks to the protection of the British and French marines was also on its way to the Yser region to reinforce the barrier which had to be created and maintained.

These moves took time. The English Army was only to come into action by Oct. 20. On the other hand, the Belgian Army, which had been fighting for three months, was momentarily lacking ammunition. Gen. Joffre ordered a new effort.

On Oct. 4 he had intrusted to Gen. Foch the mission of co-ordinating the operations of the armies in the north.

On the 18th he placed at his disposal reinforcements which, continually increasing until Nov. 12, were to form the French army of Belgium under the command of Gen. d'Urbal.

This army, in conjunction with the Belgians and an English corps, was henceforth to fight between the sea and the Lys River.

The Journal de Genève, judging this phase of the war, has written that the French General Staff, by shifting so swiftly such huge bodies of troops, gave evidence that it had the situation splendidly in hand.

The result of this effort was a total failure of the German attack in Flanders.

GERMAN OFFENSIVE CHECKED.

This attack was especially violent; twelve army corps and four cavalry corps were massed between the Lys and the sea.

The Emperor was at the head of his armies. He addressed his men, stating that a "decisive blow" was to be delivered. For three weeks the German staff hurled furious assaults in mass formation. But as early as Nov. 12 we were in a position to state that the outcome of these assaults had been a victory for the Allies.

From the sea to Dixmude the Belgian Army, Gen. Grossetti and Admiral Ronarc'h held first the railroad from Nieuport to Dixmude, then the left bank of the Yser.

A hostile army corps, which had succeeded in reaching the left bank, was forced to withdraw. It has never been able to go further than Dixmude.

More to the south, from Dixmude to the north of Ypres, a like situation.

The Germans, on Nov. 12, had crossed the river at two points, were pushed back to the other bank, thus giving Gen. Humbert the command of the bridges.

East of Ypres, Gens. Dubois, Balfourrier, and Douglas Haig had not yielded an inch of ground.

Further south the German attack, aiming at our lines of communication, had been particularly violent, but the English and the French regained all the ground that had been momentarily lost and made it impregnable.

During the second half of November the shattered German attacks weakened. The infantry engaged us less frequently and the artillery showed less activity.

The enemy, in the battle of Ypres alone, had lost at least 120,000 men.

Never had such a thoroughly prepared and spirited offensive undergone such a complete failure.

A WAR OF SIEGE.

Meanwhile, from the banks of the Lys to the ridges of the Vosges a war of siege was ceaselessly raging. The Bulletin des Armées says:

It is hardly necessary to emphasize the meritorious behavior of our troops in waging this war inch by inch, never yielding, progressing often in spite of the added difficulty of transporting important French and English contingents to the north.

In close conjunction with the armies of the north the armies of Gen. Maudhuy and Gen. de Castelnau held without flinching in the slightest the line between the Lys and Noyon, from the middle of October till the end of November.

Their progress has been continuous since the end of October; our positions in Arras and La Bassée have been strengthened, Quesnoy-en-Santerre has been captured, and in all the encounters with the enemy our artillery and infantry have constantly made gains.

Between the Oise and the Argonne the armies of Maunoury, d'Espéray, and Langle de Cary were confronted with very strong positions, viz., the heights of the Aisne, of Berru, Nogent-l'Abbesse, Moronvilliers, and the wooded hills of Western Argonne.

In September they had to resist a very violent general attack. This attack was a failure, especially east of Rheims, (Sept. 26.)

The Emperor had witnessed this check of his troops just as a week later he was to witness the failure at Ypres.

Our armies, that is to say, Sarrail's and Dubail's, fulfilled with method and success the task intrusted to them, viz., to protect our right flank against attacks on the line from Metz to Thionville; to retain in front of them the greatest possible number of German army corps; to free as far as practicable, the national territory that had been invaded, especially in the Woevre region and around Verdun.

In a first period (Sept. 13-29) the enemy had the upper hand, fortified themselves in St. Mihiel, reached the Hauts-de-Meuse, and threatened Verdun.

In the second period (Oct. 1 to Nov. 30) we regained the advantage.

We cleared the vicinity of Verdun. We advanced east of Nancy, which is now quite safe from German shells, to the north of Lunéville, and to the northeast and east of Saint-Dié.

In November we had recovered almost in its integrity the invaded territory between Belfort and the Moselle.

In brief, the situation on Dec. 1 was as follows:

In number of men, the French Army is equal to what it was on Aug. 2, as all the gaps have been filled up.

The quality of the troops is infinitely better. Our men now fight like veterans. All are deeply convinced of their superiority and have absolute faith in the final victory.

Several necessary changes were made among the commanding officers, and in the last three months none of those mistakes was committed that had been observed and punished in August.

Our supply in artillery ammunition has been largely increased. The heavy artillery which we lacked has been provided for and seen at work on the battlefield.

The English Army has been very heavily reinforced in November. It is numerically stronger than at the outset of the campaign. The Indian troops have completed their apprenticeship in European warfare.

The Belgian Army has been reorganized into six divisions. It is ready and eager to reconquer the national territory.

A SERIES OF GERMAN REVERSES.

The enemy have failed in their abrupt attack upon Nancy.

They failed in their swift march on Paris.

They failed to envelop our left wing in August.

They failed in the same attempt in November.

They failed to pierce through our centre in September.

They failed in their attack by way of the coast on Dunkirk and Calais.

They failed in their attack on Ypres.

The Bulletin des Armées concludes its account in these words:

Germany has exhausted its reserves in this fruitless effort. Her newly formed troops are raw.

Russia more and more asserts her superiority against Germany, as well as against Austria.

The German armies after this check are fatally doomed to retreat.

All this has been accomplished during the last four months. The moment had come to sum up these operations; the press is now free to comment upon them.

LONG LIVE THE ALLIES!

By CLAUDE MONET.

[From King Albert's Book.]

I FEEL myself greatly honored by the opportunity given me to express all my admiration of heroic Belgium, and to offer a like admiration to the noble and valiant King of the Belgians.

Long live Belgium! Long live the Allies! Long live France!

United States Fair to All
Disclaimer of Bias Against Germany and Austria

By William J. Bryan, American Secretary of State

The following letter is the most exhaustive document that has come from the Administration at Washington since the outbreak of the war dealing with any aspect of the relations of this country toward that conflict. Its length is due to the fact that it is intended as a categorical denial of the different charges that have been made and of the arguments current in German circles accusing the Administration of unfriendliness to Germany and Austria-Hungary. Senator Stone was interested in having these charges answered for two reasons: First, there is a large German population in St. Louis, the chief city of his State, and, second, he is Chairman of the Committee on Foreign Relations. Senator Stone wrote his letter of inquiry on Jan. 8, saying that he had received many letters from sympathizers with Germany and Austria who believed the United States Government had been showing partiality to England, France, and Russia.

WASHINGTON, Jan. 20, 1915.

Hon. William J. Stone, Chairman Committee on Foreign Relations, United States Senate, Washington, D.C.

DEAR Mr. Stone: I have received your letter of the 8th inst. referring to frequent complaints or charges made in one form or another through the press that this Government has shown partiality to Great Britain, France, and Russia against Germany and Austria during the present war and stating that you have received numerous letters to the same effect from sympathizers with the latter powers. You summarize the various grounds of these complaints and ask that you be furnished with whatever information the department may have touching these points of complaint in order that you may be informed as to what the true situation is in regard to these matters.

In order that you may have such information as the department has on the subjects referred to in your letter, I will take them up seriatim.

(1) Freedom of communication by submarine cables versus censored communication by wireless.

The reason that wireless messages and cable messages require different treatment by a neutral Government is as follows:

Communication by wireless cannot be interrupted by a belligerent. With a submarine cable it is otherwise. The possibility of cutting the cable exists, and if a belligerent possesses naval superiority the cable is cut, as was the German cable near the Azores by one of Germany's enemies, and as was the British cable near Fanning Island by a German naval force. Since a cable is subject to hostile attack, the responsibility falls upon the belligerent, and not upon the neutral, to prevent cable communication.

A more important reason, however, at least from the point of view of a neutral Government, is that messages sent out from a wireless station in neutral territory may be received by belligerent warships on the high seas. If these messages, whether plain or in cipher, direct the movements of warships or convey to them information as to the location of an enemy's public or private vessels, the neutral territory becomes a base of naval operations, to permit which would be essentially unneutral.

As a wireless message can be received by all stations and vessels within a given radius, every message in cipher, whatever its intended destination, must be censored, otherwise military information may be sent to warships off the coast of a neutral. It is manifest that a submarine cable is incapable of becoming a means of direct communication with a warship on the high seas; hence its use cannot, as a rule, make neutral territory a base for the direction of naval operations.

(2) Censorship of mails and in some cases repeated destruction of American letters on neutral vessels.

As to the censorship of mails, Germany, as well as Great Britain, has pursued this course in regard to private letters falling into their hands. The unquestioned right to adopt a measure of this sort makes objection to it inadvisable.

It has been asserted that American mail on board of Dutch steamers has been repeatedly destroyed. No evidence to this effect has been filed with the Government, and therefore no representations have been made. Until such a case is presented in concrete form this Government would not be justified in presenting the matter to the offending belligerent. Complaints have come to the department that mail on board neutral steamers has been opened and detained, but there seem to be but few cases where the mail from neutral countries has not been finally delivered. When mail is sent to belligerent countries open and is of a neutral and private character it has not been molested so far as the department is advised.

(3) Searching of American vessels for German and Austrian subjects on the high seas and in territorial waters of a belligerent.

So far as this Government has been informed, no American vessels on the high seas, with two exceptions, have been detained or searched by belligerent warships for German and Austrian subjects. One of the exceptions to which reference is made is now the subject of a rigid investigation, and vigorous representations have been made to the offending Government. The other exception, where certain German passengers were made to sign a promise not to take part in the war, has been brought to the attention of the offending Government with a declaration that such procedure, if true, is an unwarranted exercise of jurisdiction over American vessels in which this Government will not acquiesce.

An American private vessel entering voluntarily the territorial waters of a belligerent becomes subject to its municipal laws, as do the persons on board the vessel.

There have appeared in certain publications the assertion that failure to protest in these cases is an abandonment of the principle for which the United States went to war in 1812. If the failure to protest were true, which it is not, the principle involved is entirely different from the one appealed to against unjustifiable impressment of Americans in the British Navy in time of peace.

(4) Submission without protest to British violations of the rules regarding absolute and conditional contraband as laid down in The Hague Conventions, the Declaration of London, and international law.

There is no Hague Convention which deals with absolute or conditional contraband and, as the Declaration of London is not in force, the rules of international law only apply. As to the articles to be regarded as contraband, there is no general agreement between nations. It is the practice of a century, either in time of peace or after the outbreak of war, to declare the articles which it will consider as absolute or conditional contraband. It is true that a neutral Government is seriously affected by this declaration, as the rights of its subjects or citizens may be impaired. But the rights and interests of belligerents and neutrals are opposed in respect to contraband articles and trade and there is no tribunal to which questions of difference may be readily submitted.

The record of the United States in the past is not free from criticism. When neutral this Government has stood for a restricted list of absolute and conditional contraband. As a belligerent, we have contended for a liberal list, according to our conception of the necessities of the case.

The United States has made earnest representations to Great Britain in regard to the seizure and detention by the British authorities of all American ships or cargoes bona fide destined to neutral ports, on the ground that such seizures and detentions were contrary to the existing rules of international law. It will be recalled, however, that American courts have established various rules bearing on these matters. The rule of "continuous voyage" has been not only asserted by American tribunals, but extended by them.

They have exercised the right to determine from the circumstances whether the ostensible was the real destination. They have held that the shipment of articles of contraband to a neutral port "to order," from which, as a matter of fact, cargoes had been transshipped to the enemy, is corroborative evidence that the cargo is really destined to the enemy, instead of to the neutral port of delivery. It is thus seen that some of the doctrines which appear to bear harshly upon neutrals at the present time are analogous to or outgrowths from policies adopted by the United States when it was a belligerent. The Government, therefore, cannot consistently protest against the application of rules which it has followed in the past, unless they have not been practiced as heretofore.

(5) Acquiescence without protest to the inclusion of copper and other articles in the British lists of absolute contraband.

The United States has now under consideration the question of the right of a belligerent to include "copper unwrought" in its list of absolute contraband instead of in its list of conditional contraband. As the Government of the United States has in the past placed "all articles from which ammunition is manufactured" in its contraband list, and has declared copper to be among such materials, it necessarily finds some embarrassment in dealing with the subject.

Moreover, there is no instance of the United States acquiescing in Great Britain's seizure of copper shipments. In every case in which it has been done vigorous representations have been made to the British Government, and the representatives of the United States have pressed for the release of the shipments.

(6) Submission without protest to interference with American trade to neutral countries in conditional and absolute contraband.

The fact that the commerce of the United States is interrupted by Great Britain is consequent upon the superiority of her navy on the high seas. History shows that whenever a country has possessed that superiority our trade has been interrupted and that few articles essential to the prosecution of the war have been allowed to reach its enemy from this country. The department's recent note to the British Government, which has been made public, in regard to detentions and seizures of American vessels and cargoes, is a complete answer to this complaint.

Certain other complaints appear aimed at the loss of profit in trade, which must include at least in part trade in contraband with Germany, while other complaints demand the prohibition of trade in contraband, which appears to refer to trade with the Allies.

(7) Submission without protest to interruption of trade in conditional contraband consigned to private persons in Germany and Austria, thereby supporting the policy of Great Britain to cut off all supplies from Germany and Austria.

As no American vessel, so far as known, has attempted to carry conditional contraband to Germany or Austria-Hungary, no ground of complaint has arisen out of the seizure or condemnation by Great Britain of an American vessel with a belligerent destination. Until a case arises and the Government has taken action upon it, criticism is premature and unwarranted. The United States in its note of Dec. 28 to the British Government strongly contended for the principle of freedom of trade in articles of conditional contraband not destined to the belligerent's forces.

(8) Submission to British interference with trade in petroleum, rubber, leather, wool, &c.

Petrol and other petroleum products have been proclaimed by Great Britain as contraband of war. In view of the absolute necessity of such products to the use of submarines, aeroplanes, and motors, the United States Government has not yet reached the conclusion that they are improperly included in a list of contraband. Military operations today are largely a question of motive power through mechanical devices. It is therefore difficult to argue successfully against the inclusion of petroleum among the articles of contraband. As to the detention of cargoes of petroleum going to neutral countries, this Government has, thus far, successfully obtained the release in every case of detention or seizure which has been brought to its attention.

Great Britain and France have placed rubber on the absolute contraband list, and leather on the conditional contraband list. Rubber is extensively used in the manufacture and operation of motors, and, like petrol, is regarded by some authorities as essential to motive power today. Leather is even more widely used in cavalry and infantry equipment. It is understood that both rubber and leather, together with wool, have been embargoed by most of the belligerent countries. It will be recalled that the United States has in the past exercised the right of embargo upon exports of any commodity which might aid the enemy's cause.

(9) The United States has not interfered with the sale to Great Britain and her allies of arms, ammunition, horses, uniforms, and other munitions of war, although such sales prolong the conflict.

There is no power in the Executive to prevent the sale of ammunition to the belligerents. The duty of a neutral to restrict trade in munitions of war has never been imposed by international law or by municipal statute. It has never been the policy of this Government to prevent the shipment of arms or ammunition into belligerent territory, except in the case of neighboring American republics, and then only when civil strife prevailed. Even to this extent the belligerents in the present conflict, when they were neutrals, have never, so far as the records disclose, limited the sale of munitions of war. It is only necessary to point to the enormous quantities of arms and ammunition furnished by manufacturers in Germany to the belligerents in the Russo-Japanese war, and in the recent Balkan wars, to establish the general recognition of the propriety of the trade by a neutral nation.

It may be added that on the 15th of December last, the German Ambassador, by direction of his Government, presented a copy of a memorandum of the Imperial German Government which, among other things, set forth the attitude of that Government toward traffic in contraband of war by citizens of neutral countries. The Imperial Government stated that "under the general principles of international law, no exception can be taken to neutral States, letting war material go to Germany's enemies from or through neutral territory," and that the adversaries of Germany in the present war are, in the opinion of the Imperial Government, authorized to "draw on the United States contraband of war, and especially arms worth billions of marks."

These principles, as the Ambassador stated, have been accepted by the United States Government in the statement issued by the Department of State on Oct. 15 last, entitled "Neutrality and Trade in Contraband." Acting in conformity with the propositions there set forth, the United States has itself taken no part in contraband traffic, and has, so far as possible, lent its influence toward equal treatment for all belligerents in the matter of purchasing arms and ammunition of private persons in the United States.

(10) The United States has not suppressed the sale of dumdum bullets to Great Britain.

On Dec. 5 last the German Ambassador addressed a note to the department stating that the British Government had ordered from the Winchester Repeating Arms Company 20,000 "riot guns," Model 1897, and 50,000,000 "buckshot cartridges" for use in such guns. The department replied that it saw a published statement of the Winchester Company, the correctness of which the company has confirmed to the department by telegraph. In this statement the company categorically denies that it has received an order for such guns and cartridges from or made any sales of such material to the British Government, or to any other Government engaged in the present war. The Ambassador further called attention to "information, the accuracy of which is not to be doubted," that 8,000,000 cartridges fitted with "mushroom bullets" had been delivered since October of this year by the Union Metallic Cartridge Company for the armament of the English Army.

In reply the department referred to the letter of Dec. 10, 1914, of the Remington Arms-Union Metallic Cartridge Company of New York to the Ambassador, called forth by certain newspaper reports of statements alleged to have been made by the Ambassador in regard to the sales by that company of soft-nosed bullets. From this letter, a copy of which was sent to the department by the company, it appears that instead of 8,000,000 cartridges having been sold only a little over 117,000 were manufactured and 109,000 were sold.

The letter further asserts that these cartridges were made to supply a demand for a better sporting cartridge with a soft-nosed bullet than had been manufactured theretofore, and that such cartridges cannot be used in the military rifles of any foreign powers. The company adds that its statements can be substantiated and that it is ready to give the Ambassador any evidence that he may require on these points. The department further stated that it was also in receipt from the company of a complete detailed list of the persons to whom these cartridges were sold, and that from this list it appeared that the cartridges were sold to firms in lots of 20 to 2,000 and one lot each of 3,000, 4,000, and 5,000. Of these only 960 cartridges went to British North America and 100 to British East Africa.

The department added that if the Ambassador could furnish evidence that this or any other company is manufacturing and selling for the use of the contending armies in Europe cartridges whose use would contravene The Hague Conventions, the department would be glad to be furnished with this evidence, and that the President would, in case any American company is shown to be engaged in this traffic, use his influence to prevent so far as possible sales of such ammunition to the powers engaged in the European war, without regard to whether it is the duty of this Government upon legal or conventional grounds to take such action.

The substance of both the Ambassador's note and the department's reply have appeared in the press.

The department has received no other complaints of alleged sales of dumdum bullets by American citizens to belligerent Governments.

(11) British warships are permitted to lie off American ports and intercept neutral vessels.

The complaint is unjustified from the fact that representations were made to the British Government that the presence of war vessels in the vicinity of New York Harbor was offensive to this Government, and a similar complaint was made to the Japanese Government as to one of its cruisers in the vicinity of the Port of Honolulu. In both cases the warships were withdrawn.

It will be recalled that in 1863 the department took the position that captures made by its vessels after hovering about neutral ports would not be regarded as valid. In the Franco-Prussian war President Grant issued a proclamation warning belligerent warships against hovering in the vicinity of American ports for purposes of observation or hostile acts. The same policy has been maintained in the present war, and in all of the recent proclamations of neutrality the President states that such practice by belligerent warships is "unfriendly and offensive."

(12) Great Britain and her allies are allowed without protest to disregard American citizenship papers and passports.

American citizenship papers have been disregarded in a comparatively few instances by Great Britain, but the same is true of all the belligerents. Bearers of American passports have been arrested in all the countries at war. In every case of apparent illegal arrest the United States Government has entered vigorous protests with request of release. The department does not know of any cases except one or two, which are still under investigation, in which naturalized Germans have not been released upon representations by this Government. There have, however, come to the department's notice authentic cases in which American passports have been fraudulently obtained and used by certain German subjects.

The Department of Justice has recently apprehended at least four persons of German nationality who, it is alleged, obtained American passports under pretense of being American citizens, and for the purpose of returning to Germany without molestation by her enemies during the voyage. There are indications that a systematic plan had been devised to obtain American passports through fraud for the purpose of securing safe passage for German officers and reservists desiring to return to Germany.

Such fraudulent use of passports by Germans themselves can have no other effect than to cast suspicion upon American passports in general. New regulations, however, requiring among other things the attaching of a photograph of the bearer to his passport, under the seal of the Department of State, and the vigilance of the Department of Justice, will doubtless prevent further misuse of American passports.

(13) Change of policy in regard to loans to belligerents.

War loans in this country were disapproved because inconsistent with the spirit of neutrality. There is a clearly defined difference between a war loan and the purchase of arms and ammunition. The policy of disapproving of war loans affects all Governments alike, so that the disapproval is not an unneutral act. The case is entirely different in the matter of arms and ammunition because prohibition of export not only might not, but, in this case, would not, operate equally upon the nations at war. Then, too, the reason given for the disapproval of war loans is supported by other considerations which are absent in the case presented by the sale of arms and ammunition. The taking of money out of the United States during such a war as this might seriously embarrass the Government in case it needed to borrow money, and it might also seriously impair this nation's ability to assist the neutral nations which, though not participants in the war, are compelled to bear a heavy burden on account of the war, and, again, a war loan, if offered for popular subscription in the United States, would be taken up chiefly by those who are in sympathy with the belligerents seeking the loan.

The result would be that great numbers of the American people might become more earnest partisans, having material interest in the success of the belligerent whose bonds they hold. These purchasers would not be confined to a few, but would spread generally throughout the country, so that the people would be divided into groups of partisans, which would result in intense bitterness and might cause an undesirable if not a serious situation. On the other hand, contracts for and sales of contraband are mere matters of trade. The manufacturer, unless peculiarly sentimental, would sell to one belligerent as readily as he would to another. No general spirit of partisanship is aroused—no sympathies excited. The whole transaction is merely a matter of business.

This Government has not been advised that any general loans have been made by foreign Governments in this country since the President expressed his wish that loans of this character should not be made.

(14) Submission to arrest of native-born Americans on neutral vessels and in British ports and their imprisonment.

The general charge as to the arrest of American-born citizens on board neutral vessels and in British ports, the ignoring of their passports, and their confinement in jails, requires evidence to support it. That there have been cases of injustice of this sort is unquestionably true, but Americans in

Germany have suffered in this way, as Americans have in Great Britain. This Government has considered that the majority of these cases resulted from overzealousness on the part of subordinate officials in both countries. Every case which has been brought to the attention of the Department of State has been properly investigated, and if the facts warranted a demand for release has been made.

(15) Indifference to confinement of non-combatants in detention camps in England and France.

As to the detention of non-combatants confined in concentration camps, all the belligerents, with perhaps the exception of Servia and Russia, have made similar complaints, and those for whom this Government is acting have asked investigations, which representatives of this Government have made impartially. Their reports have shown that the treatment of prisoners is generally as good as possible under the conditions in all countries, and that there is no more reason to say that they are mistreated in one country than in another country, or that this Government has manifested an indifference in the matter. As this department's efforts at investigations seemed to develop bitterness between the countries, the department on Nov. 20 sent a circular instruction to its representatives not to undertake further investigation of concentration camps.

But at the special request of the German Government that Mr. Jackson, former American Minister at Bucharest, now attached to the American Embassy at Berlin, make an investigation of the prison camps in England, in addition to the investigations already made, the department has consented to dispatch Mr. Jackson on this special mission.

(16) Failure to prevent transshipment or British troops and war materials across the territory of the United States.

The department has had no specific case of the passage of convoys or troops across American territory brought to its notice. There have been rumors to this effect, but no actual facts have been presented. The transshipment of reservists of all belligerents who have requested the privilege has been permitted on condition that they travel as individuals and not as an organized, uniformed, or armed bodies. The German Embassy has advised the department that it would not be likely to avail itself of the privilege, but Germany's ally, Austria-Hungary, did so.

Only one case raising the question of the transit of war material owned by a belligerent across United States territory has come to the department's notice. This was a request on the part of the Canadian Government for permission to ship equipment across Alaska to the sea. The request was refused.

(17) Treatment and final internment of German S.S. Geier and the collier Locksun at Honolulu.

The Geier entered Honolulu on Oct. 15 in an unseaworthy condition. The commanding officer reported the necessity of extensive repairs which would require an indefinite period for completion. The vessel was allowed the generous period of three weeks, to Nov. 7, to make repairs and leave the port, or, failing to do so, to be interned. A longer period would have been contrary to international practice, which does not permit a vessel to remain for a long time in a neutral port for the purpose of repairing a generally run-down condition due to long sea service. Soon after the German cruiser arrived at Honolulu a Japanese cruiser appeared off the port, and the commander of the Geier chose to intern the vessel rather than to depart from the harbor.

Shortly after the Geier entered the Port of Honolulu the steamer Locksun arrived. It was found that this vessel had delivered coal to the Geier en route and had accompanied her toward Hawaii. As she had thus constituted herself a tender or collier to the Geier, she was accorded the same treatment and interned on Nov. 7.

(18) Unfairness to Germany in rules relative to coaling of warships in Panama Canal Zone.

By proclamation of Nov. 13, 1914, certain special restrictions were placed on the coaling of warships or their tenders or colliers in the Canal Zone. These regulations were framed through the collaboration of the State, Navy, and War Departments and without the slightest reference to favoritism to the belligerents. Before these regulations were proclaimed war vessels could procure coal of the Panama Railway in the Zone ports, but no belligerent vessels are known to have done so.

Under the proclamation fuel may be taken on by belligerent warships only with the consent of the canal authorities and in such amounts as will enable them to reach the nearest accessible neutral port; and the amount so taken on shall be deducted from the amount procurable in United States ports within three months thereafter. Now it is charged that the United States has shown partiality, because Great Britain and not Germany happens to have colonies in the near vicinity where British ships may coal, while Germany has no such coaling facilities. Thus it is intimated the United States should balance the inequalities of geographical position by refusal to allow any warships of belligerents to coal in the Canal Zone until the war is over. As no German warship has sought to obtain coal in the Canal Zone the charge of discrimination rests upon a possibility which during several months of warfare has failed to materialize.

(19) Failure to protest against the modifications of the Declaration of London by the British Government.

The German Foreign Office presented to the diplomats in Berlin a memorandum dated Oct. 10 calling attention to violations of and changes in the Declaration of London by the British Government, and inquiring as to the attitude of the United States toward such action on the part of the Allies. The substance of the memorandum was forthwith telegraphed to the department on Oct. 22, and was replied to shortly thereafter to the effect that the United States had withdrawn its suggestion, made early in the war, that for the sake of uniformity the Declaration of London should be adopted as a temporary code of naval warfare during the present war, owing to the unwillingness of the belligerents to accept the declaration without changes and modifications, and that thenceforth the United States would insist that the rights of the United States and its citizens in the war should be governed by the existing rules of international law.

As this Government is not now interested in the adoption of the Declaration of London by the belligerents, the modifications by the belligerents in that code of naval warfare are of no concern to it, except as they adversely affect the rights of the United States and those of its citizens as defined by international law. In so far as those rights have been infringed the department has made every effort to obtain redress for the losses sustained.

(20) Generally unfriendly attitude of Government toward Germany and Austria.

If any American citizens, partisans of Germany and Austria-Hungary, feel that this Administration is acting in a way injurious to the cause of those countries, this feeling results from the fact that on the high seas the German and Austro-Hungarian naval power is thus far inferior to the British. It is the business of a belligerent operating on the high seas, not the duty of a neutral, to prevent contraband from reaching an enemy.

Those in this country who sympathize with Germany and Austria-Hungary appear to assume that some obligation rests upon this Government, in the performance of its neutral duty, to prevent all trade in contraband, and thus to equalize the difference due to the relative naval strength of the belligerents. No such obligation exists; it would be an unneutral act, an act of partiality on the part of this Government to adopt such a policy if the Executive had the power to do so. If Germany and Austria-Hungary cannot import contraband from this country it is not, because of that fact, the duty of the United States to close its markets to the Allies. The markets of this country are open upon equal terms to all the world, to every nation, belligerent or neutral.

The foregoing categorical replies to specific complaints is sufficient answer to the charge of unfriendliness to Germany and Austria-Hungary. I am, my dear Senator, very sincerely yours,

W.J. BRYAN.

THE HOUSE WITH SEALED DOORS

By EDITH M. THOMAS.

... "A house with sealed doors, where a family of 7,000,000 sits in silence around a cheerless hearth.... America opened the window ... and slipped a loaf of bread into the larder."—Frederick Palmer, in THE NEW YORK TIMES.

MERCHANT ships many are on the main.
This that we send plies not for gain—
Ship of the loaves! May her course be straight,
When the starving millions her coming wait!

In a "Happy Province" beyond the sea
("Happy" by fiat—a monarch's decree!)
They have seized their lands, they have taken their stores,
They have shut them up, they have sealed the doors!

The folk within—their table is bare.
But why should the lords of the "Province" care?—
Myrmidons, myrmidons, first to feed;
Afterwards think of the people's need.

Let the arm'd men eat, let the people wait,
(Say the lords of the "Province" who parcel out fate,)
Let the arm'd men feed—that their strength endure,
That their hearts be lusty, their grasp be sure!

In that "Happy Province" beyond the sea
They are not bond and they are not free:
In silence they sit by their smoldered hearth;
But the winds bear their burden around the earth!

The winds and the waters are rolling along
The rune of their sorrow (too cruel for song!) ...

Bring food for the family robbed of its stores;
Open a window where sealed are the doors!

Merchant ships many are on the main.
This that we send plies not for gain—
Ship of the loaves!... Ye have given them lead,
Ye lords of the "Province," but we give bread!

_____

Seizures of American Cargoes

By William J. Bryan, American Secretary of State

By agreement between the Governments of the United States and Great Britain the text of the American note, printed below, setting forth the views of this Government in opposition to British interference with American trade, was made public in Washington on Dec. 31, 1914, and simultaneously in London. At the same time copies of the American communication were for the first time delivered to the Ambassadors and Ministers of all the powers at Washington, and the note was cabled by them to their respective Governments. The American communication—it is not a note, strictly speaking, because all notes are sent by mail in diplomacy and never by telegraph—sets forth clearly the conditions of which the American Government and people complain resulting from the frequent seizures and detentions by the British of American cargoes destined to neutral European ports.

The Secretary of State to the American Ambassador at London.

Department of State,
WASHINGTON, Dec. 26, 1914.

The present condition of American foreign trade resulting from the frequent seizures and detentions of American cargoes destined to neutral European ports has become so serious as to require a candid statement of the views of this Government in order that the British Government may be fully informed as to the attitude of the United States toward the policy which has been pursued by the British authorities during the present war.

You will therefore communicate the following to his Majesty's principal Secretary of State for Foreign Affairs, but in doing so you will assure him that it is done in the most friendly spirit and in the belief that frankness will better serve the continuance of cordial relations between the two countries than silence, which may be misconstrued into acquiescence in a course of conduct which this Government cannot but consider to be an infringement upon the rights of American citizens.

The Government of the United States has viewed with growing concern the large number of vessels laden with American goods destined to neutral ports in Europe which have been seized on the high seas, taken into British ports, and detained sometimes for weeks by the British authorities. During the early days of the war this Government assumed that the policy adopted by the British Government was due to the unexpected outbreak of hostilities and the necessity of immediate action to prevent contraband from reaching the enemy.

For this reason it was not disposed to judge this policy harshly, or protest it vigorously, although it was manifestly very injurious to American trade with the neutral countries of Europe. This Government, relying confidently upon the high regard which Great Britain has so often exhibited in the past for the rights of other nations, confidently awaited amendment of a course of action which denied to neutral commerce the freedom to which it was entitled by the law of nations.

COUNT LADISLAUS STADNICKI

Founder of the Polish Legion of the German Army.

(Photo from Engelbrecht.)

GENERAL VON KROBATKIN

Chief of the Austrian General Staff.

(*Photo from Paul Thompson.*)

This expectation seemed to be rendered the more assured by the statement of the Foreign Office early in November that the British Government was satisfied with guarantees offered by the Norwegian, Swedish, and Danish Governments as to non-exportation of contraband goods when consigned to named persons in the territories of those

Governments, and that orders had been given to the British fleet and customs authorities to restrict interference with neutral vessels carrying such cargoes so consigned to verification of ship's papers and cargoes.

It is therefore a matter of deep regret that, though nearly five months have passed since the war began, the British Government has not materially changed its policy and do not treat less rigorously ships and cargoes passing between neutral ports in the peaceful pursuit of lawful commerce, which belligerents should protect rather than interrupt. The greater freedom from detention and seizure which was confidently expected to result from consigning shipments to definite consignees rather than "to order" is still awaited.

It is needless to point out to his Majesty's Government, usually the champion of the freedom of the seas and the rights of trade, that peace, not war, is the normal relation between nations and that the commerce between countries which are not belligerents should not be interfered with by those at war unless such interference is manifestly an imperative necessity to protect their national safety, and then only to the extent that it is a necessity.

It is with no lack of appreciation of the momentous nature of the present struggle in which Great Britain is engaged and with no selfish desire to gain undue commercial advantage that this Government is reluctantly forced to the conclusion that the present policy of his Majesty's Government toward neutral ships and cargoes exceeds the manifest necessity of a belligerent and constitutes restrictions upon the rights of American citizens on the high seas which are not justified by the rules of international law or required under the principle of self-preservation.

The Government of the United States does not intend at this time to discuss the propriety of including certain articles in the lists of absolute and conditional contraband which have been proclaimed by his Majesty. Open to objection as some of these seem to this Government, the chief ground of present complaint is the treatment of cargoes of both classes of articles when bound to neutral ports.

Articles listed as absolute contraband, shipped from the United States and consigned to neutral countries, have been seized and detained on the ground that the countries to which they were destined have not prohibited the exportation of such articles. Unwarranted as such detentions are, in the opinion of this Government, American exporters are further perplexed by the apparent indecision of the British authorities in applying their own rules to neutral cargoes.

For example, a shipment of copper from this country to a specified consignee in Sweden was detained because, as was stated by Great Britain, Sweden had placed no embargo on copper. On the other hand, Italy not only prohibited the export of copper, but, as this Government is informed, put in force a decree that shipments to Italian consignees or "to order" which arrive in ports of Italy cannot be exported or transshipped. The only exception Italy makes is of copper which passes through that country in transit to another country. In spite of these decrees, however, the British Foreign Office has thus far declined to affirm that copper shipments consigned to Italy will not be molested on the high seas. Seizures are so numerous and delays so prolonged that exporters are afraid to send their copper to Italy, steamship lines decline to accept it, and insurers refuse to issue policies upon it. In a word, a legitimate trade is being greatly impaired through uncertainty as to the treatment which we may expect at the hands of the British authorities.

We feel that we are abundantly justified in asking for information as to the manner in which the British Government propose to carry out the policy which they have adopted in order that we may determine the steps necessary to protect our citizens engaged in foreign trade in their rights and from the serious losses to which they are liable through ignorance of the hazards to which their cargoes are exposed.

In the case of conditional contraband, the policy of Great Britain appears to this Government to be equally unjustified by the established rules of international conduct. As evidence of this, attention is directed to the fact that a number of the American cargoes which have been seized consist of foodstuffs and other articles of common use in all countries which are admittedly relative contraband. In spite of the presumption of innocent use because destined to neutral territory, the British authorities made these seizures and detentions without, so far as we are informed, being in possession of facts which warranted a reasonable belief that the shipments had in realty a belligerent destination, as that term is used in international law.

Mere suspicion is not evidence, and doubts should be resolved in favor of neutral commerce, not against it. The effect upon trade in these articles between neutral nations resulting from interrupted voyages and detained cargoes is not entirely cured by reimbursement of the owners for the damages which they have suffered, after investigation has failed to establish an enemy destination. The injury is to American commerce with neutral countries as a whole through the hazard of the enterprise and the repeated diversion of goods from establishing markets.

It also appears that cargoes of this character have been seized by the British authorities because of a belief that, though not originally so intended by the shippers, they will ultimately reach the territory of the enemies of Great Britain. Yet this belief is frequently reduced to a mere fear in view of the embargoes which have been decreed by the neutral countries to which they are destined on the articles composing the cargoes.

That a consignment "to order" of articles listed as conditional contraband and shipped to a neutral port raises a legal presumption of enemy destination appears to be directly contrary to the doctrines previously held by Great Britain and thus stated by Lord Salisbury during the South African war:

"Foodstuffs, though having a hostile destination, can be considered as contraband of war only if they are for the enemy forces; it is not sufficient that they are capable of being so used, it must be shown that this was in fact their destination at the time of their seizure."

With this statement as to conditional contraband the views of this Government are in entire accord, and upon this historic doctrine, consistently maintained by Great Britain when a belligerent as well as a neutral, American shippers were entitled to rely.

The Government of the United States readily admits the full right of a belligerent to visit and search on the high seas the vessels of American citizens or other neutral vessels carrying American goods and to detain them WHEN THERE IS SUFFICIENT EVIDENCE TO JUSTIFY A BELIEF THAT CONTRABAND ARTICLES ARE IN THEIR CARGOES; but his Majesty's Government, judging by their own experience in the past, must realize that this Government cannot without protest permit American ships or American cargoes to be taken into British ports and there detained for the purpose of searching generally for evidence of contraband or upon presumptions created by special municipal enactments which are clearly at variance with international law and practice.

This Government believes and earnestly hopes his Majesty's Government will come to the same belief, that a course of conduct more in conformity with the rules of international usage, which Great Britain has strongly sanctioned for many years, will in the end better serve the interests of belligerents as well as those of neutrals.

Not only is the situation a critical one to the commercial interests of the United States, but many of the great industries of this country are suffering because their products are denied long-established markets in European countries, which, though neutral, are contiguous to the nations at war. Producers and exporters, steamship and insurance companies, are pressing, and not without reason, for relief from the menace to transatlantic trade which is gradually but surely destroying their business and threatening them with financial disaster.

The Government of the United States, still relying upon the deep sense of justice of the British Nation, which has been so often manifested in the intercourse between the two countries during so many years of uninterrupted friendship, expresses confidently the hope that his Majesty's Government will realize the obstacles and difficulties which their present policy has placed in the way of commerce between the United States and the neutral countries of Europe and will instruct its officials to refrain from all unnecessary interference with the freedom of trade between nations which are sufferers, though not participants, in the present conflict; and will in their treatment of neutral ships and cargoes conform more closely to those rules governing the maritime relations between belligerents and neutrals which have received the sanction of the civilized world and in which Great Britain has in other wars so strongly and successfully advocated.

In conclusion, it should be impressed upon his Majesty's Government that the present condition of American trade with the neutral European countries is such that, if it does not improve, it may arouse a feeling contrary to that which has so long existed between the American and British people. Already it is becoming more and more the subject of public criticism and complaint. There is an increasing belief, doubtless not entirely unjustified, that the present British policy toward American trade is responsible for the depression in certain industries which depend upon European markets. The attention of the British Government is called to this possible result of their present policy, to show how widespread the effect is upon the industrial life of the United States and to emphasize the importance of removing the cause of complaint.

WILLIAM J. BRYAN,
Secretary of State.

GERMAN CROWN PRINCE TO AMERICA

[By The Associated Press.]

GENEVA, (via Paris,) Jan. 29.—Crown Prince Frederick William of Germany has sent to the local correspondent of The Associated Press, in response to a request for a statement on the war, the following reply, dated near Verdun, Jan. 22:

"You ask me to send a message to the American people. Being an officer and no diplomat, I have no right to do so, but if you like I will tell you three things:

"First—Every single German and Austrian is quite certain that we will come out on top, and will give his last drop of blood to this end.

"Second—We are convinced that the day will come when the people of Russia and France will find out that they are only doing the dirty work for England.

"Third—We expect from America absolutely fair play in all questions.

"These are my personal ideas, but a good many of my countrymen feel the same. Greetings.

"WILHELM, Kronprinz."

The Official British Explanation

By Sir Edward Grey, Secretary of State for Foreign Affairs of Great Britain

The State Department in Washington and the Foreign Office in London, by agreement, made public simultaneously on Jan. 10, 1915, the British reply to the American protest against the undue detention of American ships and cargoes seized for search for contraband. The answer, signed by Sir Edward Grey, the British Secretary of State for Foreign Affairs, was addressed to Walter Hines Page, the American Ambassador in London, who cabled it to Washington on Jan. 7. The note is preliminary, and was to be followed by a more detailed reply.

The British Secretary of State for Foreign Affairs to the American Ambassador.

FOREIGN OFFICE, Jan. 7, 1915.

Your Excellency: I have the honor to acknowledge receipt of your note of the 28th of December. It is being carefully examined and the points raised in it are receiving consideration, as the result of which a reply shall be addressed to your Excellency dealing in detail with the issues raised and the points to which the United States Government have drawn attention. This consideration and the preparation of the reply will necessarily require some time, and I therefore desire to send without further delay some preliminary observations which will, I trust, help to clear the ground and remove some misconceptions that seem to exist.

Let me say at once that we entirely recognize the most friendly spirit referred to by your Excellency and that we desire to reply in the same spirit and in the belief that, as your Excellency states, frankness will best serve the continuance of cordial relations between the two countries.

His Majesty's Government cordially concur in the principle enunciated by the Government of the United States that a belligerent, in dealing with trade between neutrals, should not interfere unless such interference is necessary to protect the belligerent's national safety, and then only to the extent to which this is necessary. We shall endeavor to keep our action within the limits of this principle on the understanding that it admits our right to interfere when such interference is not with "bona-fide" trade between the United States and another neutral country, but with trade in contraband destined for the enemy's country; and we are ready, whenever our action may unintentionally exceed this principle, to make redress.

We think that much misconception exists as to the extent to which we have, in practice, interfered with trade. Your Excellency's note seems to hold his Majesty's Government responsible for the present condition of trade with neutral countries, and it is stated that, through the action of his Majesty's Government, the products of the great industries of the United States have been denied long-established markets in European countries which, though neutral, are contiguous to the seat of war. Such a result is far from being the intention of his Majesty's Government, and they would exceedingly regret that it should be due to their action.

I have been unable to obtain complete or conclusive figures showing what the state of trade with these neutral countries has been recently, and I can, therefore, only ask that some further consideration should be given to the question whether United States trade with these neutral countries has been so seriously affected. The only figures as to the total volume of trade that I have seen are those for the exports from New York for the month of November, 1914, and they are as follows, compared with the month of November, 1913:

Exports from New York for November, 1913, and November, 1914, respectively: Denmark, $558,000, $7,101,000; Sweden, $377,000, $2,858,000; Norway, $477,000, $2,318,000; Italy, $2,971,000, $4,781,000; Holland, $4,389,000, $3,960,000.

It is true that there may have been a falling off in cotton exports, as to which New York figures would be no guide, but his Majesty's Government have been most careful not to interfere with cotton, and its place on the free list has been scrupulously maintained.

We do not wish to lay too much stress upon incomplete statistics; the figures above are not put forward as conclusive, and we are prepared to examine any further evidence with regard to the state of trade with these neutral countries, which may point to a different conclusion or show that it is the action of his Majesty's Government in particular and not the existence of a state of war and consequent diminution of purchasing power and shrinkage of trade, which is responsible for adverse effects upon trade with the neutral countries.

That the existence of a state of war on such a scale has had a very adverse effect upon certain great industries, such as cotton, is obvious, but it is submitted that this is due to the general cause of diminished purchasing power of such countries as France, Germany, and the United Kingdom rather than to interference with trade with neutral countries. In the matter of cotton it may be recalled that the British Government gave special assistance through the Liverpool Cotton Exchange to the renewal of

Italy and the War

By William Roscoe Thayer

[From THE NEW YORK TIMES, Jan. 17, 1915.]

William Roscoe Thayer, author of the article printed below, is one of the leading authorities on Italy in this country. His works on Italian history include "The Dawn of Italian Independence," "Italica," "A Short History of Venice," and "The Life and Times of Cavour." The last named, published three years ago, made a marked impression and won for its author an enviable place as a historian. Mr. Thayer is a graduate of Harvard and has edited the Harvard Graduates' Magazine since 1892. Since 1913 he has been a member of the Board of Overseers of Harvard College.

TOO little has been said about Italy's refusal to join Germany and Austria in their war for world power. During the past five months we have heard German apologists offer the most contradictory arguments to prove, first, that Russia, next, that France and Belgium, and, finally, that England began the struggle. The Kaiser himself, with that disdain of fact which is the privilege of autocrats, declared that the sword was forced into his hands. And all the while the mere abstention of Italy from supporting Germany and Austria gave the lie to the Germanic protestations and excuses.

By the terms of the Triple Alliance every member of it is bound to communicate at once to the other members all international diplomatic transactions which concern the alliance. Germany and Austria failed to do this during the earlier stages in July, when they were preparing for the war. Only after they had laid their train so surely that an explosion was almost inevitable did they communicate the documents to Italy and call upon her to take her place in the field with them. But Italy refused; because, after examining the evidence, she concluded that Germany and Austria were the aggressors. Now, the terms of the Triple Alliance bind its members to stand by each other only in case of attack.

Italy's verdict, therefore, threw the guilt of the war on Germany and Austria. She had testimony before her which does not appear even in the "White Papers" and other official diplomatic correspondence; and all the efforts of German zealots and casuists have not subtracted one iota from the meaning of her abstention. Germany and Austria were the aggressors—that is the Italian verdict which history will confirm.

On this side of the water the German apologists made as little as possible of Italy's withdrawal—they were too busy trying to persuade the American public that trivialities like the passage of a French aeroplane or of a French automobile with two French officers in it, across a corner of Belgium, thirty minutes before the German Army invaded Belgium, proved that the French and Belgians began the war. They sneered a little at Italian honor; they implied that scuttling off was all that could be expected of a decadent Latin people; and they hinted that, after the Kaiser had disposed of France, Belgium, England, and Russia, he would punish Italy for her "flight."

At Berlin, however, the importance—military, political, and naval—of Italy's withdrawal from the Triple Alliance was appraised at its true value. The German Foreign Office employed alternately threats and blandishments upon her. They warned her that, if she refused to back up her allies, she would be treated without mercy at the end of hostilities. When the policy of terrorizing failed, seductive promises were held out—suggestions of an addition to Italian territory and of a subsidy for military expenses. These also failed. Italy could not be induced to send her million soldiers against the Allies. Then Germany labored to prevent her from actively joining the Allies—and this effort Germany is keeping up at the present moment, under the direction of the sleek Prince von Bülow.

The Italians, who have in large measure a sense of humor, that clarifying quality which Prussianization has destroyed in the Germans, must have smiled when they heard the German envoys expatiate on the beauties of neutrality, and, although they are a polite people, they must have found it hard to keep from laughing when the agents of Dr. Bethmann-Hollweg, who had just declared that a treaty is only a scrap of paper, to be torn up at pleasure, tried to impress upon Italy the sacredness of the treaty which bound her to the Triple Alliance.

Not content with these official, or officious, manoeuvres, the German Government sent Socialist leaders into Italy to urge the Italian Socialists not to consent to a war in behalf of the Allies; but they, too, seem to have met with a chilly reception. The Italian Socialists, like the rest of the world, wondered why it was that 5,000,000 Socialists in Germany should allow themselves to be commandeered, apparently without a murmur, to uphold a war waged to preserve and extend military despotism.

In addition to these direct efforts to win Italy to their side, or at least to keep her from going over to the enemy, the Germans have been busy since early in August with their Press Bureau, which has pursued methods there similar to those they have made us familiar with here. But in Italy they have been more guarded and less truculent, and they have not, like the preposterous Bernstorff and his associates, assumed that the public they were addressing was not only ignorant of the simplest facts of recent European history, but were also morally imbecile.

Although the Italians are not less susceptible than are other peoples to be swayed by sudden political gusts, they were not at the end of July, 1914, taken by surprise. For a long time past their King and statesmen had deliberated as to what ought to be Italy's course in case Germany should carry out her well-understood purpose of humbling England. The Italians were not deceived by the increase from year to year of the German Army. They knew perfectly well what the tremendous efforts of the Germans to create a great navy meant. They had no illusions as to the purpose of the strategic railways to the Belgian frontier on the west or to the Russian border on the east. They knew how narrowly a European war was averted during the Balkan cataclysm two years ago. They did not wrong the Kaiser by supposing that the immense fund which he had recently raised from "voluntary" 5 per cent. contributions on incomes was to be given to The Hague Tribunal to promote the cause of universal peace. They logically and honorably decided that, if Germany provoked war, Italy would not support her. The bond of the Triple Alliance called for no other action on her part. Germany and Austria provoked the war; Italy stood by her agreement.

But a still further consideration influenced her. It was understood that, *if the war in which Germany and Austria engaged should involve England as an enemy, Italy's obligation to support the Triple Alliance would cease.* Since it would be suicidal for Italy to accept the liability of a *casus foederis* which should expose her to attack by the English and French Navies, her participation in the Triple Alliance always carried the proviso that it did not bind her to fight England.

Such is the substance of the statement made by the dean of Italian statesmen, in a letter I received from him two months ago. No Italian could speak from a more thorough knowledge of the facts than he possessed, and that it has long been surmised that the Triplice could not drive Italy against England appears in various publications. Gen. Bernhardi, for instance, who knew so accurately the intentions of the German General Staff and the secrets of the German Foreign Office, intimates more than once that Germany and Austria, in their war for world power, need not hope for Italy's support. Referring to Col. Boucher's book, "L'Offensive contre L'Allemagne," he says: "Modern French writers are already reckoning so confidently on the withdrawal of Italy from the Triple Alliance that they no longer think it necessary to put an army in the field against Italy, but consider that the entire forces of France are available against Germany."[4]

[Enlarge]

Why Italy made the reservation in the case of England will appear when we glance at the origin of the Triple Alliance.

In 1871 Bismarck thought that the Franco-Prussian war, by the military losses and by the immense indemnity which it inflicted on the French people, had rendered France powerless for a generation. But within four years she paid the indemnity and had so far recovered in her armament, commerce, and prosperity, that the Iron Chancellor prepared to attack her again, and this time, to quote his butcher's phrase, "to bleed her white." Only the certainty that the other powers would interfere stayed his hand then.

So he set about circumventing France by other means. A league of the three Emperors of Germany, Austria, and Russia was the combination he preferred; but Russia proved an uncertain partner, as she feared Germanization, on the one hand, and, on the other, she was the encourager of pro-Slavic aspirations which ran counter to the Germans' ambition. Bismarck, therefore, looked about him for an alternative plan.

He would keep the friendship of Russia—even though Russia declined a formal league—and he would lure Italy into the Germanic alliance. England, he knew, could not be persuaded to enter a Continental combination. Her commercial interests pointed elsewhere, and she still clung to her policy of splendid isolation. But Italy was unattached; and while she was the least formidable of the six great powers, Bismarck saw that he could make good use of her for his own purposes. The adroitness by which he drew her into his net is in direct contrast to the bovine diplomacy by which Kaiser William II. and his subservient Chancellors have succeeded, during the past twenty years, in smashing all their alliances and in alienating the sympathy of the civilized world.

After the completion of Italian unity in 1870, the new Italian Kingdom found itself harassed not only by the many details of solidifying the civil Government, but also by the perplexities of international relations. The abolition of the Pope's temporal power made her, in theory at least, an object of odium to zealous Roman Catholics throughout the world. Her nearest neighbors—France and Austria—having long been the most loyal supporters of the head of the Roman Church, Italy could not be sure that either or both of them might not intrigue against her in behalf of the restoration of the Papacy. There was also in Italy a group of patriotic Jingoes—the Irredentists—bent on "redeeming" from Austria territory whose inhabitants they claimed were Italian in language, ideals, and situation. The Irredentist propaganda naturally increased the rancor which Austria felt toward the Italians over whom she had recently despotized.

When Crispi, who was passing from his earlier character of conspirator and Radical to that of constitutional statesman, made the tour of the European Chancelleries, in 1877, he found Bismarck profuse in his expression of good-will toward Italy. If we are to believe Crispi, the Chancellor was ready then to draw up a treaty with her, and went so far as to hint that he approved of Italy's aspirations. Among these were the possession of Tunis and a foothold on the east coast of the Adriatic. The next year, at the Berlin Congress, however, Italy's interests were ignored, and, instead, Austria was encouraged to extend her dominion south of the Balkans, and the French were at least not discouraged from coveting a stronger position in the Mediterranean.

Finally, in 1882, France seized Tunis, to the immense indignation of the Italians, who had come to regard that as their predestined province. For it lay only a few hours by steamer from the southern coast of Sicily; it commanded the passage between the western and eastern Mediterranean; and, above all, it was the symbol of Italy's colonial ambition. To have a colony, if not several, was then regarded as the sign of being a first-class power; and that Italy should be tricked out of Tunis seemed to advertise to the world that she was not a first-class power. For her protests availed nothing.

The Italians did not know then, nor for a long time afterward, that *the French seizure of Tunis was directly due to Bismarck's instigation.* Lord Salisbury, also, who seems to have been in the plot, approved it for his own reasons. Bismarck's motives were plain—he wished to entangle France further in African colonial ventures. It had taken forty years, many thousand soldiers' lives, and great expenditures for France to make Algiers reasonably safe. As Tunis would increase the French burdens, it followed that every regiment needed there would diminish the strength of the armies with which France guarded herself from a German attack on her eastern frontier.

Having roused the Italians to wrath by this ruse, Bismarck had no difficulty in persuading them to join the Triple Alliance. He hardly needed to suggest that, if they had felt anxious at the possibility of French hostile pressure before, they had an even greater reason for such anxiety now that the French controlled the Mediterranean south of them. We may suspect also that Bismarck pointed out, as a special inducement, that, if Italy joined the alliance, she would be free from the likelihood of an attack by Austria.

Accordingly, in 1882, Italy entered into partnership with Germany and Austria for mutual defense. The only powers likely to assail them at that time were France and Russia; for England was still isolated, and Bismarck, although he felt a strong antipathy toward the English, was too shrewd a statesman either to scorn or to provoke them. As late as 1889, he approved of Italy's seeking an *entente* with England.

At the time Italy joined the Triplice she felt, no doubt, an unwonted sense of security. Were not two powerful empires standing by, ready to defend her? Her wounded pride, also, was solaced by her admission on equal terms into such a league. Neither France nor any other could henceforth taunt her with being a second-rate power.

The immediate result of the alliance was the spread of German commercial and financial enterprises throughout the peninsula, and the steady growth of Italian bad feeling toward France. A large group of Italians made Gallophobia their guiding principle. They remembered that, in the sixties, Napoleon III. had maintained at Rome that French garrison which prevented them from emancipating the States of the Church from Papal control, and from completing the unification of Italy. They remembered that Napoleon annexed Nice—Garibaldi's birthplace—to France, and that the French *chassepots* at Mentana dispersed Garibaldi and his red shirts bent on capturing the Eternal City. In the eighties, the Italians had good reason to suspect that the French Clericals were busy devising some imbroglio through which the Pope might be restored to the temporal power.

A convinced Gallophobe and crafty intriguer like Crispi, therefore, easily inflamed Italian indignation, so recently excited by the seizure of Tunis and by Clerical intrigues, and he counted it a gay feather in his cap when, in 1889, he declared a tariff war on France. Hard times for Italy followed; the commerce of the country was dislocated, and although Crispi tried to get compensation by negotiating special terms for trade with Germany and Austria, the new customers did not make up for the old. Germany could not furnish capital as France had done. Paris was, and is, the financial capital of the European Continent.

On this side Italy lost and Bismarck gained by the Triple Alliance—for he had attained his purpose of splitting France and Italy apart. What advantage did the Italians derive from the agreement? The reply commonly given is, protection. But, we ask, protection from whom? Not from France, because it is clear enough that, whether the Triplice existed or not, Germany would have attacked the French, if they had attacked the Italians; so that Italy had in Germany a logical protector, to whom she need not have sacrificed her initiative.

Her only other possible assailant was Austria, and it may fairly be argued that the alliance restrained Austria from attack; but Austria permitted herself every other unfriendly act toward Italy except open war; and Germany looked placidly on.

The fact that Germany, the chief Protestant nation in Europe, was the ally of Italy, might also be regarded as a support to the Italians in their long conflict with Papal pretensions; but how little Germany cared for Italy's welfare in this struggle appeared in 1903, when Kaiser Wilhelm prevented the election of Cardinal Rampolla as Pope. Rampolla, if not a Liberal, was a devoted Italian; Sarti, who defeated him, was a Reactionary, controlled by the Jesuits, hostile to Italy.

When we look at Germany's action in other affairs we find pleasant words but no tangible profit. From her geographical position Italy claimed an interest in the status of the Balkan Peninsula, and particularly in the eastern shore of the Adriatic. Germany pretended to favor her interests—according to Crispi, Bismarck even went so far as to ask, "Why don't you take Albania?"—but it was Austria that Germany steadily pushed on into the Balkans; and in 1908, when Austria, with Germany's connivance, appropriated Bosnia and Herzegovina, the Italians realized that they had been tricked again, as they were in the case of Tunis.

Since 1908 the Teutonic partners, growing more and more arrogant, have shown indifference to the concerns of their Italian ally, who, seeing no future for her in Europe, swooped down on Tripoli, the only stretch of North African littoral not already possessed by the French and by the English. Persons on the inside at Rome whispered that, if Italy had not occupied Tripoli when she did, Germany would have forestalled her; for the Kaiser, furious at being thwarted in Morocco and at having failed to bully France into submission, as he had done in 1905, had determined to seize Tripoli, come what might. More than one Foreign Office has ample proof to settle this assertion. Its plausibility is patent—Germany was already in close league with Turkey, and, looking forward to a war on England, she saw the advantage of owning territory and a naval base within easy reach of the Suez Canal.

Certain it is that both Germany and Austria frowned on Italy's Libyan enterprise, and that, in their intrigues in the Balkan Peninsula, in 1912 and 1913, they ignored their Italian partner.

And yet as long ago as 1895 Germany admitted that Italy was hardly getting a fair return from her bargain with her Teutonic allies. On March 5, 1895, Senator Lanza reported an interview he had just had with Emperor William, who said; "He had found Count Kálnoky (the Austrian Premier) ... still uneasy lest we (Italy) may come to consider the Triple Alliance insufficiently advantageous, merely because it cannot supply us, at once and in times of peace, with the necessary means of satisfying our desires with regard to the territories of Northern Africa and others as well. His Majesty ... added: 'Wait patiently. Let the occasion but present itself and you shall have whatever you wish.'"[5]

In spite of the Kaiser's assurance, Italy has got less and less return from the Triple Alliance every year since 1895.

It appears, therefore, that Italy long ago opened her eyes as to the real profit the alliance brought her. When England loomed up as the objective which Germany resolved to destroy, Italy quite logically let it be understood that she would not engage in a fight against England. Over thirty years of political alliance had created no sympathy among the Italians for the Germans. Like all other Europeans, they resented the arrogance of the Teutons who strode over their country.

But deeper, far deeper than personal dislike of bad manners was the fundamental antagonism between the Italian and the Prussian ideal. The Italians were pledged to Liberty, the Germans to Autocracy, bulwarked by militarism. In their long struggle for independence the Italians had had the sympathy of the best Englishmen, and in Palmerston, and especially in Lord John Russell, they found very powerful political helpers. But never since Bismarck took the helm of Prussia had one word in behalf of Democracy and Freedom been lisped by Monarch or Minister. For Italy to abandon her democratic ideal and to revert to the feudal-despotic ideal of the Pan-Germanists is unthinkable.

If she goes into the war, as now seems probable, it will be to uphold the Allies, who are fighting against Teutonic ambition inspired by despotic aims. Self-preservation demands that choice—because, should Germany win, she will not spare Italy. A stronger reason than self-interest, or than fear, however, will guide the Italians. In their past civilization and in their modern ideals they belong with the Western powers. They know the origin of their national independence. And if any Ministry should attempt to send them to replenish the wasting armies of Germany and of Austria, they would invoke the memory of Victor Emmanuel and of Garibaldi, of Mazzini and of Cavour, and refuse to be partners in schemes to aggrandize the Hapsburgs and the Hohenzollerns.

"I am the son of Liberty," said Cavour; "to her I owe all that I am." That, too, is Italy's motto, which she will not deny.

HE HEARD THE BUGLES CALLING

BY CAREY C.D. BRIGGS

THERE'S an old red mill at the foot of the hill;
Hear the mill-wheel turning, turning
To the drip of tears through the long, long years
Of my heart's relentless yearning—
Oh, the tender note of the catch in his throat,
Oh, the tear that he dried with laughter;
"I'll be back some day—
Mind the mill while I'm away,"
And he waved one last kiss floating after.
Gone is the miller boy,
Gone from the mill;
Gone up the winding road,
Gone o'er the hill;
Gone with the drum-beat up over the hill,
Where he heard the bugles calling.

There's no grist for the mill or siller for the till,
But I've kept the mill-wheel turning
To the rumble and the beat of a million marching feet,
And my sad heart's muffled yearning.
Oh, the road his brave feet trod, lit with glory up to God,
Oh, the courage of his call shames my sorrow;
"I'll be back some day—
Mind the mill while I'm away,"
And I caught one last kiss for tomorrow.
Gone is the miller boy,
Gone from the mill;
Gone up the winding road,
Gone o'er the hill;
Gone with the drum-beat up over the hill,
Where he heard the bugles calling.

German Soldiers Write Home
Letter of Prince Joachim

The following letter was written by Prince Joachim of Prussia, son of the Kaiser, to Sergt. Karl Kummer of a Prussian Regiment of Guards, who had been sent, badly wounded, to his sister at Teplitz, and whom the Prince had known for years.

MY Dear Kummer: How sincerely I rejoiced to receive your very solicitous letter. I was sure of Kummer for that—that no one could hold him back when the time came to do some thrashing! God grant that you may speedily recover, so that you can enter Potsdam, crowned with glory, admired and envied. Who is nursing you?

The old proud First Guard Regiment has proved that it was ready to conquer and to die. Kummer, if I can in any way help you I shall gladly do so by providing anything that will make you comfortable. You know how happy I have always been for your devotion to the service, and how we two always were for action (Schwung.) I, too, am proud to have been wounded for our beloved Fatherland, and I regret only that I am not permitted to be with the regiment. Well, may God take care of you. Your devoted,

JOACHIM OF PRUSSIA.

Letter of Rudolf Herzog

The following letter, written from the field by Rudolf Herzog, one of the leading German novelists and poets, was published in rhymed verse in No. 41 of Die Woche.

IT had been a wild week. The storm wind swept with its broom of rain; it lashed us and splashed us, thrashed noses and ears, whistled through our clothing, penetrated the pores of our skin. And in the deluge—sights that made us shudder—gaunt skeleton churches, cracked walls, smoking ruins, piled hillock high; cities and villages—judged, annihilated.

Over there a stone pit; faces grown like the faces of beasts, a picked-up rabble of assassins. A short command. A howling of death. Squarely across the road we surge. A bloody grappling coil; batteries broken and shattered; iron and wood and bits of clothing and bones.

And upon the just and the unjust alike, the lashing rain for days and nights.

We rushed through the gray Ardennes woods, the Chief Lieutenant and I, racing along day after day, wrapped up tightly, our rifles ready, through wood and marsh. No time to lose! No time to lose! Down into the valley of the Meuse!

Of twenty bridges, there remained but beams rolled up by the waters— and yawning gaps.

Now comes the order: In three days new bridges must be finished!

Haste, men! Haste! Rain or no rain, it must be done!

Pioneers and railway builders working together, hunt up material, drag and hammer and ram it together; take the rain for the sweat of their brows; look like fat toiling devils; hang along the banks, lie in the water—after all, in this weather, no one can get any wetter! They speak very little, and never laugh. Three days are short. Nothing, nothing but duty!

Not a thought remained for the distant homeland and dear ones far away; the only thought, by day and by night—on to the enemy, come what may! No mind intent on any other goal. No time to lose! No time to lose! Haste! Haste!

And forward and backward and criss-cross through the gray Ardennes, the Chief Lieutenant and I, racing day after day. Laughter, when we tried it, died sickly on our lips. The bridges! the bridges! and nothing but the bridges! Empty belly, and limbs like lead. Once more, now; all together for a last great heave!

There lies Fumay on the smooth-flowing river; and next to the old bridge, a newly built one stretches from shore to shore—a German roadway, a roadway to good fortune!

Captain of the Guard! You? From the Staff Headquarters?

He shouts my name as he approaches.

"Congratulations! Congratulations!"

And he waves a paper above a hundred heads.

"Telegram from home! Make way there, you rascal! At the home of our poet—I've just learned it—a little war girl has arrived!"

I hold the paper in my outstretched hand. Has the sun broken suddenly into the enemy's land? Light and life on all the ruins?...

I see a new bridge reaching on—

Springtime scatters the shuddering Autumn dreariness.

My little girl! I have a little girl in my home!...

You bring back my smile to me in a heavy time....

I gaze up at the sky and am silent. And far and near the busy, noisy swarm of workers is silent. Every one looks up, seeking some point in the far sky. Officers and men for a single heart-throb listen as to a distant song from the lips of children and from a mother's mouth—stand there and smile around me, in blissful pensiveness, as if there were no longer an enemy. Every one seems to feel the sun, the sun of olden happiness.

And yet, it had merely chanced that on the German Rhine, in an old castle lost amid trees, a dear little German girl was born.

(Written Sept. 17, 1914, in the field.)

Letter of the Duke of Altenburg

From a letter written from the front by the Duke of Altenburg on Sept. 5, and published in the Altenburger Zeitung.

WE have lived through a great deal and done a great deal, marching, marching continually, without rest or respite. On Aug. 10 we reached Willdorf, near Jülich, by train, and from the 12th of August we marched without a single day of rest except Aug. 16, which we spent in a Belgian village near Liége, until today, when we reached ———. Those have been army marches such as history has never known.

DJEMAL PASHA

The Turkish Minister of Marine, Who Shares with Enver Pasha the Control of Turkish Affairs.

(Photo © International News Service.)

EMIR ALI PASHA

**Vice President of the Turkish Parliament, Who Was Sent to Berlin to Take
Back to Turkey Mohammedan Prisoners Captured from the Allies.**

(*Photo from Press Illustrating Co.*)

The weather was fine, except that a broiling heat blazed down upon us. The regiment can point back to several days' marches of fifty kilometers ——. Everywhere our arrival created great amazement, in Louvain as well as in Brussels, into which the entire —— marched at one time. At first we were taken for Englishmen in almost every village, and we still are, because the inhabitants cannot realize that we have arrived so early. The Belgians, moreover, in the last few days almost invariably set fire to their own villages.

On Aug. 24 we first entered battle; I led a combined brigade consisting of ——. The regiment fought splendidly, and in spite of the gigantic strain put upon it, it is in the best of spirits and full of the joy of battle. On that day I was for a long time in the sharpest rifle and artillery fire. Since that time there have been almost daily skirmishes and continual long marches; the enemy stalks ahead of us in seven-league boots. On Aug. 26 we put behind us a march of exactly twenty-three hours, from 6:30 o'clock in the morning till 5:30 the next morning. With all that, I was supposed to lead my regiment across a bridge to take a position guarding a new bridge in course of construction; but the bridge, as we discovered in the nick of time, was mined; twenty minutes later it flew into the air.

After resting for three hours in a field of stubble, and after we had all eaten in common with the men in a field kitchen—as we usually do—we continued marching till dark.

The spirit among our men is excellent. Tonight I am to have a real bed—the fourth, I believe, since the war began. Today I undressed for the first time in eight days.

———————————————

Letter of Paul Oskar Höcker

The German novelist, Paul Oskar Höcker is a Captain of the Landwehr.

I WANTED to write to you from the village of D., which we captured by storm. Hundreds of Frenchmen, upon the retreat of their troops, preferred to flee to the cellars, where they promptly transformed themselves into civilians. Our battalion had orders to conduct investigations, arrest those apparently liable to military service, and to take possession of all arms. Unexpectedly large stores of ammunition thus fell into our hands. Among these seizures were many chests containing dumdum bullets and bearing the stamp of the ammunition factory where they were made. The cartridges were intended for use in carabines. Accordingly, it would seem to be chiefly a question of the unlawful use of these missiles, repulsive to the laws of nations, by bicycle and scout corps.

These bullets lay also in a factory package in a writing desk next to a draft of the last will and testament which Monsieur le Capitaine wrote out on the first day of mobilization: He bequeathed his cash fortune of 110,000 francs, as well as his household furniture and his two hunting dogs, to Mme. Isabelle H. The forsaken Mme. Isabelle, who sought distant and clearer skies two days before our entry into the village, does not, however, seem to have been very fond of animals; for out of the forsaken house there rose piteously the whimpering and whining of the half-starved setters.

But what are the thousand bright recollections of the captured town, what are all the experiences of this campaign, compared to the heavy, heavy days of fighting which our battalion had to battle through near L.!

On Sunday, Oct. 4 the detachment marched from D. in the direction of L. It had been known for some time that the enemy was attempting a movement around our extreme right flank. Continual detrainments of French troops were taking place at L. A further advance was to be permitted to them under no conditions. The march toward L. took place on various roads. A cavalry division cleared the territory north of the city, and dispatched, simultaneously with our own advance, a company of Jaegers and a company of bicycle men against L.

At 1 o'clock we received fire. The point of our column returns it. As ever in small towns and suburbs the skill of the French is great in street fighting, turning to best advantage every protruding corner and extension of a building, and utilizing every alley of trees for firing attacks. Then the Frenchman clears these spaces quickly and hurries for protection to the next block of houses, till he has lured the foe far enough forward to surprise him with a carefully prepared fire from the side.

By leaps and bounds we advance along the broad road to the heights of the two suburbs F. and R. Here for the first time there is a matching of fighting forces. Undoubtedly the foe is far superior to us numerically; and he seems firmly determined not to allow himself to be crowded out of his excellent sheltered positions.

Our battery rolls up, and lets her brazen tongue speak. The infantry fight ceases, until the foremost buildings are set aflame on all three sides. Troop at a time, the French now take to flight, most of them abandoning their cartridges, as is evidenced by the rattle of exploding ammunition on every floor of the buildings.

But R. holds out, while F., at the right of the roadway, and the houses afire on the road toward Lille itself are quickly cleared of the enemy. The bicycle patrol, which has undertaken a determined advance to F., meets no further foe.

But upon the two companies engaged on my right there is poured a murderous fire that presently exacts heavy toll; and in the rough country hereabout it is impossible to discover the masked positions of the sharpshooters and machine guns. The Frenchman is an expert in the location of excellent hiding places, wire entanglements, and the like. He even puts forth infinite efforts to make his fortified positions extremely comfortable nests from which he can enjoy a view of all the points at which, in the irregular lay of the land, the enemy must necessarily halt; and thereupon the Frenchman meets the hesitating column of attack with his concentrated fire.

Four guns are nibbling at the edge of the village with their shells. Perhaps the machine guns, whose monotonous rattle lashes our nerves to the snapping point, may be hidden there in the church tower. But the battery commander hesitates to damage the house of God. So he leaves a gap there, and sweeps the smaller houses. Suddenly one of the machine guns ceases—it must have been concealed in the hedge close to the church; the gun squad serving it must have been found by the fire of our gunners; for presently there is noticeable in that quarter a foot race of red-trousered infantrymen. In the moaning of the shells there mingles the rattling of shrapnel. A whole group tumbles pell-mell; yonder one of them dashes madly this way and that, until a new load strikes him—they move like dolls in a miniature theatre; it is hard to realize at this distance that human lives are being crushed out here.

But an hour later we entered R. Night has fallen. Through the mighty gaps in the gabled roofs of the houses of the narrow street on which we enter shines the moon. Four men of the bicycle corps stand silent at the entrance to the village; the prisoners in their midst, infantrymen in uniform or in rapidly donned civil garb—the tell-tale red of the trousers shows under the short vest of one of them. In the streets lie curious bundles, the corpses of those who have fallen here. A wounded soldier drags wearily up to the subaltern officer's post, with hands raised above his head; it is a Frenchman who has thrown away his blue coat, but still wears his cap. The steps of the incoming battalion ring out on the village pavement. Otherwise an icy silence, night, and the smell of blood and burning.

And now horror creeps over us. We greet Death. He greets us.

In R. scarcely a single house is still inhabited. All have fled to L. In the street that has been assigned to my company, I must have almost every house opened by force, in order that the men, worn out with marching and fighting, may rest. Here and there, in answer to prolonged knocking, one of the inhabitants comes to the door. When the shell fire began they took refuge in their cellars.

In the brightly tiled hall of a pretty house that has escaped damage I sit with the gentlemen for several hours over glasses of mulled wine. We are waiting for orders for the next day. The orders reach us at 1 o'clock that night; the detachment is to take its stand at 7 o'clock beside the church at R., in order to continue the advance toward L.

But during the hours of the night many changes have taken place. The troops driven out of R. have sent their patrols, the black scouts, to the very edge of the suburb again, under cover of darkness; and reports of our cavalry and bicycle men tell that during the night heavy detachments of troops sent from the north have reached L. They talk of 40,000 to 50,000 men, chiefly newly enlisted forces and territorials; but Englishmen, too, are said to be among them. Our assigned task does not include fighting a destructive battle. We are simply to compel the enemy to unfold his forces, for certain strategic reasons the nature of which, of course, we do not know. Accordingly, our small detachment must risk everything in order to lure upon itself as many as possible of the enemy's troops. That, too, is just what happened.

We take our former positions. The cavalry division has departed, with its artillery, its bicycle corps, its Jaegers, and its machine guns. New problems are in store on the right wing for the brave division which has already distinguished itself throughout the entire campaign. We remain alone with our battery—the third battalion of the active regiment and our provincial Landwehr battalion.

It is going to be a heavy, heavy, heavy day of fighting.

Patrols establish the fact that F. is free of the enemy's forces. But as we enter the road toward L. the French machine guns at once announce themselves. They sing and whistle and whirr above our heads. After yesterday's losses (half a column of the Fifth Company is still busy burying our dead, laying our wounded in automobiles and wagons to be sent to the hospitals) our artillery will first shoot breaches in the enemy's lines before we advance.

But at midday the field artillery of the Frenchmen already replies to ours. They must have transshipped, at night, from their positions on the canal to L., in the belief that mighty forces were being assembled here for a further tremendous blow. The object of our assignment would in that case already have been for the most part accomplished. But all of us subordinate officers—who neither possess nor should possess an insight into the strategic movement—we have but a single desire: Forward!

For a few minutes, after the first thundering crash of the French artillery, there is deep silence. It seems as if nature itself were holding its breath. The crash had fallen in the alley of poplars along the road. The roadway is strewn with branches and twigs. Just beside the northern column of our battery the monstrous shell has buried itself in the clay soil. A hail of earth-crumbs has rained upon us. We cannot note any other damage. But all the companies that are still in closed formation spread out in order to offer no compact target.

For hours, now, there continues this terrible cannonading backward and forward, this dreadful argument of batteries. Horrible as is the devastation which such an instrument of murder can wreak, you gradually grow accustomed to the roaring storm. And you almost smile because you still lower your head each time. Until you remember: We greet Death, and he greets us.

"Near the church tower southeast of L. where the railway bridge can be seen, are hostile riflemen, strength several companies."

Our cavalry patrol disappears again—a French machine gun fires at it without hitting—and the battalion commander calls to me:

"Company left across the road, right and left of the farmhouse, developing a column on each side, with wide intervals between!"

Quickly the right wing column darts across. My Turkish professor, the Chief Lieutenant, manages it beautifully. One sharpshooter always darts ahead, throws himself on his belly, creeps on; a second follows. At one, two kilometers, scarcely a headpiece is visible. The left column is less successful.

Over the heads of the sharpshooters there at once whistle shells. They feel the air pressure; the tremendous noise grips them.

"Dodge! Lie down! Forward only one at a time, with long pauses! You'll betray our positions, fellows!"

And at this moment there is a clattering sound in the air above. A French airman!

"An airman, Captain!"

"Yes, yes, I've heard him."

The only thing that can help us is to keep from looking up. Only the rows of flesh-colored oval faces, that immediately turn up to greet each flight of an airman, permit the strength of forces to be estimated at such great distances.

Beyond any doubt the foe has overestimated our strength tenfold. Otherwise he would not have put forth these tremendous efforts. His strength, in such fortified positions, would have sufficed to hold an entire army corps in check. And our poor weak brigade?

I lie on my belly, creeping forward. To remain standing would be suicide.

Sst-sst-teewheet—boom-buzz—tsha! Tacktack-tacktack-tack!

It's a bad music. We are being rained upon with iron. We hear it whistle past our ears, we feel it whizz over our helmets. Our artillery covers us in front, so that we cannot fire at the single bodies of advance riflemen. They are drawing to the left toward the entrance to F. Soon the infantry bullets are striking close among us.

Nothing to be seen! Nothing to be seen!

"We must advance further!" I shout into the line of sharpshooters. The battalion commander shouts it at the same time. He wouldn't let any one rob him of the honor of advancing in the foremost row of riflemen. We crawl forward on all fours. After thirty meters, halt. Still nothing to be seen. The land rises in front of us. Fifty meters further; eighty; a hundred. At last we have a clear view ahead. Rifles are advanced.

"Half way to the left, at the entrance to F., sharpshooters, stand!"

A few shots from our ranks. The blue figures falter, fall. But at the same time we have betrayed our position. And now the hail begins anew.

"They all shoot too high! Aim well, men! Every shot a bullseye!"

My voice reaches only the rows of riflemen nearest to me. The clatter and crashing is tremendous, but even more horrible is this singing and whizzing past of shells, especially when the enemy's machine guns sweep us.

"Are those some of our men?" my bugler beside me asks. "They're already standing half way down the road back of us!"

A shiver of horror creeps over us. Yes, they have enticed and held us fast in the midst of their artillery—and on the left their infantry, well protected, has advanced under cover to our flank. And now the French machine gun patters on our right, in monotonous rhythm, in this concert of hell.

Behind us there is no longer a sign of life. Our battery is gone; it must have shot away its ammunition.

"Order of the Brigade Commander: Company retire slowly!" A man at the end of our serried line near the roadside has called the order to me. The order travels by word of mouth along our line. It is a long time before it reaches the riflemen furthest left. And as soon as the slightest movement is noticeable in the beet fields, the deadly hail rattles down upon us again.

My eyeglass is covered with sweat and dirt. I tear it away. Now, as the shells strike, clouds of dirt fly into my eyes. I close them. At my left, a rifleman crawling along, nudges me:

"The dogs!" he mutters: "Now they've got us in a hell of a pinch!"

I can speak no more. We go crawling along another 500 meters. My revolver bangs along on the ground at my left; my fieldglass at my right. For a moment I think of the droll problem given to the officer at the military examination: "What would you do if you saw artillery unfold before you, infantry on your left, and artillery against your flank on the right?" Answer: "I'd order: Take off helmets and pray!"

Take off helmets and pray! Yes, there is now no help for it. Now it's a case of dying decently like gentlemen.

"No running away, men! We're no Frenchmen!"

A minute's stop to take breath, at yon hay-rick on the left. So, there they're advancing, in a gay company, the blue-frocks!

"Left, riflemen, along the church yard wall, stand! Rifle fire!"

And two groups are daring enough to stand upright and fire, although the machine gun fire is sweeping us again. The man next to me is loading his gun; suddenly he throws up an arm:

"Hell! That's pretty warm!" A bullet has passed midway through the cover of his rifle barrel.

"Go on! Slowly! One at a time! Don't crowd!"

On the road we find a man of the second column, pressed against a tree.

"Where is the battalion?"

He points in the direction of R.

"There they are, still fighting, Captain."

Yes, there still stand some riflemen in a rifle fight. An officer with them.

"Forward!" and I point in their direction.

But over there the witches' caldron is boiling more fiercely. The machine guns are nearer there. After a short consultation with the leader of the division I order: "Retire. Singly."

The narrow road through which we retire is swept continually with fire. I climb up to the ridge. Now nothing further matters. Only not to fall alive in the hands of those over there! To die! I stumble over a ridge in the field. A few moments of unconsciousness. Then again the tacktack-tacktack of the machine guns. God, our Lord, Thou art our refuge forever and aye! I pray Thee, I pray Thee, let me die an honest soldier's death. And not suffer long. Now, dear Lord, please; now! If only my fellows don't begin to run!

"Slowly, men; slowly. Halt at the brown stretch of field."

Panting, we lie there. "Rifles in position! Take aim! Fire!"

As soon as a few shots have been fired, there ensues a pause in the firing over there. We make good use of it. Then, "Down on your bellies again!"

I cannot go further.

"Go ahead without me, boys. Greet my people for me. God with you. You've fought well. Damn you, fellow, run, I tell you! Down on your faces! Take breath. Fire!"

When, long ago, I went to my confirmation lesson, the Superintendent once said—ah, what a remarkable man that was!—"I would like only to take a single look at my little garden. I'm a city child, and have grown so fond of the flowers, this little bit of earth!"—Hui! hui! there it whistles over our heads again. I greet Death. And my lips touch the ridge of the field furrow.

Of dust thou art; to dust thou shalt return.

"Boys, you're not afraid? Eh?" And I try to laugh.

"The apes over there! They don't know how to shoot. Such clowns! They'll hit the sky!"

Hui! hui! tack-a-tack-tacktack! Run on! The patent-leathered lackeys can't hit us!

But there lies one of the other company. Dead.

"Don't run! Keep halting! Fire!"

From the village a hail of shrapnel. From the opposite side, the same. But now nobody runs with lowered head. We are now used to the benediction of bullets. Further on, further on!

Of the brigade there's not a trace. When the artillery had shot away its ammunition, the order was given: "Retire, all!" It reached me, in front there with the rifle lines, fully an hour later than the rest.

Scattered stragglers join me.

"Where is our Chief Lieutenant?"

"Wounded in the neck; only a glancing bullet. Has returned slowly on an artillery horse. Midway among the shrapnels. Great fellow."

Nobody knows where the point of reunion is. I lead the rest of the battalion after the other companies. Night is falling. Somewhere a cavalry patrol tells us: They're to bivouac over there at the fort.

We march toward that. Bicycle men come to meet us. We hear from them—no one believed that a single man of us could escape that devil's caldron alive. My orderly (Bursche) comes riding to meet me. His eyes are wet.

"My Captain! My Captain!"

I must press many hands. I warm myself at the bivouac fire. The Quartermaster has brought me a half flask of champagne. There's red wine for the men in the baggage division. It has already been mulled. A plate of rice soup. The earth-crumb is still sticking to my lips. I swallow it down with the first draught of foaming wine: "I greet thee, Life! I greet thee, Earth!" And comrades come up and are glad to see me, old monster, again.

Thank God, my company has suffered only few losses! When I order the Sergeant Major to read the list, only a few are missing. But this one or that one has been seen by some one of his comrades after the fight. Well, then they are only scattered, and will find their way back by and by. The battalion in these two days of fighting lost thirty-eight dead and sixty-six wounded. That includes some light wounds from glancing bullets.

It all lies behind me like a confused dream. We are bivouacking in the casemates of the fort. I awake several times in terror. Deep, deep silence.

Only the pacing to and fro of the sentinel on guard. To and fro, to and fro. He is cold.

I creep deeper into the straw. Poor fellow, the sentinel. How soft I've got it! So warm here! I have hot eyes and hot cheeks, but ice-cold hands.

I pity all those who know life and death only from books. War is a great teacher. We learn to love the earth. And thus our homeland becomes so sacred to us.

———————————————————————

Damp Humor of the Night Watch

From a field postcard written by a German soldier in the Franco-Prussian war and sent home by one who recalled it under similar circumstances in the present one.

> I guard this shed,
> But who guards me?
> Around my head
> But night I see.
> This only comfort sweet is mine,
> To soothe my graveyard cough:
> "This town will pay a lovely fine
> If some one picks me off."

War Correspondence
The Place of Tombs

By Perceval Gibbon.

[Special Cable to THE NEW YORK TIMES.]

ZYRDDOW, Poland, Received in London Jan. 19.—There is a spot above the river which must not be indicated too explicitly, but whose name signifies in Russian the place of tombs. It is thus christened by the troops who camp in a great forest which shadows the whole position. It is a point at which the new German plan of thrusting toward the railway instead of as hitherto toward the road has produced fighting of more than Homeric quality.

The Russians, who never misjudge the value of ground, were established here in well-made trenches, with the shelter of the forest at their backs for reserves and supports. Upon this iron front the Germans spent themselves in fruitless attacks, incurring crippling losses. It was only after repeated and disastrous failure of these tactics that they began a different method of approach.

Here, as everywhere else, they have a large amount of artillery, and under incessant shell fire they proceeded to sap their way toward the Russian trenches. Incidentally they expended shells enough to last an army through the whole of a small war, and where formerly six acres of trees projected from the main forest there are now no trees at all.

The parapet of their trench is only thirty-five paces from the Russian parapet, and the men crouching behind their shelter can hear the voices of their enemies. None dare lift head or hand to even the loopholes on the breastworks, since the worst shot in the world can send bullet after bullet through any loophole at that distance. The Russians are able to throw hand grenades, with which their trenches are supplied, clear into the German trenches, while the German shelling has had to cease since their own men are in equal danger from any shell aimed at the Russian trenches.

I rode down through the forest in an effort to reach one of the trenches two nights ago, passing from the pale shine of the snow upon the bare fields to sheer darkness. I found the staff established in a spacious dugout some 400 yards behind the actual first line. Here, as always, was a straw-padded, candle-lit interior, with an orderly waiting, with telephone to ear, and all those rough-and-ready contrivances by which men live who have death forever at their elbow. Here, too, their faces disguised by weeks of beard and grimed with the smirch of war, were burly Russian officers, those adequate and quietly confident men who are the strength and inspiration of the Russian Army.

In all the gloom, where all life was balanced on a hair, one thing was steadfast and cordial, and that was the unshaken assurance of these cheerful, expert fighting men in their power to hold the Germans and presently to resume the offensive, to which each one of them looks forward, and advance at last toward the frontier of Germany. None underestimates the enemy. They criticise him in a spirit of absolute professional impartiality, admiring quite frankly the organization and courage of the German infantry, but condemning the artillery and pooh-poohing the cavalry.

Yesterday morning the Germans renewed their bombardment of the positions at Radziwillow, where the fine Russian trench is practically impregnable, and has already cost them huge losses in their attempts to assault it.

I had an illustration of their lack of system in artillery fire while returning along the rear of this position. Their shells sailed up across the woods to the south of the railway, bursting on an empty stretch of fields about a thousand yards away, and turned seven or eight hundred acres of virgin snow into an inferno of smoke and torn earth, but no single shell fell nearer than a thousand yards to any living soul.

During the last day or two I have seen a change in the nature of the fighting on this front. The German procedure has no longer its old character of desperate decision but has become more desultory and their pressure flickers up and down the line as though in a panic of effort to find some point at which the defense is weak.

I learned here from prisoners that the Germans lately have been celebrating victories. Berlin and other cities are said to be gay with flags, and Gen. von Hindenburg has been acclaimed as a national hero. I can only keep my eyes on the small portion of the long front limited by Socahczew on the north and Msczonow on the south, but in regard to this region I can offer my personal testimony that at no point have the Germans gained anything in the nature of a success nor made any attack which has not been immensely more costly in lives to them than to the Russians.

Shelled Tsing-tao With Wireless Aid

By Jefferson Jones,

Staff Correspondent of The Minneapolis Journal and Japan Advertiser.

[From THE NEW YORK TIMES, Jan. 24, 1915.]

TOKIO, Dec. 15.—Far out in the Yellow Sea busy gunners on a Japanese battleship aimed a 12-inch gun at one of the German forts in Tsing-tao. Opening the breech, they removed the smoking cartridge case, put in another loaded one, and waited to learn whether the projectile had scattered death among the enemy or exploded harmlessly in soft earth. They were five or six miles from their target.

The gunners gazed toward the battleship's wireless masts. Presently came a sputter and crackle of electric sparks. An officer appeared in the turret and said, perhaps, "Very good. Put some more in the same place," or, "That one was fifty feet to the right or sixty feet too high." He had received a wireless message from the shore telling exactly where the shell had struck, probably for the first time since naval warfare began.

At the rear of the Japanese lines, where a naval lookout had been erected, I saw several marines focusing horned telescopes on the besieged forts. As soon as a shell landed one of the men would telephone the exact location to the naval wireless station at Sesheco, which relayed the message to the warships.

The fourth day of the siege was the most severe of the whole siege of Tsing-tao. Gen. Johoji on the extreme left, with Gen. Barnardiston of the British expeditionary force, was pressing the intrenched Germans near Moltke Fort. Early in the morning Gen. Johoji had sent a detachment against the triangular pumping station fort, as it was deemed wise not to turn the siege guns on the place, because the fort might be destroyed and the supply of water be cut off in the city when the troops entered. The detachment approached the fort without any resistance from the Germans, and, surrounding it, discovered that there was a small garrison, which had barred itself inside. The Japanese commanded the men to surrender, threatening to dynamite the place. The steel door was opened and twenty-three Germans walked out.

The capture of this fort was the key for the final attack of the Japanese, as it left the central fort and redoubts exposed to fire.

Late in the afternoon the fire became extremely heavy. The Germans seemed to be making sharp resistance to the Japanese, lest they advance within the quarter-mile zone of the redoubt walls. The Japanese infantry, however, were sapping away, and as dusk settled over the field we saw the bright flash of bursting shrapnel from the German forts. It was the first shrapnel sent out by the Germans during the siege.

Ten, twelve, fifteen, and sometimes even twenty shrapnel shells could be counted bursting at one time, all in a straight line, over the Japanese front line, and then the big German searchlights would flash about the field. They would fall on fifteen or twenty Japanese sappers on the top of their trenches placing sandbags, and then the flash would disappear.

Thursday, Nov. 5, seemed only a repetition of what we had seen the day before. All night long the firing kept up, and it was evident that the German garrison at Tsing-tao was making stubborn and gallant resistance.

That night the Japanese forces advanced 200 yards under a heavy shrapnel fire from the Germans. A snowstorm, followed by rain, had filled the trenches with water a foot deep, and it was in these that the Japanese and British forces found themselves during the closing days of the siege.

Friday, Nov. 6, was a bitter morning. A forty-mile gale was blowing off the Yellow Sea, and with the thermometer at 2 below zero it was not any too comfortable, even for those of us who were fortunate enough to get near a charcoal burner.

Toward midnight Gen. Yamada, whose men were intrenched in front of Forts 2 and 3, sent out a detachment to learn the condition of the German garrison opposing him. The men approached the redoubt walls of the forts, climbed ten feet to the bottom, and found themselves face to face with wire entanglements twenty yards wide and running the length of the wall. No Germans were seen. Reinforcements were called for while the scouts were cutting the entanglements. At 1 A.M., Nov. 7, Gen. Yamada with more than 300 men was behind the redoubt walls of Fort 3.

In the meantime, heavily protected on all sides by planks and sandbags, a detachment of 200 Germans with machine guns was watching the approach of Gen. Barnardiston's men, who had been stationed to the right of Gen. Yamada. The Germans were unaware that the Japanese had gained the wall, when suddenly a sentry heard Japanese voices. The signal was given and the Germans rushed from their sandbag houses into the shadow of the wall, hoping to reach their comrades, stationed 500 yards back along the casement walls. Some, perhaps, reached their destination, but the majority of the men were shot down by the Japanese infantry.

The capture of Forts 2 and 3 by Gen. Yamada was quickly reported to Gen. Horiuchi, and within an hour his men had captured Forts 4 and 5 with very little resistance. Gen. Johoji, on the extreme left, with Gen. Barnardiston of the British force, also advanced with the news of the capture of the positions, but the Germans put up a stubborn resistance, and it was not until 6:30 A.M. that the attackers gained the coast fort and Fort 1.

With the capture of the redoubt fortifications there still remained the mountainous forts, Iltis, Bismarck, and Moltke, a quarter of a mile back toward Tsing-tao. With detachments of engineers and infantrymen, Gens. Horiuchi and Yamada ordered the general attack. The men rushed from their trenches for the base of the forts. It was to be a hand-to-hand bayonet attack.

But two guns on the Iltis fort had already been silenced, the four big 28-centimeter mortars on the same fort were useless for use at the base of Iltis, while the other guns had been so placed and sandbagged at the rear of the fort that they could not be quickly brought forward and utilized for work along the steep slopes leading to the forts. Rifles and machine guns were resorted to.

The Japanese, as they charged up the slope, were mowed down by the machine guns, but on they came from all sides—17,000 men against 3,800. The German garrison could not hold out, and the white flag was hoisted from Fort C, close to Gov. Gen. Meyer Waldeck's residence. The surrender came at 7:05 A.M.

THE BROKEN ROSE

(TO KING ALBERT)

By ANNIE VIVANTI CHARTRES.

[From King Albert's Book.]

SHY, youthful, silent—and misunderstood,
In the white glare of Kinghood thou didst stand.
The sceptre in thy hand
Seemed but a flower the Fates had tossed to thee,
And thou wert called, perchance half scornfully,
Albert the Good.

Today thou standest on a blackened grave,
Thy broken sword still lifted to the skies.
Thy pure and fearless eyes
Gaze into Death's grim visage unappalled
And by the storm-swept nations thou art called
Albert the Brave.

Tossed on a blood-red sea of rage and hate
The frenzied world rolls forward to its doom.
But high above the gloom
Flashes the fulgent beacon of thy fame,
The nations thou hast saved exalt thy name—
Albert the Great!

* * * * * *

Albert the good, the brave, the great, thy land
Lies at thy feet, a crushed and morient rose
Trampled and desecrated by thy foes.
One day a greater Belgium will be born,
But what of this dead Belgium wracked and torn?
What of this rose flung out upon the sand?

Behold! Afar where sky and waters meet
A white-robed Figure walketh on the sea

(Peace goes before Him and her face is sweet.)
As once He trod the waves of Galilee
He comes again—the tumult sinks to rest,
The stormy waters shine beneath His feet.

He sees the dead rose lying in the sand,
He lifts the dead rose in His holy hand
And lays it at His breast.

O broken rose of Belgium, thou art blest!

The Emden at Penang
Pen Picture by a Times Correspondent of the Havoc She Wrought

[From THE NEW YORK TIMES Correspondent in Penang.]

PENANG, STRAITS SETTLEMENTS, Oct. 29.—The German cruiser Emden called here yesterday and departed, leaving death and destruction behind her. You will doubtless have learned long before this story of her visit, carried by the slow mails of the Far East, is read in the United States some account of the Emden's raid, but the cable can hardly carry a detailed picture of the destruction wrought in a brief hour or so yesterday in this busy harbor, and it seems worth while to describe for you how this sudden vision of war burst on Penang.

For those who do not know, the City of Penang lies on the western coast of the Malay Peninsula, just below the Siamese border. It is the shipping point of the Federated Malay States, where 65 per cent. of the world's tin is produced, as well as a great amount of rubber and copra. With a population of 246,000, it is growing by leaps and bounds and gives every indication of soon becoming one of the largest ports in the Far East.

The thing that makes this city a point of importance in the present war is the fact that it is the last port of call for ships going from China and Japan to Colombo and Europe. As a result, it has been made more or less of a naval base by the English Government. Large stores of Admiralty coal have been collected and all vessels have been commanded to stop here for orders before crossing the Bay of Bengal.

It was probably with the idea of crippling this base, from which her pursuers were radiating, that the Emden made her raid here. Had she found it temporarily undefended she could at one blow seriously have embarrassed the English cruisers patrolling these waters and at the same time cause a terrific loss to English commerce by sinking the many merchantmen at anchor in the harbor.

It was early on Wednesday morning that the Emden, with a dummy fourth funnel and flying the British ensign, in some inexplicable fashion sneaked past the French torpedo boat Mosquet, which was on patrol duty outside, and entered the outer harbor of Penang. Across the channel leading to the inner harbor lay the Russian cruiser Jemtchug. Inside were the French torpedo boats Fronde and Pistolet and the torpedo boat destroyer D'Iberville. The torpedo boats lay beside the long Government wharf, while the D'Iberville rode at anchor between two tramp steamers.

At full speed the Emden steamed straight for the Jemtchug and the inner harbor. In the semi-darkness of the early morning the Russian took her for the British cruiser Yarmouth, which had been in and out two or three times during the previous week and did not even "query" her. Suddenly, when less than 400 yards away, the Emden emptied her bow guns into the Jemtchug and came on at a terrific pace, with all the guns she could bring to bear in action. When she had come within 250 yards she changed her course slightly, and as she passed the Jemtchug poured two broadsides into her, as well as a torpedo, which entered the engine room but did comparatively little damage.

The Russian cruiser was taken completely by surprise and was badly crippled before she realized what was happening. The fact that her Captain was spending the night ashore and that there was no one on board who seemed capable of acting energetically completed the demoralization. She was defeated before the battle began. However, her men finally manned the light guns and brought them into action.

In the meantime the Emden was well inside the inner harbor and among the shipping. She saw the French torpedo boats there, and apparently realized at once that unless she could get out before they joined in the action her fate was sealed. At such close quarters (the range was never more than 450 yards) their torpedoes would have proved deadly. Accordingly, she turned sharply and made for the Jemtchug once more.

All the time she had been in the harbor the Russian had been bombarding her with shrapnel, but, owing to the notoriously bad marksmanship prevalent in the Czar's navy, had succeeded for the most part only in peppering every merchant ship within range. As the Emden neared the Jemtchug again both ships were actually spitting fire. The range was practically point-blank. Less than 150 yards away the Emden passed the Russian, and as she did so torpedoed her amidships, striking the magazine. There was a tremendous detonation, paling into insignificance by its volume all the previous din; a heavy black column of smoke arose and the Jemtchug sank in less than ten seconds, while the Emden steamed behind the point to safety.

No sooner had she done so, however, than she sighted the torpedo boat Mosquet, which had heard the firing and was coming in at top speed. The Emden immediately opened up on her, thereby causing her to turn around in an endeavor to escape. It was too late. After a running fight of twenty minutes the Mosquet seemed to be hit by three shells simultaneously and sank very rapidly. The German had got a second victim.

It was here that the chivalrous bravery of the Emden's Captain, which has been many times in evidence throughout her meteoric career, was again shown. If the French boats were coming out, every moment was of priceless value to him. Nevertheless, utterly disregarding this, he stopped, lowered boats, and picked up the survivors from the Mosquet before steaming on his way.

The English here now say of him, admiringly, "He played the game."

Meantime, boats of all descriptions had started toward the place where the Russian cruiser had last been seen. The water was covered with débris of all sorts, to which the survivors were clinging. They presented a horrible sight when they were landed on Victoria Pier, which the ambulance corps of the Sikh garrison turned into a temporary hospital. Almost all of them had wounds of one sort or another. Many were covered with them. Their blood-stained and, for the most part, naked bodies were enough to send shivers through even the most cold-blooded person. It was a sight I shall not forget for many a day. Out of a crew of 334 men 142 were picked up wounded. Only 94 were found practically untouched. Ninety-eight were "missing." It is not yet known how many of the crew of the 78 of the Mosquet were rescued by the Emden.

So much of the story I am able to write from personal observation and investigation. Here, however, is an account of what occurred from an officer who saw it all from closer range and more intimate conditions, for he was on the French torpedo boat destroyer Pistolet. I tell his story exactly as he told it to me:

"The Captain of the Pistolet had invited Capt. T. and myself to have a game of bridge whist on board. His ship was lying alongside the Government wharf, just inside the inner harbor. The game proved a most interesting one and time flew by unnoticed. Finally, just before 1 A.M., it came to a close, but, owing to the fact that our going home at that hour of the morning would mean a rikisha ride of over two miles, the Captain stretched a point and invited us to remain on board, which we did. Little did we know what our decision was to mean to us.

"At 5:25 the next morning, just as day was breaking, I was awakened by a deafening crash, followed by two others in rapid succession. Without waiting for more, I pulled my ducks over my pajamas and hurried on deck. Right before us, at the entrance to the inner harbor, lay the Russian cruiser Jemtchug. Steaming toward her at full speed came the German cruiser Emden, her bow guns belching forth vast clouds of smoke, through which the flash of the guns could just be distinguished. She was less than half a mile away. After what seemed to me an interminable delay, the surprised

Jemtchug started to reply with her small guns, and the din grew greater and greater.

"As the Emden came on she swerved slightly out of her course and steamed down the far side of the channel, thus bringing her broadside guns to bear on the Jemtchug, which by this time was literally spitting fire. The range now was less than 300 yards, and the execution being done must have been terrible. We noticed, however, that the greater number of the Russian shells were 'carrying over.'

"The Emden now changed her course again, to the right, and disappeared behind a group of several tramp steamers so as to enable her to turn around without unduly exposing herself. While she was doing this the firing diminished greatly, owing to the disinclination on the part of either, I imagine, wantonly to damage harmless merchant vessels. No sooner had she started on her way out of the harbor, however, than the din arose once more.

"Just at this time the French torpedo boat Fronde dropped back from her position alongside us and started in to take part in the mêlée with a machine gun. This caused the Emden to devote part of her time to us, and we were made the objective of a severe machine-gun fire which, owing to our position in the shadow of the pier and of the fact that the light was very poor, did little or no damage. Nevertheless, it was rather disconcerting to hear the rattle of lead on the corrugated iron sheds behind us.

"By this time the Emden must have realized that at such close quarters she was subject to the danger of a torpedo attack, (although as a matter of fact no effort seemed to have been made along these lines,) and she accordingly started up the north channel toward the outer harbor at full speed, firing broadside after broadside at the Jemtchug, now badly crippled.

"Suddenly, as the two cruisers were abreast and no more than 150 yards from one another, there was a tremendous crash. The Jemtchug heaved up amidships, there was another detonation even louder than the first, and she sank before I could realize what had happened. All that remained was a large pillar of smoke to mark the spot where she had been. A German torpedo had found its mark, and the Emden sailed around the point without firing another shot.

"By this time—less than thirty minutes after the first shot had been fired—the Pistolet had cast off and we started across the harbor toward the place where we had last seen the Jemtchug, with the Fronde close behind us. It was slow work, as we had very little steam.

"As we neared the scene of the disaster I received my first impression of the horror of modern naval warfare. The water was strewn with wreckage, amid which heads were popping up and down like corks in a lily pond. It seemed as if it were alive with men. They were everywhere, hanging on to pieces of wood, clutching life preservers, clinging to débris of all kinds.

"When we reached them we immediately started in getting them aboard by means of boats, ropes looped at the end, by hand, and in any way possible. They were indeed a most terrible sight. Most of them were wounded, and those that were were bleeding profusely. Practically none were wearing more than a pair of trousers, and a considerable number did not even have that. A few were frightfully lacerated, and we recovered one man who had had his leg blown off below the knee—he died five minutes after we got him on board. It was like living a frightful nightmare. Everywhere you turned you met a groaning, greasy mass of humanity.

"Discipline was thrown aside and Captain and men alike toiled in their efforts to alleviate the suffering of the Jemtchug's survivors. My partner at bridge the previous night, the doctor, asked my assistance, and together we went from man to man doing what emergency work we could. My pajama-decked costume was rapidly covered with blood. It was a case of everybody helping everybody else.

"Finally, when numerous launches of all sizes and makes had put out to relieve us, we returned to the Victoria jetty, which the ambulance corps of the Sikh garrison, aided by volunteers and local doctors, had turned into a temporary hospital. Here were removed what remained of the Jemtchug.

"While the last few men were taken off the Pistolet, another cannonading was heard. I hurried ashore, with no feeling of regret, I might say, and took a rikisha to the outer sea wall to see whatever fighting was going on. The ships were so far away that it was hard to tell with the naked eye exactly what was going on. We could see the little torpedo boat Mosquet trying to get beyond the range of the Emden's guns while the shells were throwing up water all around her. The chase had kept on for twenty minutes, I should say, when we saw the little craft sink by the bow. The Emden lowered boats to pick up any possible survivors, but, from the short time they were down, I imagine most of the crew were lost.

"I have tried to give you some little idea in the foregoing of the frightful encounter I have witnessed. It seemed like a nightmare afterward, although while it was actually going on you felt as if you were looking at a sham battle. Even when the bullets started in to rattle on the iron-covered sheds above our heads there was nothing terrifying about it. After the effect of the first few shots had worn off I felt as if I were watching a play. That quiet, staid Penang with her shaded streets and sampan covered harbor should be the scene of a naval engagement such as I witnessed today is almost unbelievable. Yet the sordid aftereffects are before our eyes.

"Only the masterly manoeuvring of that gentleman of the German fleet—the Captain of the Emden—prevented the city from being the scene of a terrible carnage. His refusal to sink unarmed vessels while the crews were on board, his refraining from bombarding the town, his stopping to pick up the crew of the Mosquet, although every minute was valuable to him, at once made him 'that gentleman, the Captain of the Emden.' On all sides you heard 'I hope they sink the Emden, but it will be a shame if any of her crew are lost.'

"While steaming away from Penang he met the tramp Glen. Instead of capturing her, he sent her into Penang with the message: 'I tried not to hit the town. If I did so, I am very sorry, indeed.' Well, he 'played the game,' and he has made me, for one, feel extremely doubtful whether the much-talked-of German 'atrocities' are true, except where the exigencies of war have made them unavoidable."

Here you have the story of an engagement which will go down in history as a demonstration that, even under the conditions of modern naval warfare, it is possible for two ships of almost equal armament to fight by daylight at almost point-blank range without resulting in the disabling of both. A sight similar to that witnessed yesterday would be considered by most naval critics as impossible, or, rather, suicidal.

The sad, or, rather, disgraceful, part of the story has yet to be told. It was true that the Jemtchug was caught unprepared. Her Captain was spending the night ashore, her decks were not cleared, she was slow to get into action, and when she did so her marksmanship was poor. All this could hardly be excused, but it becomes insignificant when we consider the case of the French torpedo boats and the D'Iberville, whose help the Jemtchug had a right to expect. Here they lay in a harbor with fully ten minutes' warning that a hostile ship was approaching, yet they allowed that ship to enter the harbor, steam around it, turn, and make her escape without so much as firing a shot, when, if they had gone into action, the Emden could hardly have escaped. The range was everything they could have desired.

What was the matter? Why did they remain silent? The answer is this: Although it was a time of war, a large percentage of the officers of these ships had been allowed to remain ashore over night. Not one of the ships had steam up. Their decks were not even cleared for action. Yet, even taking this into consideration, it is inexplicable that, when two or three torpedoes from any one of them would have saved the day, none was fired. The ships need not have moved an inch to have done so. The range was ridiculously short—less than 200 yards at one time. But surprise, lack of discipline, and general inefficiency seemed to hold them paralyzed.

The prevailing opinion here is that they did not wish to draw the Emden's fire on themselves—although one did use her machine gun toward the end of the engagement. Whatever is said, however, it is impossible to get away from the fact that the French Navy yesterday sustained a blow to its efficiency that it will take a long time to wipe out. Theirs was a "masterly inaction" caused by something which they do not attempt themselves to define. Both army and navy commanders here are one in their contemptuous condemnation of such a spectacle.

The Belgian Soldier

[From The London Times, Oct. 17, 1914. By its Special Correspondent lately in Antwerp.]

BEFORE it fades I would like to record my impression of the Belgian soldier as I have seen him day after day through the two months ending with the fall of Antwerp.

I have seen him on every kind of duty and off, on the roads, in cabarets, in camp and barrack, on the march, in trenches, fighting from behind all sorts of cover or from none, on foot, on horseback, on bicycles, mounted proudly on his auto-mitrailleuse, or running behind his gun-team of dogs, each dog pulling and barking as if it would tear the whole German Army to pieces. I have seen him wounded on battlefields, by the roadside, and in hospitals; I have seen him, in the later days at Antwerp, brought back from the forts and from those terrible advanced trenches unwounded, but from sheer exhaustion in almost more serious plight than any of his comrades whom the shells had hit. And I have seen him dead.

As a result there has grown up in me an extraordinary affection for him. Greater even than my admiration of his careless courage is my liking for the man. For all his manhood he has so much of the child in him; he is such a chatterbox and so full of laughter, and never are his laugh and badinage so quick as when he has the sternest work on hand. Unshaven, mud-bespattered, hungry, so tired that he can hardly walk or lift his rifle to his shoulder, he will bear himself with a gallant gayety which, I think, is quite his own and is altogether fascinating.

As time goes on perhaps it will be the faces of the dead and wounded that will live most clearly in the memory, but at present the pictures of the Belgian soldier which stand out sharpest are less lugubrious and more commonplace.

I walked one day back toward Antwerp, along that awful road which ran by Contich and Waerloos to Waelhem. Daily along that road the German shells fell nearer to the city, so that whenever one went out to the place that he had visited yesterday he was likely to find himself disagreeably surprised. One day I found myself, (I would not have been there had I known it,) perhaps a mile inside the range of the enemy's guns. A Red Cross car had dropped me and picked up wounded men instead, and there was nothing for it but to walk back along the road.

Along the road from the foremost trenches came a dozen Belgian soldiers, just relieved after twenty-four hours of what it is difficult to describe otherwise than as hell. Muddied from head to heel, they could hardly drag their feet along, and, glad of any company, I fell in and walked with the last straggler of the little band, while the shrapnel with its long-drawn scream—whew-ew-ew-ew-bang!—broke on either side of us.

At every whew-ew-ew-ew which came too near I dived for cover. If there was no friendly wall or vehicle or tree trunk at hand the ditch beside the road was always there. And every time I dived my companion stood in the middle of the road and shook with laughter—not unkindly, but in the utmost friendliness and good humor—waiting till I rejoined him and we resumed our walk.

A little man, shockingly bedraggled, worn out almost to the point of collapse, utterly indifferent to his own danger, and taking a huge, childlike delight in my care for my personal safety, the picture of him as he stood and laughed all alone in the bare road amid the bursting shells seems to me curiously typical of the whole Belgian Army.

Another picture also—a composite photograph—I shall never forget. It is the same man—sometimes blonde, sometimes dark, but always the same smallish man—as, on picket duty, he stops you to examine your papers. He does not understand the papers in the least. The British passport begins with the words, "We, Sir Edward Grey, a Baronet of the United Kingdom...." Sternly he wrinkles his brow over the formidable document, earnestly trying to do his duty. At last, "Votre nom, Edouard Gra-ee?" he asks. You explain that you wish that it was and call attention to the place where your own insignificant name is mentioned lower down. To his immense relief he has mastered the central fact, namely, that you are English. And his face lights up with the smile which one has come to know so well; a smile of real pleasure and good-will.

Sometimes he speaks a word of English, and with what pride he uses it! "All ri'!" "Good night!" "How do?" And you go on into the night feeling that you are leaving a friend behind whom you would like to stop and talk to. And he, you know, has been cheered in his lonely duty by the mere contact with an ally.

THE HEROIC LANGUAGE

By ALICE MEYNELL.

[From King Albert's Book.]

WHEN our now living languages are "dead,"
Which in the classes shall be treasured?
Which will the masters teach?
Kepler's, and Shakespeare's, and thy word, thy phrase,
Thy grammar, thou heroic, for all days,
O little Flemish speech!

Cheerful Spirits in Trench Inferno

[Special Cable to THE NEW YORK TIMES.]

NORTHERN FRANCE, Dec. 20, (Dispatch to The London Daily News.)—This week—a week of many significant things—has ended in the wildest whirl of weather imaginable. The rains have been terrific, blinding, tropical in their almost ceaseless roar and fury. Surely only madmen or fiends would fight in such an elemental maelstrom. We may be both, and perhaps we are, now that the whole world is topsy-turvy; for we are going savagely on at this dread business, half blind and wholly desperate. If the furious sky were to rain red-hot pitchforks the contending armies would still be undismayed and would crawl, if not fly, at one another's throats.

But there is no romance in trench fighting; it is sickening, demoralizing. Ask any soldier who has been at it for a time. He will pour a few plain truths into your shocked ear. Down at the railroad terminal today I met some of them—a queer mixture. There was a batch of German prisoners; there was a squad of wounded Belgians, and there were four lost, stolen, or strayed British soldiers from the Seventh Division—a Sergeant and three men. They were all so plastered over with dirt that it was difficult to sort out their nationality.

What struck me most was their absolute and undisguised cheerfulness. I have lively recollection of the first German prisoners I saw in the early days of the war. They were in a gray funk, which is several degrees more sheer than a blue funk. They absolutely believed that the next moment or two would be their last on this woeful earth and that they would be shot out of hand.

The young Prussians I met today said that they had been having a very thin time recently; that their food was bad, and getting worse and more scanty every day; that pneumonia and rheumatism were rife in their trenches, to say nothing of the dreaded typhoid, and that they were tremendously glad to be out of it all. They understood that they were going to England. Anyway, they hoped so fervently.

The Belgian soldiers were all slightly wounded, mostly in the legs and arms. The mud and slime of the trenches north of Furnes had not yet dried upon their sodden clothes. They were cold and benumbed and desperately hungry, for their train had been held up for hours while certain private and confidential military scene changing was going on. In spite of the pain their hurriedly dressed wounds were giving them they, too, were cheerful.

French Amenities

[From The London Times, Dec. 18, 1914.]

An officer in the R.A.M.C. writes:

FIGURE to yourself (as Wells says, isn't it?) a country of flat plowed field, pollard willows and deep muddy ditches. Then we come along, and in military parlance "dig ourselves in." That is, with the sweat of the brows of hundreds of Tommies working by night deep narrow trenches five feet deep and at least with the earth thrown up another two and a half feet as a bank on top. These trenches are one and a half to two feet wide, and curl and twist about in a maddening manner to make them safer from shell-fire. Little caves are scooped in the walls of the trenches, where the men live about four to a hole, and slightly bigger dugouts where two officers live. All the soil is clay, stickier and greasier than one could believe possible. It's like almost solid paint, and the least rain makes the sides of the trenches slimy, and the bottom a perfect sea of mud—pulls the heels off your boots almost. One feels like Gulliver walking along a Lilliputian town all the time. The front line of trenches—the firing line—have scientific loopholes and lookout places in them for seeing and firing from, and a dropping fire goes on from both sides all day long, but is very harmless.

Dec. 3, 1914.—I was just starting for my daily constitutional "on top" when the enemy began their bombarding, nearly one and a half hours earlier than usual, so I will postpone my little walk and finish this instead. Yesterday we had one man killed and two wounded, the first casualties for over a week. The story of one of the wounded is worth telling to show you the pluck of these men. He told me he noticed some new digging going on on the side of the enemy in front of his firing post. One can see the spadefuls of earth coming up from below the ground level when new trenches are being dug. Although this was in broad daylight, our man thought he would go and see what the Germans were up to, so he hops over the side of his trench and runs forward thirty yards to a ditch and crawls along it some hundred yards or so. He then spots a large shell-hole in the field on one side of the ditch, so doubles off and gets into that and has a good look around. Not satisfied with the point of view, he sprints to a line of willows nearer still to the enemy—within 250 yards of them indeed—and proceeds to climb up one of them. While doing this he gets shot through the shoulder. He told me he thought he had ricked his arm at first, as it felt numb and useless. Meanwhile a great pal of his in the regiment, hearing that he had gone out like this, hops over the parapet and sets off to look for him, and comes up just as he gets hit. The second man upbraids the first roundly for being a fool, carries his rifle for him, and brings him back. All this is done quite in the day's work and "sub rosa," as they would get punished for leaving the trench like that in the daytime if it was spotted. The pluck of these men is perfectly extraordinary, and the placid way life goes on under the risk of being sniped or shelled any moment is, until one gets used to seeing it, quite past belief. I must say the officers set the men a magnificent example.

A young officer attached to the Yorkshire Light Infantry writes on Dec. 6:

One wonders when one sees a German face to face, is this really one of those devils who wrought such devastation—for devastation they have surely wrought. You can hardly believe it, for he seems much the same as other soldiers. I can assure you that there is none of that insensate hatred that one hears about, out here. We are out to kill, and kill we do, at any and every opportunity. But, when all is done and the battle is over, the splendid universal "soldier spirit" comes over all the men, and we cannot help thinking that Kipling must have been in the firing line when he wrote that "East is East and West is West" thing. Just to give you some idea of what I mean, the other night four German snipers were shot on our wire. The next night our men went out and brought one in who was near and getatable and buried him. They did it with just the same reverence and sadness as they do to our own dear fellows. I went to look at the grave the next morning, and one of the most uncouth-looking men in my company had placed a cross at the head of the grave, and had written on it:

Here lies a German,
We don't know his name,
He died bravely fighting
For his Fatherland.

And under that, "got mit uns," (sic,) that being the highest effort of all the men at German. Not bad for a bloodthirsty Briton, eh? Really, that shows the spirit.

I don't believe there is a man living who, when first interviewing an 11-inch howitzer shell, is not pink with funk. After the first ten, one gets quite used to them, but really, they are terrible! They hit a house. You can see the great shell—a black streak—just before it strikes, then, before you hear the explosion, the whole house simply lifts up into the air, apparently quite silently; then you hear the roar, and the whole earth shakes. In the place where the house was there is a huge fountain-spout of what looks like pink fluff. It is the pulverized bricks. Then a monstrous shoot of black smoke towering up a hundred feet or more, and, finally, there is a curious willow-like formation, and then—you duck, as huge pieces of shell, and house, and earth, and haystack tumble over your head. And yet, do you know, it is really remarkable how little damage they do against earth trenches. With a whole morning's shelling, not a single man of my company was killed, although not a single shell missed what it had aimed at by more than fifty yards. That makes all the difference, that fifty yards. If you only keep your head down, you are as safe as houses; exactly, you will remark, "as safe as houses."

The Things the Wounded Talk About

[A British Surgeon, in The London Times, Dec. 22, 1914.]

IF you would realize fully what the war, as an event in the procession of events, means you must come to France and visit a military hospital. You must make this visit not as a sightseer, nor yet in the spirit of a philanthropist, but only as a friend. You must come prepared to listen to stories that have no relation to war and the affairs of war—most soldiers, I think, are reluctant to speak of the things they have seen—to stories that concern home ties and the doings, real and conjectured, of children—queer, sentimental stories woven around old ideas like the Christmas idea and the idea of home.

They will fill you with wonder at first, those unwarlike tales, because they belong to the truly unexpected, against which it is impossible to be prepared. It would not be an exaggeration to describe the first effect of them as startling. They kill so many illusions and they discredit so many beliefs. War, rendered thus the background of life, assumes a new proportion and a new meaning. Or, rather, it becomes vague and meaningless, like a darkness.

A few days ago I sat by the bedside of a wounded sapper—a reservist—and heard the story of life in a signal-box on a branch line in the North of England. The man was dying. I think he knew it. But the zest of his everyday life was still strong in him. He described the manner in which, on leaving the army originally, he had obtained his post on the railway. He told me that there were three trains each way in the day, and mentioned that on Winter nights the last train was frequently very late. This meant a late supper, but his wife saw to it that everything was kept hot. Sometimes his wife came to the box to meet him if it was a dry night.

In the next bed there was a young Scotsman from a Highland district which I know very well. We were friends so soon as he learned that I knew his home. He was a roadman, and we talked of his roads and the changes which had been wrought in them of late years by motor traffic. He recalled a great storm, during which the sea wall around a certain harbor was washed away and the highway rendered impassable. Then, rather diffidently, he confessed that he had lost a foot and would be handicapped in his work—"at Ypres."

At the far end of the ward there was a German who spoke a little English. He was a married man and came from Saxony. His wife and children, he said, would miss him at Christmas. We spoke a long time on the subject of Christmas. I suppose by all the orthodox canons that this German should have told me that he was glad to be a prisoner or else should have declared his conviction that the German Army would speedily carry everything before it to victory. But somehow he forgot to say these things and I forgot to ask him about them. These things seemed far away in the quiet ward, even—and for this I beg forgiveness—grotesque and uninteresting.

I had the curiosity to return to the young Scot and to ask him if he regretted the decision which had led to his being maimed for life. He shook his head. "No, because I've had a good home. A man with a good home should fight for it." He added that his father had advised him very strongly to enlist.

By the touchstone of the men it has broken this war is judged, and the makers of this war. And more than ruined villages and desecrated churches these soldiers pronounce condemnation. They, who have given so much, are, in a sense, without joy and without enthusiasm; rather they shun recollection. There is no zest in the killing of men. Their thoughts, especially at this season, are directed away from the dull, mechanic force which labors against its bonds across Europe, and dwell in the homes it has threatened. The war is revealed as a thing gross and dull-witted, a crime even against the ancient, chivalrous spirit of war.

Three Dying Foes Made Friends

[From The Hartford Courant, Jan. 14, 1915.]

To the Editor of The Courant:

I have read nothing more tender and moving than the subjoined letter found by a Red Cross agent at the side of a dead officer and forwarded to the person to whom it was addressed. The writer was a French cavalry officer engaged to a young American girl in Paris. It was written as he lay dying from wounds received in a cavalry charge. Let it speak for itself.

E.P.P.

THERE are two other men lying near me, and I do not think there is much hope for them either. One is an officer of a Scottish regiment and the other a private in the Uhlans. They were struck down after me, and when I came to myself, I found them bending over me, rendering first aid.

The Britisher was pouring water down my throat from his flask, while the German was endeavoring to stanch my wound with an antiseptic preparation served out to them by their medical corps. The Highlander had one of his legs shattered, and the German had several pieces of shrapnel buried in his side.

In spite of their own sufferings they were trying to help me, and when I was fully conscious again the German gave us a morphia injection and took one himself. His medical corps had also provided him with the injection and the needle, together with printed instructions for its use.

After the injection, feeling wonderfully at ease, we spoke of the lives we had lived before the war. We all spoke English, and we talked of the women we had left at home. Both the German and the Britisher had only been married a year....

I wondered, and I supposed the others did, why we had fought each other at all. I looked at the Highlander, who was falling to sleep, exhausted, and in spite of his drawn face and mud-stained uniform, he looked the embodiment of freedom. Then I thought of the Tricolor of France and all that France had done for liberty. Then I watched the German, who had ceased to speak. He had taken a Prayer Book from his knapsack and was trying to read a service for soldiers wounded in battle.

And ... while I watched him, I realized what we were fighting for.... He was dying in vain, while the Britisher and myself, by our deaths, would probably contribute something toward the cause of civilization and peace.

[The letter ends with a reference to the failing light and the roar of guns.]

Chronology of the War
Showing Progress of Campaigns on All Fronts and Collateral Events from Jan. 7 to and Including Jan. 31, 1915

CAMPAIGN IN EASTERN EUROPE

[Continued from the Last Number.]

Jan. 8—Germans are trying to carry the Russian lines near Bolinow by the use of steel shields to protect riflemen.

Jan. 9—Germans renew offensive from direction of Mlawa; fighting on the Rawka and in the north; Russians enter Transylvania; Austrians meet delays near Nida River.

Jan. 11—Russians are strengthening their lines.

Jan. 12—Russians are pressing the Austrians near the Nida; Austrians are fleeing from Bukowina.

Jan. 13—Russians occupy several villages in the Masurian Lake region and threaten Mlawa; Austrians state that Russians lost heavily in Przemysl siege.

Jan. 14—Russians push north from Warsaw; Germans retake several positions on Bzura River; it is reported that Germans are short of supplies.

Jan. 15—New Russian army marches north in Poland; Germans near Mlawa are in peril; von Hindenburg declared in danger.

Jan. 16—Austrians bring up heavy artillery to hold the Donajec River; Germans are on way to Budapest.

Jan. 17—Russians take Kirlibaba Pass and progress along right bank of the Vistula; Germans pushed back on Plock.

Jan. 18—Germans occupy Kielce; Russians fall back to Radom; Russian capture of Kirlibaba Pass flanks Austrians; Germans out of Plock.

Jan. 20—Russians drive Austrians back in Hungary and march on Jacobeni.

Jan. 21—Russians renew offensive against Mlawa; Austrians rout Russians from intrenchments on Donajec River.

Jan. 22—New Russian army nears Prussia; invasion of Hungary halted; Russian advance is causing alarm in Budapest.

Jan. 23—Germans are massing in Hungary; Russians advance in the north.

Jan. 24—Russians checked in Transylvania.

Jan. 25—Armies are deadlocked in Central Poland; Austrians declare that Transylvania is safe; fierce fighting in Bukowina; Russians forced from trenches south of Tarnow.

Jan. 27—Austrians report the recapture of Uzsok Pass; Russians seize Pilkalen; ten army corps are gathered in Southern Hungary, with many Germans in them.

Jan. 28—Great struggle for the Carpathians is opening; Austro-German forces advance on eighty-mile front.

Jan. 29—Russian wings advance in East Prussia and the Carpathians; Russians close in on Insterburg; Tilsit surrounded.

Jan. 30—Russians cut railway between Memel and Tilsit, and enter Hungary.

Jan. 31—Russians gain in Carpathians.

CAMPAIGN IN WESTERN EUROPE.

Jan. 8—Allies gain north of Soissons, near Rheims, and in Alsace; French Alpine troops use skis in gaining an advantage in Alsace.

Jan. 9—Germans retake Steinbach and Burnhaupt; French take Perthes and gain near Soupir.

Jan. 10—French cut German railway lines to prevent reserves from coming to the relief of Altkirch.

Jan. 11—Allies, attacking from Perthes, are trying to cut German rail communications.

Jan. 12—French attempt offensive near Soissons and Perthes; they are checked in Alsace; British forces at the front are steadily increasing in number.

Jan. 13—Germans, reinforced, win victory at Soissons, forcing French to abandon five miles of trenches and to cross the Aisne, leaving guns and wounded; heights of Vregny are won in this fight by the Germans under the eyes of the Kaiser; Germans take 3,150 prisoners and fourteen guns in two days' fighting.

Jan. 15—French are calm over the Soissons defeat; British gain near La Bassée.

Jan. 17—Allies take trenches in Belgium; deadlock at La Bassée; Allies closing on Lille.

Jan. 18—Fierce fighting at La Boisselle; both sides are claiming success at Tracy-le-Val.

Jan. 19—French advance in attempt to cut off St. Mihiel.

Jan. 20—French are nearer Metz; British take Freylinghuysen.

Jan. 21—Germans repulsed in Ardennes woods by French and Belgians; French retake trenches at Notre Dame de Lorette; Germans retake Le Pretre woods; it is learned that the Soissons battle was won by von Kluck's veterans, and that the Germans granted a half-hour truce while French Red Cross aided wounded.

Jan. 22—Fierce fighting in Hartmanns-Weiler region.

Jan. 23—Germans renew activity near Ypres and bombard left wing of Allies; fighting in Argonne region.

Jan. 24—Germans are bombarding Flanders towns; Allies leave St. Georges.

Jan. 25—Kaiser sends Prince Eitel Friedrich to capture Thann and direct fighting in Alsace; French gain toward Altkirch and destroy bridges over the Meuse at St. Mihiel; Germans forced to abandon Dixmude trenches because of floods.

Jan. 26—Another battle on at La Bassée; Germans gain ground by vigorous offensive near Craonne and in Alsace.

Jan. 27—Germans attack between La Bassée and Bethune, this being the Kaiser's birthday; the French claim that the German loss is 20,000; indecisive fighting near Ypres.

Jan. 28—French defeated at Craonne; Germans make gains in the Vosges and Upper Alsace.

Jan. 29—Germans checked in two attempts to cross the Aisne; they drain the Yser flood area.

Jan. 30—Germans win in the Argonne.

Jan. 31—Kaiser directs German assault on La Bassée; zouaves and Indians win the Great Dune west of Lombaertzyde.

CAMPAIGN IN AFRICA.

Jan. 9—French win in Kamerun.

Jan. 15—British take Swakopmund.

CAMPAIGN IN ASIA MINOR AND EGYPT.

Jan. 9—Turks hasten construction of railway lines across Sinai peninsula.

Jan. 10—Turks are marching on Egypt; reserve Turkish army, trying to save Erzerum, repulsed at frontier.

Jan. 12—Erzerum road is being fought for; Noury Bey captured by Russians.

Jan. 13—Turks occupy Tabriz and report Arab victory over British troops on the lower Tigris.

Jan. 14—Armenian refugees cross Russian frontier; Turkish invasion of Persia continues.

Jan. 15—Turks advance in Persia.

Jan. 17—Turkish corps cut to pieces in the Caucasus.

Jan. 18—Turkish soldiers are being frozen to death.

Jan. 21—Turks are pushing plans for a strategic railway to the Egyptian frontier.

Jan. 24—Russians check Turkish advance on Erzerum.

Jan. 27—British defeat Turkish advance guard toward El Kantara on the Suez Canal; three Turkish army corps now marching on Egypt; British win at Korna.

Jan. 28—Turks, reinforced, attack Russians in the Caucasus.

Jan. 29—Turks fortify Erzerum, and order civilians to depart.

Jan. 30—Russians take Tabriz.

Jan. 31—Turks defeated near Sari-Kamysh.

NAVAL RECORD.

Jan. 11—Report from Vienna that French dreadnought Courbet has been sunk.

Jan. 12—Japanese cruisers are hunting the German converted cruiser Prince Eitel Friedrich off the coast of Peru.

Jan. 13—Dover forts drive off two German submarines; bombardment of the Dardanelles by the allied fleets continues.

Jan. 16—French submarine Saphir sunk by Turkish mine at the Dardanelles; Italian gunboat Coatit damaged in the Adriatic.

Jan. 20—Dutch naval patrol boat sunk by a mine, five men being lost.

Jan. 21—German cruiser Karlsruhe reported off Porto Rico.

Jan. 22—German submarine U-19 sinks British freighter Durward.

Jan. 23—German supply ship sunk by Australian cruiser.

Jan. 24—British patrolling squadron under Vice Admiral Beatty defeats German squadron attempting to reach English coast; German battle cruiser Blücher sunk and two other German battle cruisers damaged; British battle cruisers Lion and Tiger damaged; Germans claim three British ships were sunk.

Jan. 28—British Admiralty denies that any British ship was sunk.

Jan. 30—German submarine sinks three British steamers in Irish Channel and chases Liverpool passenger boat.

Jan. 31—German submarine sinks two British steamers in English Channel; third steamer escapes.

AERIAL RECORD.

Jan. 10—German aeroplanes threw thirty bombs on Dunkirk, damaging several houses; Belgian aviators give battle to the Germans at great altitude and finally drive them off; German aviator shot down by French near Amiens.

Jan. 16—German hydroaeroplane lost in North Sea; nine aviators of the Allies drop bombs on Ostend.

Jan. 19—German airships drop bombs on Yarmouth, King's Lynn, and other English towns; four persons are killed, ten wounded, and considerable property damage is done; it is reported that the German plant at Friedrichshafen produces a super-Zeppelin every three weeks.

Jan. 21—Allies drop bombs on Essen.

Jan. 22—Holland is to investigate a report that a Zeppelin violated her neutrality by flying over her territory.

Jan. 23—Germans drop bombs on Dunkirk; it is reported that the American Consulate is damaged.

Jan. 25—It is reported from Amsterdam that 400 German war automobiles were destroyed in the raid on Essen.

Jan. 26—Russians bring down German airship that bombarded Libau.

Jan. 28—Crew of German airship that bombarded Libau will be tried by military court and will not be treated as prisoners of war; bomb dropped on Belgrade.

AMERICAN INTERESTS.

Jan. 24—Administration makes public in Washington a letter written by Secretary Bryan to Senator Stone of Missouri in which discrimination against Germany and Austria-Hungary is denied; twenty charges made by pro-Germans are taken up and the Administration's position and action on each are stated in detail.

AUSTRIA-HUNGARY.

Jan. 17—Anti-war demonstrations in Vienna; Czech editor executed for treason.

Jan. 20—Governor of Cracow orders partial evacuation of the city.

Jan. 21—Archduke Charles Francis, the Austrian Crown Prince, is in Berlin, where he will be joined shortly by Baron Burian, the new Austro-Hungarian Minister of Foreign Affairs; plans of campaign against Russia are to be discussed with German officials.

Jan. 23—Baron Burian leaves Berlin for German Army Headquarters to confer with the Kaiser.

Jan. 25—Riots in many parts of Hungary.

Jan. 28—Riot among Southern Slavs because of mobilization order.

Jan. 29—Prisoners of war are to be employed in farm work.

Jan. 30—Warning is sent to Rumania against agitation among Rumanian population of Transylvania.

BELGIUM.

Jan. 8—Cardinal Mercier has been placed under restraint by the German authorities because of his pastoral, read in the churches on Jan. 3, in which he told the Belgians that they owe German authority "neither respect, nor attachment, nor obedience."

Jan. 9—It is reported that Cardinal Mercier was arrested, but the report is denied by the Military Governor of Belgium; circulation of the Mercier pastoral is not being permitted.

Jan. 10—The Mercier pastoral is read in English churches; Belgian refugees are proving a problem in England and Holland.

Jan. 11—Admiration for Cardinal Mercier expressed by King Albert in a letter to the Pope.

Jan. 12—It is reported from Rome that the Vatican has asked Germany for an explanation regarding the acts with reference to Cardinal Mercier.

Jan. 22—Full text of the Mercier pastoral is printed in THE NEW YORK TIMES.

CANADA.

Jan. 22—Major General Hughes, Minister of Militia and Defense, arrives in Vancouver to arrange for enlistment of third contingent.

Jan. 30—First detachment of Canadian troops is in France; other detachments are en route; nine German prisoners escape from Halifax citadel; war fund of $1,500,000 raised in five days in Montreal.

Jan. 31—Six Canadians, including two officers, killed in La Bassée fight.

EGYPT.

Jan. 10—Abbas Hilmi, deposed Khédive, calls upon Egyptians and Sudanese to rise against England.

ENGLAND.

Jan. 8—House of Lords adjourns after discussion of recruiting and other phases of the war.

Jan. 12—Government appeals to women to induce men to enlist.

Jan. 15—War Office issues statement that letters destined for hostile countries will be held up unless they are unsealed.

Jan. 16—Seven British naval officers, interned in Holland, escape, but five are recaptured.

Jan. 23—Statement shows that total casualty list of officers up to Jan. 12 was 4,344, of whom 1,266 were killed, the rest being wounded and missing; many interned Germans and Austrians released on parole.

Jan. 27—Two Hindu soldiers win Victoria Crosses; London financial papers deprecate a joint loan for the Allies.

Jan. 28—Many Oxford "blues" are serving in the army.

Jan. 31—There are 178 peers serving in the army.

FRANCE.

Jan. 10—Government will surrender German surgeons and nurses held as prisoners of war only in equal exchange.

Jan. 14—Socialist Senator demands postponement of war discussion in Parliament and says speeches must give way to voice of cannon.

Jan. 18—Paris darkened by police order.

Jan. 22—Capt. Uhde, stated to be a relative of the Kaiser, is sent to concentration camp after being accused of having spied on the French fleet at Toulon.

Jan. 27—Many doctors have been killed, wounded, and taken prisoner, the reason for lengthy casualty list being stated to be that the French doctors do not desert their wounded on approach of the enemy.

Jan. 29—Officer stops Mrs. Asquith and party on way to the front for a weekend.

GERMANY.

Jan. 8—Government charges that San Marino has been encouraging espionage by its wireless station.

Jan. 9—Tobacco sent to French prisoners to be admitted free of duty.

Jan. 10—Retired Belgian General and Lieutenant sentenced to life imprisonment for aiding Belgians to escape to Holland; it is said that the Landsturm can still furnish 5,000,000 men; Socialist meeting prohibited in Saxony.

Jan. 11—Reports from Russia state that German women in men's uniform have been taken prisoners in bayonet charges recently and that some of them are wounded and in hospital; sale of blankets forbidden in Berlin and Brandenburg; the stocks are to be placed at the disposal of the military authorities; French women and children taken from occupied territory are being sent home.

Jan. 12—The Pope is negotiating for better treatment of clerical prisoners.

Jan. 17—Official reports state that the prisoners of war held by Germany and Austria are now 800,000.

Jan. 22—Escaped British officer charges cruelty toward British prisoners.

Jan. 23—Money prizes are offered to the first invaders of England.

Jan. 25—Secretary Bryan makes public the text of German Government's notification of cancellation of exequaturs granted by Belgian Government to foreign Consular representatives, and the reply of the United States.

Jan. 27—Prince von Bülow tells Italian statesmen that Italy's preparations for war are resented and that an ultimatum may be sent; French charge that German soldiers reverse bullets for short-range fighting; wife of Greek Consul at Liége sentenced to prison for aiding Belgians to escape; all neutrals to be expelled from Upper Alsace; Gen. von Bissing orders all Englishmen in Belgium sent to Germany.

Jan. 30—Value of French territory occupied by the Germans is estimated at $1,900,000,000 by the Inspector General of the Crédit Foncier, or 7.2 per cent., of the total value of all France; according to the census of 1911 3,255,000 persons, or 8.2 per cent. of the population of France, live in this territory; Berlin night life is under the war ban, yet the opera and theatres are open.

ITALY.

Jan. 11—Troops sent to garrison the Italian islands in the Aegean.

Jan. 12—Demonstration when the body of Constantino Garibaldi, killed while serving with the French, arrives in Rome; many applications for nationality by Germans are being refused; Committee of National Defense formed at Milan.

Jan. 13—Italians in all parts of the world are offering to enlist in event of war; a special police census shows 700,000 Austrians and Germans in the country; embassies advise them to leave.

Jan. 23—Vice Consul at Liége dismissed for aiding Belgians; prominent Italians appeal to neutral countries to take steps to preserve art treasures in belligerent countries.

Jan. 25—Radicals want war.

Jan. 29—Soldiers of the First and Third Categories are called to the colors; retired officers fit for service are liable to be recalled.

Jan. 30—Contracts for army and navy supplies are placed in the United States.

Jan. 31—Riots in Rome against neutralists.

RUMANIA.

Jan. 8—The nation is mobilizing 750,000 men, of whom 500,000 form the field army.

Jan. 11—London experts think that Rumania will soon enter war on side of Allies, her army linking with the extreme Russian left.

Jan. 16—Students in Switzerland summoned home because of mobilization.

Jan. 22—Orders are placed with Swiss firms for medical supplies.

Jan. 26—Exportation of army supplies to Hungary recommenced.

RUSSIA.

Jan. 9—Girl fights with Cossacks and wins Cross of St. George.

Jan. 10—Only half the number of this year's recruits liable for military service are called out.

Jan. 20—It is reported that some members of the imperial family are opposed to the war.

Jan. 21—Troops are warned against bogus proclamations, bearing Czar's name, circulated by Austrians.

Jan. 22—Orders issued for expulsion of Austrian and German subjects.

Jan. 26—Foreign Minister Sazonof says there will be no peace while a single soldier of the enemy remains on Russian soil.

Jan. 29—Poles form legion at Warsaw.

RELIEF WORK.

Jan. 8—California's relief cargo is on the way to Rotterdam.

Jan. 9—To date the value of cargoes of food, clothing, and medical supplies delivered, in transit on the Atlantic, or arranged for from the United States to Belgium amount to more than $14,000,000; milk and sugar are scarce in Belgium, the babies feeling the influence of the food crisis.

Jan. 10—Antwerp Council passes resolution of thanks to Americans, whose help "is literally saving us."

Jan. 11—American party sent to relieve German and Austrian prisoners in Russia is halted by the Russian Government pending negotiations.

Jan. 15—Large consignment of supplies is sent to Saloniki by American Red Cross; Virginia and Maryland send Belgian relief ships; Georgia is raising funds for a ship.

Jan. 21—American Red Cross issues report of its European activities from Aug. 1 to Jan. 9; war fund thus far amounts to $1,188,000; forty-five American Red Cross surgeons and 150 nurses are on war duty in Europe; Sing Sing prisoners are to knit socks for Polish destitute.

Jan. 23—Mme. Grouitch, wife of the Secretary General for Foreign Affairs of Servia, arrives in New York seeking funds for seeds for the Servian Spring planting; Dr. Wickliffe Rose and Ernest Bicknell, who have been in Russian Poland for the American Red Cross, report from Berlin that conditions in Poland are worse, if anything, than those in Belgium.

Jan. 24—Commission for Relief in Belgium has thirty-five chartered steamships running between American ports and Rotterdam carrying supplies.

Jan. 26—American Red Cross ships large consignment of supplies for Constantinople and Servia.

Jan. 27—Commission for Relief in Belgium states that 76,000 tons of food, in addition to supplies in sight, are needed for next three months; there are now 1,400,000 destitute, and the number is increasing daily.

Jan. 28—Committee of prominent American educators plans to have the 20,000,000 children of the United States help war sufferers through a new fund, to be called the Children of America's Fund.

Jan. 31—Rockefeller Foundation denies that it has withdrawn from Belgium relief work.

TO HIS MAJESTY KING ALBERT

By WILLIAM WATSON.

[From King Albert's Book.]

RECEIVE, from one who hath not lavished praise
On many Princes, nor was ever awed
By empire such as groveling slaves applaud,
Who cast their souls into its altar-blaze—
Receive the homage that a freeman pays
To Kinghood flowering out of Manhood broad,
Kinghood that toils uncovetous of laud,
Loves whom it rules, and serves the realm it sways.

For when Your people, caught in agony's net,
Rose as one dauntless heart, their King was found
Worthy on such a throne to have been set,
Worthy by such as They to have been crowned;
And loftier praise than this did never yet
On mortal ears from lips of mortals sound.

FOOTNOTES

[1] This is similar to the manner in which the English entente with France was arranged. The British Parliament and the British Cabinet were kept in ignorance of the fact that English and French naval experts were consulting together. The British Minister for Foreign Affairs, Sir Edward Grey, repeatedly assured the country that Great Britain's hands were free. Yet, when the crisis came, this quite unofficial exchange of military views and plans, this mere gentleman's agreement, revealed itself, of course, as a binding obligation. Nations do not reveal their military secrets to each other except on the clear understanding that an alliance is in force.

[2] The report of Sir Edward Goschen, British Ambassador to Berlin, on the severance of diplomatic connections between England and Germany, was published by the British Foreign Office as a "White Paper" on Aug. 27, 1914. Sir Edward said that in pursuance of instructions from Downing Street, he went on Aug. 3 to see Gottlieb von Jagow, the German Foreign Minister, and asked if Germany would promise to respect Belgian neutrality. Herr von Jagow replied that it was too late, as German troops had already crossed the Belgian border, and explained the military necessity of this step.

After remonstrance, Sir Edward withdrew, but made another visit the same afternoon and warned von Jagow that unless the German Government at once withdrew its troops from Belgian soil he must demand his passports. Herr von Jagow repeated that withdrawal was impossible; and, seeing that war was now certain, expressed his deep regret at the failure of the policy by which he and the Chancellor, Dr. von Bethmann-Hollweg, had been trying to get into more friendly relations with England and through her with France.

The Ambassador, after mutual expressions of personal regard, withdrew and visited the Imperial Chancellor, who, according to Sir Edward's story, "began a harangue, which lasted about twenty minutes. Just for a word, 'neutrality'—a word which in war was so often disregarded—just for a scrap of paper, Great Britain was going to make war on a kindred nation. The policy to which he had devoted himself had tumbled like a house of cards. What Great Britain had done was unthinkable—it was like striking a man in the back when he was fighting for his life against two assailants."

Sir Edward said that he protested strongly against this and told the Chancellor that, while an advance through Belgium might be a matter of life and death for Germany, the defense of Belgian neutrality, in compliance with her solemn engagement, was a matter of life and death for the honor of Great Britain.

"The Chancellor said," Sir Edward continued: "'But at what a price will that compact have been kept! Has the British Government thought of that?' I hinted to his Excellency as plainly as I could that fear of consequences could hardly be regarded as an excuse for breaking a solemn engagement. But his Excellency was so excited, so little disposed to hear reason, so evidently overcome by the news of our action, that I refrained from adding fuel to the flame by further argument."

[3] In his address at Cardiff, appearing in Vol. 1, No. 2, of THE NEW YORK TIMES CURRENT HISTORY, Premier Asquith said:

In a communication to the German Government in 1912 regarding her future policy Great Britain declared that she would neither make nor join in any unprovoked attack upon Germany. But that was not enough for German statesmanship.

Germany wanted us to go further and pledge ourselves to absolute neutrality in the event of Germany being engaged in war. To that demand there was but one answer, and that was the answer which the Government gave.

[4] Bernhardi: "Germany and the Next War." English popular edition, Page 138.

[5] Crispi's "Memoirs," iii., 326-7.